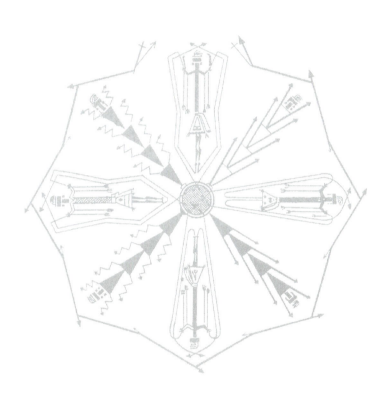

Essence *of* ARIZONA

The Visitors Guidebook

Krzysztof Gaj and Janet Wandrey

PAPER TOUCH PUBLISHING

ACKNOWLEDGEMENTS

The creation of this book was facilitated by the cooperation of Chambers of Commerce, Offices of Tourism, museums, art galleries, private businesses, and individuals to whom we express our gratitude. We also thank our families for their patience, support, and interest in our work.

PHOTO AND ILLUSTRATION CREDITS

Book and cover design, maps, photos, and illustrations are by Krzysztof Gaj and Janet Wandrey unless otherwise stated below.

- Tom Darro, part of painting, *The Desert Mother*, front cover
- Dover Publications, pages i, vi, ix, 26, 33, 34, 68, 86, 91, 95, 100, 111, 124, 129, 181, 194, 208, 234, 304
- Jennifer Wandrey, page 16
- Brian Winter, pages 30, 31, 45
- Gene Balzar, page 35
- Al Richmond, page 48
- Bonnie Furlong, pages 62, 63
- Willis Peterson, pages 78, 189
- Bill McLemore, pages 88, 92
- Jeff Noble, page 89
- Horizons West, page 108
- Jeffrey Crespi, page 110
- John Andresen, page 156
- Frank McCarthy, page 161
- Stacy Kollar, page 174
- Finn Foto, page 287

Library of Congress Catalog Card Number: 99-61430

ISBN 0-9646499-2-6

First edition published in 1995 by Paper Touch Publishing.

The publisher and authors assume no responsibility for any personal injury or personal property loss or damage while the user of this book is visiting or en route to places mentioned in this book. Please use your own judgement to assure your own safety.

Paper Touch Publishing
6981 W. Rose Garden Lane, Glendale, Arizona 85308

ABOUT THIS BOOK

It is our pleasure to welcome all visitors and readers of this book to Arizona, a state of incredible beauty and excitement, where history and adventure interact with leisure in modern society. Visitors will capture the essence of Arizona by experiencing its diverse cultures, exploring the grandeur of its land, and basking in its beautiful climate. For the traveler's convenience the book is divided into Northern, Central, and Southern sections, beginning with places of interest in and around the major Arizona cities—Flagstaff, Phoenix, and Tucson.

The content of this book includes more than two hundred places to visit, well documented with photographs, numerous charts and maps, travel directions, plus special interest sections such as Arizona Outdoors, Desert Survival, Indian Reservations, Indian Art, Airport, Ghost Towns, Petroglyphs, Rockhounding Tips, Annual Events, and a Postcard Gallery.

Our postcard section depicts Arizona as seen through the eyes of artists. The original art work is on display in major Arizona museums and art galleries. We hope you will enjoy and make use of the *Essence of Arizona Postcard Gallery* which is located at the back of this book and includes:

- *Zoroaster's Temple at Sunset*, oil painting by Thomas Moran, courtesy of the Phoenix Art Museum
- *Hopi Spotted Corn Kachina*, E9646, photo by Gene Balzar, courtesy of Northern Arizona Museum, Flagstaff
- *Bend of the River*, acrylic painting by W. H. Ford, courtesy of the Wickenburg Gallery, Wickenburg
- *Contemporary Deer Kachina* carving by Alvin Navarie, photo by Bill McLemore, courtesy of Gilbert Ortega Galleries, Scottsdale
- Navajo Rugs, courtesy of the Heard Museum, Phoenix
- *Fancy Dancer*, oil painting by John Nieto, courtesy of the Heard Museum, Phoenix
- *The Vaquero,* oil painting by Frederic Remington, courtesy of Desert Caballeros Western Museum, Wickenburg
- *Beautiful Burden,* oil painting by Ted DeGrazia, courtesy of DeGrazia Gallery in the Sun, Tucson
- *Eatin' Dust,* acrylic painting by W. H. Ford, courtesy of The Wickenburg Gallery, Wickenburg
- *The Desert Mother,* oil painting by Tom Darro, courtesy of The Overland Gallery, Scottsdale

TABLE OF CONTENTS

ARIZONA

Visitors come to Arizona by the millions each year to enjoy the beautiful climate, to marvel at spectacular geologic formations, and to explore Arizona's history. They go on self-guided and guided tours of old Indian ruins. They take pictures of the empty weather-eroded dwellings on top of mesas, under overhanging cliffs, in canyon walls, and on desert plateaus. Many descendants of the people who lived in these dwellings now choose to live on reservations, cherishing their heritage and passing it down to their children.

The most documented tourist attractions in Arizona are Indian ruins, petroglyphs, and Indian artifacts. Arts and crafts of present-day American Indians and the spectacular land forma-tions located on reservations appeal to the different interests of modern visitors. The Indian people (Native Americans) and their culture play an important role in present-day Arizona.

Spanish heritage and today's Hispanic population also play an important role in Arizona lifestyle. Tourists visit old Spanish missions in the southern part of the state and take part in Spanish/Mexican festivities, watch folklorico dancers, listen to mariachi music, as well as delight in savory Mexican cuisine.

Many early settlers came to Arizona to farm, raise livestock, and establish settlements. Others came when gold and copper were discovered. As a result, mining became a major source of income for many Arizonans. Mining was, and still is, an impor-tant part of the state's economy. A large part of America's supply of copper comes from Arizona. Silver, gold, turquoise, and other beautiful and useful minerals are also mined in the state. Like other western states, Arizona still has ranchers and cowboys combining old western traditions with modern methods of ranching. Arizona's economy has changed in the last fifty years. Today, much of Arizona's economy is based on manufacturing and services and only a small percent on mining and agriculture. Arizona has recently been referred to as a high-technology state and is often called the "Silicon Desert".

On Valentine's Day in 1912, Arizona became the forty-eighth state of the nation. The capital was moved several times and finally established in Phoenix, the largest and most central city of the state. The main metropolitan areas of Arizona hustled and bustled to keep up with modern technology and to provide an attractive lifestyle for their residents and visitors.

The railroad providing transportation, and canals and dams assuring a supply of water to the desert, have done the most to create population growth in Arizona. Today's Arizona, the sixth largest state in the nation, has a population of 3,700,000 residents. The most densely populated areas are the Phoenix metropolitan area, Tucson, Flagstaff, and Yuma. This leaves plenty of room for the smaller, unique communities and beautiful, wide-open space, both flat and mountainous. Some of the space—one fourth of the state—is covered with ponderosa pines. Other areas are used by agriculturists for growing cotton, citrus, and produce.

The history of Arizona was made by early prospectors, miners, cowboys, Indians, and outlaws. Today's Arizona doesn't look anything like it does in old western movies; and residents have switched their occupations from gold prospectors and bounty hunters to more sophisticated professions.

Modern, tall glass buildings of our cities, beautiful landscapes, a vast number of swimming pools, and unlimited sunshine make Arizona irresistible to world travelers. Arizona is a safe place to visit. It isn't frequented by earthquakes, hurricanes, mud slides, or tornados. Each year, millions of visitors enjoy the beautiful climate, magnificent scenery, unique flora and fauna, and warm hospitality. Going home in the middle of winter with a golden suntan is what many visitors enjoy most. The essence of Arizona is a combination of adventure, history, and cultural diversity, all in harmony with Arizona's majestic beauty.

Drawing of Anasazi pottery

MILEAGE AND STATISTICS

	Ajo	Benson	Bisbee	Casa Grande	Clifton	Coolidge	Douglas	Flagstaff	Gila Bend	Glendale	Globe	Grand Canyon	Havasu City
Ajo		175	225	99	290	120	249	256	42	116	188	337	245
Benson	175		49	115	115	112	74	301	172	169	150	382	362
Bisbee	225	49		164	164	161	24	351	221	218	200	431	412
Casa Grande	99	115	164		198	21	188	190	57	58	89	271	249
Clifton	290	115	164	198		179	156	302	259	208	111	383	401
Coolidge	120	112	161	21	179		185	197	80	65	68	278	256
Douglas	249	74	24	188	156	185		376	242	244	200	457	437
Flagstaff	256	301	351	190	302	197	376		209	144	173	81	204
Gila Bend	42	172	221	57	259	80	242	209		74	146	288	203
Glendale	116	169	218	58	208	65	244	144	74		97	225	193
Globe	188	150	200	89	111	68	200	173	146	97		254	293
Grand Canyon	337	382	431	271	383	278	457	81	288	225	254		231
Havasu City	245	262	412	249	401	256	437	204	203	193	293	231	
Holbrook	301	286	335	207	213	204	335	91	256	231	135	172	296
Hoover Dam	369	415	464	304	457	311	488	216	320	246	346	243	135
Kingman	296	342	391	231	383	238	415	143	247	172	273	170	61
Mesa	125	153	202	32	183	41	226	161	83	24	72	241	221
Miami	180	157	206	82	117	61	207	194	148	89	7	275	286
Nogales	194	73	89	134	198	139	112	320	187	188	169	401	381
Page	392	437	487	328	438	334	511	136	343	280	309	137	340
Payson	203	228	280	117	190	119	282	91	161	102	82	172	299
Phoenix	110	156	205	45	207	51	229	146	68	13	87	226	206
Prescott	212	257	307	146	299	153	331	87	163	100	189	126	192
Sedona	222	275	325	164	297	171	349	28	180	117	142	108	332
Superior	173	147	196	68	135	44	220	209	131	72	24	289	269
Tempe	120	156	205	45	188	47	229	155	78	18	78	236	215
Tombstone	201	26	24	141	141	137	48	327	194	194	176	408	388
Tuba City	335	380	430	269	381	281	455	79	278	223	254	79	283
Tucson	131	45	94	70	159	67	118	257	124	124	106	338	317
Wickenburg	168	214	263	103	256	114	287	150	119	44	145	186	148
Willcox	211	36	86	151	82	148	74	337	205	205	126	398	398
Williams	273	333	383	203	234	229	407	32	231	176	205	59	172
Yuma	158	284	334	174	381	192	358	307	116	192	271	316	156
Elevation (feet)	1,798	3,580	5,350	1,400	3,500	1,400	4,000	6,900	737	1,100	3,500	6,800	482
Summer Average Daytime Temp.	108	97	90	107	90	112	96	81	109	104	98	96	110
Winter Average Daytime Temp.	66	67	61	71	66	66	66	44	74	69	62	61	60
Population	2,919	3,824	6,288	19,082	2,840	6,927	12,822	45,857	1,747	148,134	6,062	------	24,363

Holbrook	Hoover Dam	Kingman	Mesa	Miami	Nogales	Page	Payson	Phoenix	Prescott	Sedona	Superior	Tempe	Tombstone	Tuba City	Tucson	Wickenburg	Willcox	Williams	Yuma
301	369	296	125	180	194	392	203	110	212	222	173	120	201	335	131	168	211	273	158
286	415	342	153	157	73	437	228	156	257	275	147	156	26	380	45	214	36	333	284
335	464	391	202	206	89	487	280	205	307	325	196	205	24	430	94	263	86	383	334
207	304	231	32	82	134	328	117	45	146	164	68	45	141	269	70	103	151	203	174
213	457	383	183	117	198	438	190	207	299	297	135	188	141	381	159	256	82	334	381
204	311	238	41	61	139	334	119	51	153	171	44	47	137	281	67	114	148	229	192
335	488	415	226	207	112	511	282	229	331	349	220	229	48	455	118	287	74	407	358
91	216	143	161	194	320	136	91	146	87	28	209	155	327	79	257	150	337	32	307
256	320	247	83	148	187	343	181	68	163	180	131	78	194	278	124	119	205	231	116
231	246	172	24	89	188	280	102	13	100	117	72	18	194	223	124	44	205	176	192
135	346	273	72	7	169	309	82	87	189	142	24	78	176	254	106	145	126	205	271
172	243	170	241	275	401	137	172	226	126	108	289	236	408	79	338	186	398	59	316
296	135	61	221	286	381	340	299	206	192	232	269	215	388	283	317	148	398	172	156
	308	234	175	142	304	215	98	191	174	120	159	181	311	162	241	251	261	123	374
308		73	270	339	434	326	307	259	217	244	322	268	441	295	370	201	451	184	290
234	73		197	266	360	279	234	186	144	171	249	195	367	222	297	128	378	111	216
175	270	197		65	169	297	78	15	117	135	48	6	176	240	106	73	186	193	199
142	339	266	65		176	334	83	80	182	193	18	72	183	277	112	138	134	228	264
304	434	360	169	176		456	247	175	276	294	165	175	71	399	63	233	107	352	303
215	326	279	297	334	456		227	282	228	264	345	291	463	77	393	279	474	169	446
98	307	234	78	83	247	227		93	190	86	106	84	266	170	183	151	208	123	277
191	259	186	15	80	175	282	93		102	119	63	9	181	225	111	58	192	170	184
174	217	144	117	182	276	228	190	102		60	165	111	283	161	213	61	294	67	218
120	244	171	135	193	294	164	86	119	60		182	129	301	107	230	120	311	60	288
159	322	249	48	18	165	345	106	63	165	182		54	172	288	102	121	150	233	238
181	268	195	6	72	175	291	84	9	111	129	54		182	234	112	63	192	179	193
311	441	367	176	183	71	463	266	181	283	301	172	182		406	70	239	62	351	310
162	295	222	240	277	399	77	170	225	161	107	288	234	406		336	222	417	111	380
241	370	297	106	112	63	393	183	111	213	230	102	112	70	336		169	81	281	240
251	201	128	73	138	233	279	151	58	61	120	121	63	239	222	169		250	128	174
261	451	378	186	134	107	474	208	182	294	311	150	192	62	417	81	250		362	320
123	184	111	193	228	352	169	123	170	167	60	233	179	351	111	281	128	362		285
374	290	216	199	264	303	446	277	184	218	288	238	193	310	380	240	174	320	285	
5,075	1,232	3,333	1,225	3,603	3,800	4,380	4,848	1,083	5,410	4,300	2,995	1,150	1,540	6,120	2,410	2,070	4,200	6,750	138
94	102	98	103	97	95	98	90	104	89	94	97	101	93	92	100	102	94	84	106
55	70	60	69	60	67	50	77	69	54	54	65	70	63	54	68	67	62	47	72
4,686	-------	12,722	288,091	2,018	19,489	6,598	8,377	983,403	26,455	7,720	3,468	141,865	1,220	7,323	405,390	4,515	3,122	2,532	54,923

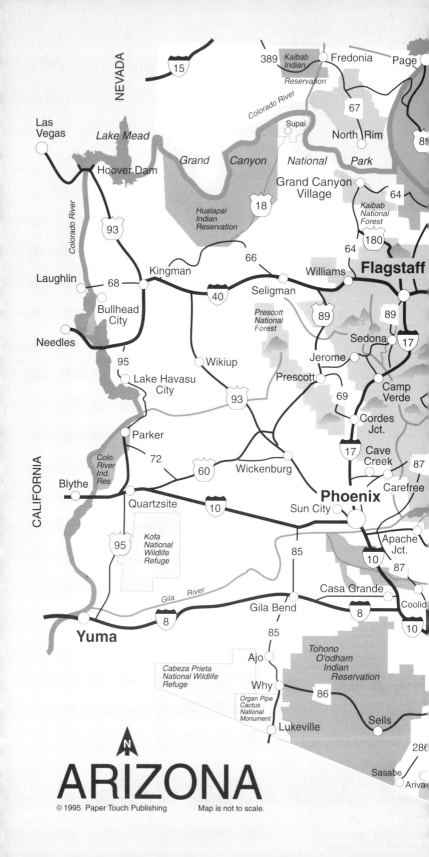

UTAH

Lake Powell 163

Navajo Indian Reservation

98
160 Kayenta

Navajo Hopi joint use area

Hopi Indian Reservation

Canyon de Chelly Natl. Mon.

Chinle

Tuba City

191

264

Ganado

Navajo Indian Reservation

40

40 87
Winslow Holbrook

Petrified Forest National Park

87

Heber

77

260

61 St. Johns

Payson Show Low 60

Springerville

Roosevelt Lake

Salt River

73 Fort Apache Indian Reservation

60

Alpine

88

San Carlos Indian Reservation

ortilla Miami
Flat Globe

Superior

666

177

70 Morenci

lorence Clifton

77 Safford

89 Oracle

666

Tucson Willcox

Saguaro National Monument

10

19

186 Chircahua Natl. Mon.

reen 83 Benson
alley

90

Sonoita 82 Tombstone

Tubac 666

Nogales Sierra Vista 92 Bisbee Douglas

MEXICO

Arizona State Flag

Official State Symbols

Flower - saguaro cactus
Tree - palo verde
Bird - cactus wren
Mammal - ringtailed cat
Reptile - rattlesnake
Fossil - petrified wood
Neckwear - bola tie
Gemstone - turquoise

Interesting State Facts

Motto - God Enriches
(Ditat Deus)
Located on 35th parallel
Lowest elevation - 70 ft.
Highest elevation - 12,356 ft.
Highest temperature ever
recorded - 127 degrees F.
Indian reservations comprise
27% of the state's land.
There are 303 lakes in Arizona
The Grand Canyon is
277 miles long.
Valley of the Sun is the
popular name for the
Phoenix metropolitan area.
World's tallest saguaro - 58 ft.
Century plant blooms
every 25 years.
World's largest rose bush
is in Tombstone.
Gila monster is the only
poisonous lizard in U.S.

Famous Arizona People

Barry Goldwater - U.S. senator
Bob McCall - space artist
Erma Bombeck - author
Steven Spielberg - movie pro-
ducer, director
Wyatt Earp - legendary sheriff
Frank Lloyd Wright - architect
Sandra Day O'Connor - U.S.
Supreme Court judge
Frank Borman - astronaut
Bruce Babbit - U.S. Secretary
of Interior
Jesse Owens - Olympic athlete
Fritz Sholder - artist

ARIZONA PARKS

◆ - National Monument
■ - State Park
▲ - Campsites

Park	Phone	Entrance Fee	Tours	Tents and RV Sites	Visitors Center	Museum and Exhibits	Picnic Area	Boating	Hiking	Hotel, Motel	Restaurant-snack	Restrooms
1 Alamo Lake ▲■	520-669-2088	●		●	●		●	●	●	●		●
2 Boyce Th. Arbr. ■	520-689-2811	●			●	●	●					●
3 Canyon de Chelly ◆	520-674-5436		●	●	●	●	●		●	●	●	●
4 Casa Grande ◆	520-723-3172	●	●		●	●	●					●
5 Catalina ▲■	520-628-5798	●		●	●		●		●			●
6 Chiricahua ▲◆	520-364-3468	●		●	●	●	●		●			●
7 Coronado ◆	520-458-4333	●			●	●	●		●			
8 Dead Horse ▲■	520-634-5283	●		●	●		●		●			●
9 Fort Bowie ◆	520-847-2500		●			●			●			
10 Fort Verde ■	520-567-3275	●			●	●	●					●
11 Glen Canyon ▲	520-645-2313		●	●	●	●	●	●	●	●		●
12 Grand Canyon ▲◆	520-638-2401	●	●	●	●	●	●		●	●	●	●
13 Hubbell Trd. Pst. ◆	520-755-3475		●		●	●						
14 Jerome ■	520-634-5381	●					●					
15 Lake Havasu ▲■	520-855-7851	●		●	●		●	●	●	●		●
16 Lake Mead ▲	520-767-3401		●	●	●		●	●	●	●	●	●
17 Lees Ferry ▲	520-335-2234		●	●			●	●				
18 Lost Dutchman ▲■	520-982-4485	●	●	●	●				●			●
19 McDowell Mt. ▲	602-971-1160			●			●		●			
20 Montezuma C. ◆	520-567-3322	●	●		●	●	●					●
21 Navajo ▲◆	520-672-2366	●		●	●		●		●			●
22 Organ Pipe ▲◆	520-387-6849	●	●	●	●		●					●
23 Painted Rock ▲■	520-683-2151	●	●	●	●		●	●	●			●
24 Patagonia L. ▲■	520-287-6965	●	●	●	●		●	●	●		●	●
25 Petrified Fst. ◆	520-524-6228	●	●		●	●	●		●		●	●
26 Picacho Peak ▲■	520-466-3183	●	●	●	●		●		●			●
27 Pipe Spring ◆	520-643-7105	●	●		●	●	●					●
28 Roper Lake ▲■	520-428-6760	●	●	●	●		●	●	●			●
29 Saguaro ◆	520-883-1380	●	●		●	●	●		●			●
30 Sunset Crater ◆	520-527-7042		●		●	●	●		●			
31 Tombstone ■	520-457-3311	●		●	●	●	●			●	●	●
32 Tonto ◆	520-474-2269	●	●		●	●	●					●
33 Tubac Presidio ■	520-398-2252	●			●	●	●					●
34 Tumacacori ◆	520-398-2341	●	●		●	●	●					●
35 Tuzigoot ◆	520-634-5564	●	●		●	●						●
36 Wahweap ▲	520-645-8883		●				●	●		●	●	●
37 Walnut Canyon ◆	520-526-3367	●	●		●	●			●			●
38 White Tanks ▲	602-262-3711			●					●			
39 Wupatki ◆	520-527-7040		●		●	●	●					●
40 Yuma Terr. Pris. ■	520-783-4771	●	●		●	●	●					●

OUTDOOR ARIZONA

Arizona, with its unparalleled beauty and climate, is the only state that allows you to view changes in vegetation and temperature from alpine to low desert during a two-hour drive. Arizona visitors, taking advantage of this unique environment, enjoy outdoor activities throughout the year, from skiing in April to engaging in water sports in the middle of winter. The wide-open land of our state, with huge areas of desert and mountains invite people to seek challenges in hiking and mountain climbing. For water and fishing enthusiasts, Arizona provides a great variety of lakes with unprecedented beauty. Many visitors, for weeks at a time, explore magnificent scenery and history hidden in lakeshore caves and canyons. Because of its natural resources, Arizona is rapidly becoming one of the most popular states to

ARIZONA
PARKS

visit. The unlimited variety of outdoor activities makes Arizona a state of endless adventure.

HIKING

The most enjoyed and least demanding outdoor activities, for local residents as well as for tourists, are hiking and backpacking on more than eleven million acres of national forest land in Arizona. Countless hiking trails (many are mentioned in this book) provide a range of difficulty to satisfy needs and expectations of all hikers. In many of Arizona's national parks hiking is necessary to fully enjoy and appreciate the enormous beauty of the land. You can pick up detailed maps of hiking trails at most of the visitor centers and at sporting goods stores.

CAMPING

At high elevations, which residents call "the green country", campgrounds are filled in the summer. In the winter time, when

A student from Germany exploring the desert.

these areas are covered with snow, desert campgrounds, with their warm temperatures, are filled quickly with outdoor enthusiasts. Easy access to most of the campgrounds, which are located only a short drive from the major cities, adds to the popularity of this form of recreation. It is advisable to make reservations if you are planning to camp during major holiday weekends. Most of Arizona's campgrounds are well-equipped facilities.

ROCKHOUNDING

Arizona is the best state in the nation for rockhounding. People from all over the world come to Arizona to prospect for their favorite minerals. Most of the sites are located on public land but for a small fee you can often engage in rockhounding on private land. Arizona has more gem and mineral shows than any other state. Rockhounds exchange, buy, and sell their findings, which include fire agate, onyx in many colors, quartz crystals, jasper, turquoise, petrified wood, tourmaline, and more. For more information about rock and gem shows refer to the Annual Events section of this book.

HUNTING

Other visitors, attracted to Arizona's wilderness by a wide range of hunting opportunities, are amateur as well as experienced hunters. The large selection of birds and animals in Arizona provides open seasons for hunting almost year-round. Game species include deer, javelina, squirrel, bear, elk, and antelope. Bighorn sheep and buffalo can be successfully hunted only once by each hunter—another permit will not be issued. For hunting permits, terrain maps, and information on hunting seasons contact the *Arizona Game and Fish Department at 2221 W. Greenway Road, Phoenix, AZ 85023, 602-942-3000.*

WILDLIFE WATCHING

People from all over the world come to Arizona to engage in bird watching. Because of our state's desert areas with their unique microclimates, many unusual species of birds can be spotted. Ornithologists, bird watchers, as well as tourists take part in this relaxing activity. Occasionally outdoor enthusiasts can witness a mountain lion lying peacefully in the sun, beautiful, distinctive

antelope leaping across the terrain or a javelina mother leading her piglets to a pool of water. Wildlife watching is a form of hunting in which your prey is captured by camera.

WATER SPORTS

Many visitors are surprised to find so many bodies of water in the form of lakes and rivers in a desert region. Originally the lakes were created for the purpose of generating power and storing the water necessary for state survival, but then water- sports enthusiasts gave the lakes another purpose. The most popular and most scenic is Lake Powell with its ninety-six canyons which can be explored by boat. Boat renting is a full-scale operation at the marinas on Lake Powell. If you love water and if you like to spend time on a houseboat, this is the place.

The awesome Colorado River not only gives us the Grand Canyon, but still provides today's adventurers with breathtaking experiences while white-water rafting. Where the river becomes calm and blue again, it forms Lake Mead, controlled by the spectacular Hoover Dam. As it continues its journey south from Hoover Dam, the Colorado River forms the western border of Arizona, providing many more areas for water sports participation and wildlife watching.

A series of lakes created by the damming of the Salt River provides escape from the desert heat and enjoyment of water sports for central Arizona residents and visitors. Not quite as large as Lake Powell or Lake Mead—lakes Roosevelt, Apache, Canyon, and Saguaro are picturesque and deliver everything that water enthusiasts may want. During the summer months, the Salt River becomes very popular among Arizonans, for its tubing-down-the-river excursions.

There are numerous small natural lakes scattered throughout central and southern Arizona, offering excellent recreational opportunities including fishing.

FISHING

Fishing in Arizona is a year-round sport. Arizona's lakes and rivers support habitat for more than twenty game fish including varieties of bass, trout, catfish, bluegill, crappie, bullhead, sunfish, pike, tilapia, and perch. You can obtain more information on rules and regulations from bait and tackle shops or the *Arizona Game and Fish Department at 2221 W. Greenway Road, Phoenix, AZ 85023, 602-942-3000.*

WINTER SPORTS

To make this state a full paradise, only snow is needed. Yes, we do get up to 250 inches of snow annually in the higher elevations, which transform usually sleepy communities into vibrant, colorful ski resorts. Skiing and other winter sports are becoming more popular among out-of-state visitors. Skiing season in Arizona begins in mid–November and lasts until mid–April. Our state has four excellent downhill ski areas.

Sunrise, the largest and most luxurious ski resort in Arizona, has more than sixty runs, varying in difficulty. The resort provides eleven lifts to elevate skiers to 11,000 feet. The biggest vertical drop is 1,800 feet. Besides downhill skiing, Sunrise is a perfect place for family enjoyment of snowmobiling, snowboarding, cross-country, and telemark skiing. The resort is on the Fort Apache Indian Reservation, owned and operated by the White Mountain Apache Tribe. *Sunrise Park Resort, P.O. Box 217, McNary, Arizona 85930, 480-735-7676.*

Snowbowl, located comfortably only fourteen miles north of Flagstaff, uses a slope of Agassiz's Peak, which was formed by volcanic eruption more than three million years ago. Skiing season ranges from mid–December to mid–April with more than 200 inches of snowfall annually. The altitude ranges from 11,500 feet to 9,200 feet with a vertical drop of 2,300 feet. The ski area is serviced by four chair lifts and two full-service day lodges. Because of its location, Snowbowl is very popular among Flagstaff and Phoenix families seeking playtime in the snow, which includes snowmobiling, tubing, cross-country skiing, snowboarding, and old-fashioned snow games. *Arizona Snowbowl, P.O. Box 40, Flagstaff AZ, 86002, 520-779-1951.*

Mount Lemmon. The biggest advantage of this skiing spot is its closeness to a metropolitan area. After sunbathing and swimming in the pool, you can take a few-minute drive to position yourself in perfect skiing conditions with a gorgeous overlook of sun-drenched Tucson. This is a perfect example of the unparalleled beauty and climate of this state. Mount Lemmon ski area reaches the elevation of 9,000 feet and has a vertical drop of 870 feet. One chair lift and two bar lifts service the skiers. For family fun and enjoyment Mount Lemmon also offers tobogganing, snowboarding, and cross-country skiing. The skiing season ranges from mid–December to the end of March. Mount Lemmon skiing facilities are located thirty-five miles north of Tucson. *Mount Lemmon Ski Valley, 520-576-1400.*

Williams Ski Area, located near the town of Williams (famous for its Grand Canyon Train excursions), provides fine skiing opportunities and snow games for local residents as well as visitors. The highest peak reaches 8,050 feet providing a vertical drop of 450 feet. The area is serviced by one tow lift and one bar lift. The surrounding forest with its many trails, provides excellent conditions for cross-country skiing. Snowmobiling, tubing, and sledding satisfy every family's needs. *Williams Ski Area, 520-635-9330.*

As you can see, Arizona provides many opportunities to enjoy winter sports. Besides downhill skiing in our major ski areas, many snow lovers take advantage of wide-open spaces to push themselves to the limit by cross-country skiing. Today, in our mechanized society, snowmobiling is becoming more and more popular. Higher speed, greater distances, possibilities of competition, and enjoyment of unlimited scenery, make this way to play in the snow an adventure for the whole family.

After the snowstorm

DESERT SURVIVAL

Arizona's elevation ranges from sea level to more than 12,000 feet, and with that goes extreme variation in climate and temperature. Temperatures range from below freezing during the winter at higher elevations to more than 120 degrees during the summer in desert valleys. Survival in Arizona's beautiful desert should not be taken for granted. Always tell someone where you are going and when you expect to return. Possible heat exhaustion, dehydration, and venomous creature bites are the main concerns. A special note of caution—during the summer months, do not leave small children or pets in a car during the heat of the day, even for a few minutes. Offer children and pets more water than they normally consume in other climates.

In the paragraphs below you will find life-saving suggestions to help prevent these misfortunes from happening to you.

PREPARING YOUR CAR FOR BACK ROAD TRAVEL

Before you venture forth, be sure your vehicle is in good condition. Check battery, hoses, belts, and tires. Pack the following items in your car: radiator water, jumper cables, car jack, shovel, old rug, tow rope, tool kit, extra gasoline, and roll of duct tape.

PREPARING FOR YOUR OWN SAFETY

Prepare a special container for these useful items: flares, drinking water, extra matches, flashlight, bar of soap, pocket knife, blanket, compass, bandanna, signal mirror, needle, antiseptic, area map, first-aid kit, nylon cord, whistle, and aluminum foil.

SURVIVING IN THE DESERT

If stranded in the desert, protect your safety by raising both hood and trunk lids, turning on flashing hazard lights and/or tying a cloth to the antenna. Stay with your car unless help is in sight. Drink water and protect yourself from the sun. Breath through your nose, and do not talk, eat, smoke, drink alcohol, or eat salt. These precautions all help prevent dehydration.

Build three signal fires in a triangle to signal that you are lost or need help. Create smoke during the day and a bright fire at night. Rest ten minutes or more each hour, if you are walking.

REACTING TO SPECIAL WEATHER CONDITIONS

Severe thunderstorms can bring lightning and floods. When there are threats of lightning avoid being the tallest object in the area. Take shelter under a grove of small trees, when in the forest. Stay away from telephone poles, single trees, hilltops, and small buildings out in the open. Crouch in a ravine if you cannot find appropriate shelter; do not lie flat. Stay away from your metal equipment, such as camera tripods, golf cubs, golf shoes, bicycles, and carts.

Flash floods, occurring easily in Arizona, are created from heavy rains sending water rushing down gullies, streams, and dry washes. Rivers, that are normally waterless during most of the year, can develop heavy currents and be life-threatening during heavy storms. It is possible to be camped in a low area and suddenly be washed away by the flood waters from a distant storm in the mountains. Take precautions by camping on high ground or moving quickly to high ground when there are flash flood warnings. Do not drive through already flooded areas. Do not wade through a rapidly flowing stream.

Dust storms, coming usually from the south, occur as thunderstorms pick up the dust of the desert. Visibility on the highway can be cut to almost zero causing hazardous driving. To prevent accidents take the following precautions. Turn on headlights and reduce speed, exit from the freeway as soon as possible, and pull off the roadway if visibility is very poor. Turn off your lights. Wait until the storm subsides before going on.

ENJOYING CACTI

The cactus flower is often quite beautiful and the cactus fruit can be an edible treat. These unique and beautiful plants, native to the southwest, can cause great pain to the unsuspecting visitor who gets too close. To protect yourself wear sturdy shoes and long pants when walking near cacti. Some respond to your closeness and their burrs seem to jump onto you. Never let the pets you are traveling with run free in the desert. A dog unfamiliar with cacti can panic and be covered with cacti burrs in a matter of seconds. Lift a cactus burr off with a fine tooth comb and remove any imbedded needles with tweezers. The needles can work their way deep under the skin.

AVOIDING VENOMOUS CREATURES

Scorpions, rattlesnakes, coral snakes, black widow spiders, and gila monsters are the most well-known venomous creatures found in Arizona. They can be avoided by learning about them.

Scorpions can be found under rocks near a lake, in the bark of certain trees, and in areas of new home construction where their nests have been disturbed. The most venomous scorpion makes its home in the bark of the cottonwood tree along river banks. To avoid scorpions, when camping or when in an old cabin, empty your shoes before putting them on. Also check your sleeping bag before crawling into it and never put your hand under a rock. Multiple scorpion stings can be dangerous to the average person and a single sting can be dangerous to a highly allergic person. Emergency treatment is to remain calm and seek medical attention as soon as possible.

Rattlesnakes begin coming out of hibernation in March to catch the warm sun. They will generally crawl away when they hear you coming but if they feel threatened they will sound their rattles and strike. During the summer they often lie in the shade of small bushes. Keep your eyes open and wear protective shoes or boots. If bitten by a rattlesnake, don't panic. Get medical attention as soon as possible. People rarely die from rattlesnake bites.

Arizona coral snakes, beautifully banded with red and black rings, are found in the southern half of the state. They spend most of their time in rodent burrows, come out mostly at night, and are quite venomous. If bitten, seek medical attention quickly.

Gila monsters are large, colorful, slow-moving lizards, who are quite venomous but will only hurt you if you back them into a corner and stick your hand in their mouth. If you see one, don't touch it. Just enjoy watching it as it slowly moves away.

Black widow spiders are found often around old buildings, wood piles, and gardens. They come out of hiding and sit in their strong messy webs in the evening, hoping to catch the bugs attracted by a nearby light. Avoid them by staying away from their webs and by wearing gloves when gardening or handling fire wood. A black widow bite can be serious to a small child. Multiple bites can be serious to the average person. A single bite may itch and become red and swollen a day after the bite occurs. Seek medical attention particularly if you are old, very young, allergic, or have some other medical condition.

Following pages: Western Diamondback Rattlesnake,
courtesy of Arizona-Sonora Desert Museum

NORTHERN
ARIZONA

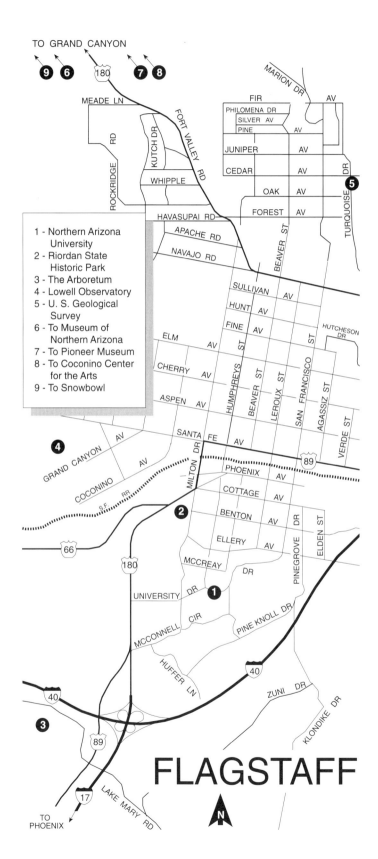

FLAGSTAFF

Historians generally agree that Flagstaff derived its name from a flag-raising ceremony held on the Fourth of July, 1876. New England settlers chose a tall pine, trimmed its branches, and attached a flag to the top, in observance of the nation's centennial. It is thought that the original flagstaff served as a trail marker for wagon trains headed west to California. Eventually the area evolved into the city of Flagstaff and the trail became the famous Route 66. After the Santa Fe railroad was laid, the Flagstaff population grew rapidly, and the town became an important lumbering center. Today, it is known for its fresh air, scientific community, cultural opportunities, and outdoor activities.

Flagstaff's popularity among tourists stems from its location—right in the center of well-preserved documents of history. The area around Flagstaff, the Colorado Plateau, was once largely populated by the Sinaguas (without water) which is evidenced by a large number of prehistoric ruins that have endured the travesty of time, weather, and explorers.

Another reason for its popularity is its elevation. Flagstaff is located at the base of the eroded crater rim of an extinct volcano in the Coconino National Forest, at an elevation of 7,000 feet. Mount Humphreys, formed by this volcano, is the highest point in Arizona and towers above Flagstaff at 12,643 feet. It is snow-capped most of the year.

The 50,000 residents enjoy a four-season climate with many days of sunshine. In winter, Flagstaff is popular for its cross-country and downhill skiing, snow tubing, sledding, and sled-dog races. *Winterfest*, occurring annually, provides excitement and entertainment for residents and visitors alike. Summer's special event is Flagstaff's *Festival of the Arts* which provides a month of cultural events among the cool pines. Flagstaff is a cool oasis for desert-valley dwellers. In addition to its recreational resources, the city is the home of Northern Arizona University, and is proud of cultural amenities uncommon in a community of its size.

Many visitors to northern Arizona use Flagstaff as their base from which to explore the many nearby attractions. After a busy day of sightseeing, the city provides excellent food and lodging.

For information call 1-800-842-7293 or 520-774-9541.

Following pages:: San Francisco Peaks towering above Flagstaff,
courtesy of Flagstaff Convention and Visitors Bureau

RIORDAN MANSION HISTORIC PARK

Successful turn-of-the-century businessmen in lumbering and merchandising, Timothy and Michael Riordan, constructed a forty-room mansion which was shared by their two families.

It was built of fieldstone and wooden siding. This large solid-looking structure stands today in the middle of a pine-shaded park in central Flagstaff, affording tourists the opportunity to catch a glimpse of how wealthy residents of the city lived during the early 1900s.

Inside the mansion the outstanding collection of American Craftsman furnishings helps you picture what life was like at that time. It becomes easy to feel that you have known the Riordan family, and to believe those who think they have seen a family ghost or two. Visitors are amazed at the early photographs sandwiched between glass window panes, and the book-lined living room with its light green porch swing. Numerous unique features make this house a memorable part of your visit to Flagstaff. The lower level of the house is accessible to the physically challenged. Popular tours are conducted a number of times each day. There is a small tour charge of $4.00 for adults. There is no admission charge for children eleven and under. It is recommended that you call ahead for tour reservations. The park is open daily from 8:00 A.M. to 5:00 P.M., May through September and from 11:00 A.M. to 5:00 P.M., October through April. The Visitor Center presents a slide show and caters to children by providing them with a touchable exhibit.

If you are traveling from Phoenix, take Interstate 17 north into Flagstaff to the junction with Interstate 40. Continue north on Milton Road to Chambers Drive and turn right. Turn left when you reach Riordan Ranch Street.

For information call 520-779-4395.

THE ARBORETUM AT FLAGSTAFF

The best place to learn about flora of this area is The Arboretum at Flagstaff. Occupying two hundred acres of ponderosa pine forest, high desert, and alpine tundra, The Arboretum provides visitors with the opportunity to wander through a large collection of wildflowers, grasses, trees, bushes, and other plants. This is an excellent place to view fall color changes.

Conservation of rare and endangered plants is one of the national programs The Arboretum supports. As a result, horticulture research is conducted on the outside acreage as well as inside the large horticulture center and greenhouse.

This is a place for relaxing, enjoying the beauty of nature, and enriching your appreciation of the Colorado Plateau region. The Arboretum is located four miles south of Highway 66 off Woody Mountain Road. Guided tours are available and admission is free. The Arboretum is open 10:00 A.M. to 3:00 P.M., Monday through Saturday and starting in May it is open from noon to 3:00 P.M. on Sunday.

For information call 520 -774-1442

LOWELL OBSERVATORY

A popular attraction near downtown Flagstaff is Lowell Observatory, on top of Mars Hill at an altitude of 7, 246 feet. Opened in 1894 by Boston businessman and scientist, Percival Lowell, for the purpose of studying Mars, it is considered the home of many scientific findings, including the 1930 discovery of the solar system's ninth planet, Pluto. The Lowell Observatory takes credit for first observations of the red shifts of galaxies, one of the findings that led to the theory of the expanding universe.

The observatory continues to be an active institution in astrophysics and solar system research. It is also active in providing programs for the public. The evening observing sessions have become increasingly popular with residents and tourists.

The Visitor Center houses Lowell's early astronomical equipment. It is open daily from noon to 5:00 P.M., April through October. *Night Sky* programs are Friday and Saturday evenings at 7:30 P.M. It is advisable to call ahead for current hours, tours, and programs. Adult admission is $3.50.

For information call 520-774-2096 or 520-774-3358.

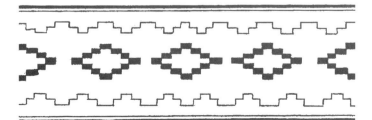

Drawing of Navajo sandpainting

MUSEUM OF NORTHERN ARIZONA

The internationally recognized Museum of Northern Arizona specializes in researching the Colorado Plateau—a massive land of river, rock, and sky. The Plateau encompasses northern Arizona and the Four Corners region including Grand Canyon, Bryce and Zion national parks as well as the Hopi and Navajo Indian reservations. The museum has comfortable study rooms and extensive resource materials.

Its outstanding educational programs and exhibits are devoted to geology, biology, anthropology, and fine arts of the area. An award winning exhibit, *Native Peoples of the Colorado Plateau*, documents twelve thousand years of human existence in that region, showing development from the Anasazi people to present day Native Americans. This is an exhibit that is well worth your time.

The museum honors the creativity of the Native American and builds its summer schedule to include Zuni, Hopi, and Navajo artist demonstrations and native dance performances. The demonstrations feature all phases of artistry in creating rugs, jewelry, fetishes, Kachina dolls, pottery, beadwork, silver-smithing, and more. We suggest you call to get the current schedule of demonstrations and exhibits.

For your enjoyment the museum provides a large selection of Indian arts and crafts, books, and other items in its gift shop. The museum is open from 9:00 A.M. to 5:00 P.M. daily. It is closed Thanksgiving, Christmas, and New Year's Day. Adult admission is $5.00 and admission for children under seven is free.

To reach the museum, drive three miles north from downtown Flagstaff on Highway 180 (Fort Valley Road).

For information call 520-774-5211.

Drawing of designs from a Hopi Shawl

Spotted Corn Kachina,
courtesy of Northern Arizona Museum

COCONINO CENTER FOR THE ARTS

The Coconino Center for the Arts, offers a variety of visual, performing, and literary arts programs. Folk, ethnic, classical, and jazz music, dance, and drama presentations are accommodated in the center's amphitheater.

The center annually offers eight art exhibitions in its four-thousand-square-foot gallery. Exhibits include contemporary and traditional fine arts and crafts in addition to reflecting the unique cultural heritage of northern Arizona. The nationally recognized show, *Trappings of the American West*, is the center's most popular event. It is a tribute to the life of the modern cowboy and spotlights arts and crafts by artists from the western United States and Canada.

The Gallery Shop offers unique handcrafted work including pottery, woodworking, jewelry, and wearable art.

The center is located off Fort Valley Road two miles west of Highway 180, north of Flagstaff. It is open Tuesday through Sunday from 10:00 A.M. to 5:00 P.M. Admission is free.

For information call 520-779-6921.

ARIZONA HISTORICAL SOCIETY
PIONEER MUSEUM

The museum is housed in a building which was constructed of volcanic cinder blocks in the very early 1900s. After serving as the County Hospital for a number of years, it became a boarding house and then the museum.

Inside you will find photographs, clothing, branding irons, etc. There is a special exhibit of Percival Lowell's memorabilia and relics of Emery Kolb, the Grand Canyon photographer. Outside the museum you will find three additional buildings which house examples of early transportation and provide a center for craft demonstrations.

If you are visiting in the winter months when the annual exhibit, *Playthings of the Past* is on display, you will relive your childhood memories of times when a little wooden train or doll provided all the happiness you needed.

Another memory-stirring attraction is the display of office and medical equipment used in the early days of Flagstaff. The museum's main goals are the preservation and interpretation of

early history of northern Arizona. Pioneer Museum is located north of Flagstaff off Highway 180, at 2340 N. Fort Valley Road. It is open from 9:00 A.M. to 5:00 P.M., Monday through Saturday. Closed Sunday, Thanksgiving, and Christmas. Admission is free.
   For information call 520-774-6272.

ADVENTURE TOURS FROM FLAGSTAFF

Enjoy this beautiful land. Get out into it. Here we suggest a few of the many opportunities to take tours, experience a white-water river trip, backpack the Grand Canyon, or participate in an archaeological expedition.

MUSEUM OF NORTHERN ARIZONA VENTURES

Ventures groups are small and permit great interaction between participants and leaders. Participants are from diverse backgrounds, and each has come for a different reason. One of the joys of a Ventures trip is meeting new people and sharing experiences. Ventures trips can be a backpacking trip down into the Grand Canyon, a river rafting trip down one of several beautiful rivers, a day hike, a houseboat adventure, the opportunity to meet with Native American artisans, to explore Indian ruins, and much more. Some trips are almost a week long and range in price. The trips take place at various times during the year. For information and registration write to Museum of Northern Arizona Ventures, *Attn: Education Department, Route 4, Box 720, Flagstaff, AZ 86001.*
   Call 520-774-5213, ext. 203.

HITCHIN POST STABLES

The whole family can enjoy horseback riding through beautiful scenery around Flagstaff participating in trail rides that range from one to four hours into Fay Canyon and to the mouth of Walnut Canyon. There are rides taking you a greater distance through gorgeous country where you might see Arizona wildlife. The horse's temperament will be matched to your riding skills. In the wintertime delight in a horse-drawn sleigh ride. Hitchin Post Stables is located at 448 Lake Mary Road.
   For information call 520-774-1719.

Downhill at Snowbowl

ARIZONA SNOWBOWL

Explore the San Francisco Peaks and the Snowbowl, in winter and summer, for plenty of adventure for the whole family. In winter (mid–December through mid–April), skiing, snowmobiling, and other snow sports are very popular with tourists and residents. In summer, the Scenic Skyride transports you to the top of Agassiz Peak from where you can see the Grand Canyon. A hike back down makes for a great day in outdoor Arizona.

The Snowbowl is located seven miles north of Flagstaff off Highway 180.

For information call 520-779-1951.

SKIING

There are many miles of trails for both down-hill and cross-country skiers. From Christmas to mid–March you can enjoy the crisp snow and usually sunny weather as you explore the scenery of northern Arizona. Ask about participating in special events. Your skiing adventure begins when you contact:

Flagstaff Nordic Center at *520-779-1951*
Mormon Lake Ski Center at *520-354-2240*
Ski Chalet in Phoenix at *602-955-3939*

Biking around Flagstaff, courtesy of Flagstaff Convention and Visitors Bureau

HIKING AROUND FLAGSTAFF

Flagstaff is completely surrounded by the woods, meadows lakes, and canyons of the Coconino National Forest. Pleasant weather and the change of seasons encourage people to get out to enjoy the hiking opportunities provided by more than 320 miles of trails. The San Francisco Peaks, standing tall above Flagstaff, offer all-season beauty for visitors to enjoy, and trails to challenge any hiker. In September and early October enjoy the glorious fall colors of aspen groves, sumac, oak, and other trees.

Humphreys Peak Trail. Four-and-a-half miles long one way, this is the most popular trail for hiking in the "Peaks" from June through September. The easy-to-follow trail is well marked and takes you to Humphreys Peak at an altitude of 12,643 feet, from which you will have a spectacular view of the Kachina Peaks Wilderness and northern Arizona. The trail begins at Snowbowl.

If you are not experienced in climbing at high altitudes, you may feel some discomfort. We caution you to stay on the trail and build fires only in existing fire rings—and only if necessary. Avoid hiking these mountains when there is danger of lightning. Be prepared for winds which traditionally blow through the San Francisco Peaks and, of course, take your own drinking water.

To reach the trailhead, take Highway 180 five miles north of

Flagstaff to the turnoff for the Snowbowl then drive eight miles to the upper lodge.

For information call 520-526-0866.

Snowbowl Scenic Skyride. During the summer months, you can enjoy a twenty-five minute ride to the top of the San Francisco Peaks in a chairlift which takes you to an elevation of 11,500 feet, providing magnificent scenery and enabling you to penetrate Humphreys Peak and Kachina trails at their highest altitude. Lunch is available at the lodge. Make sure you bring warm clothes and appropriate hiking shoes. The Snowbowl Scenic Skyride is open daily, 10:00 A.M. to 4:00 P.M. from mid–June until Labor Day.

For information call 520-779-1951.

Lockett Meadow. Glorious yellow colors of aspen leaves in the fall make this a very popular hike among photographers. Lockett Meadow, with an elevation of 8,000 feet, is a milder climb than Humphreys Peak, and gives you an opportunity to see the beautiful scenery of the San Francisco Peaks mountain range. To get there take the Sunset Crater National Monument turnoff and go past a cinder mine to the gravel road that winds up Sugar Loaf Mountain for four or five miles to the meadow.

WALNUT CANYON NATIONAL MONUMENT

One of the best preserved cliff dwellings of the Sinagua people can be viewed up close from the well maintained Island Trail. The trail leads you right into two-dozen ruins and often along the edge of a cliff. Well-preserved structures located under natural overhangs of limestone or sandstone enable you to admire the Sinaguas' advanced construction skills and imagine their lifestyle. The Sinagua closed off the exposed sides of their dwellings with stones and clay used as mortar. Originally three hundred rooms were built into the canyon walls and under the cliffs, with twenty-five rooms remaining today. As you stand in one of the rooms under the overhanging cliff and gaze across the canyon you can see the long-abandoned ruins of other dwellings tucked into crevices in the canyon walls. The 350-foot deep Walnut Canyon, created by the once-flowing water of Walnut Creek, sheltered a whole community of people who lived in family groups and farmed land along the canyon rim. For 150

Six thousand feet above the desert

years they lived a fairly tranquil lifestyle, farming, hunting, and gathering foods that grew naturally within the canyon.

The Visitor Center provides tourists with scientific information about the prehistoric Sinagua people, and displays original pottery and artifacts. For those of you who want to enrich your knowledge of the first residents of this area, there is a good selection of written material that you may purchase. From the Visitor Center you descend about 250 steps to the trail. There are handrails and places to rest, which are appreciated for the uphill climb back out.

The monument is open from 8:00 A.M. to 5:00 P.M. September through May, and from 8:00 A.M. to 6:00 P.M. June through August. It is closed on Christmas. There is an admission charge of $3.00 per person. The monument is located off Interstate 40, ten miles east of Flagstaff.

For information call 520-526-3367.

Ancient Sinagua dwellings in Walnut Canyon

SUNSET CRATER NATIONAL MONUMENT

When this volcano erupted more than nine hundred years ago, spewing ash for eight hundred square miles, it drove away the Sinagua people. The dark red cinder cone, formed as a result of the eruption, stands more than 1,000 feet high and was named Sunset Crater by John Wesley Powell, the Colorado River navigator. Sometimes the red cinder appears to be on fire because its color is so bright in the light of the setting sun. The Hopi have attached importance to the crater by believing the wind god, Yaponcha and friendly Kana'a spirit live there.

A sight almost more interesting than the crater itself is the vast area of lava flow, solidified into black motionless rivers. Rugged layers give an excellent picture of the catastrophic effects of volcanic eruptions—the incredible power of the massive lava flow destroying everything in its path. Today this peaceful monument of nature's power, sporadically colored with golden aspen trees is a beautiful sight. In 1930, a motion picture company planned to create a landslide by dynamiting the cinder cone. The protests of local citizens put a stop to this and the crater

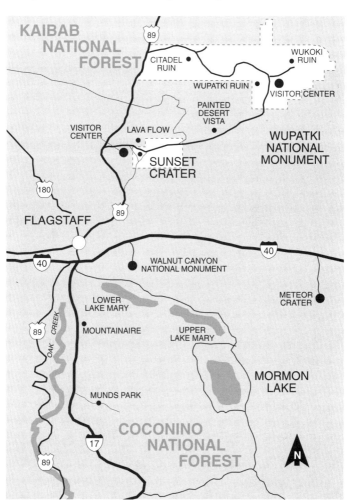

gained federal protection. Sunset Crater is located fifteen miles northeast of Flagstaff off Highway 89, and is open from 8:00 A.M. to 5:00 P.M. daily in winter, and 8:00 A.M. to 6:00 P.M. daily in summer, closed Christmas and New Year's Day.

For information call 520-526-0502.

WUPATKI NATIONAL MONUMENT

Of all the ruins of our ancient people, Wupatki is one of the most interesting. It is four stories high and once housed one hundred twenty-five people in one hundred rooms. The rear ballcourt proves that life was not all work for the Sinagua who lived here.

There are many ancient, red sandstone ruins in the 35,693-acre National Monument. In 1064 the volcanic eruption of Sunset Crater forced the inhabitants to evacuate, but they returned a few decades later after discovering that the volcanic ash had made the ground more fertile. The Sinagua left the area again in the late 1200s. Some Hopi may have lived there later, because present-day Hopi consider Wupatki to be an ancestral home.

You will want to spend most of the day seeing as many ruins as you can. They are especially picturesque in early morning or late afternoon light.

The ruins are located thirty miles north of Flagstaff off

Remains of Sinagua civilization - Wupatki National Monument

Highway 89 and are open 8:00 A.M. to 5:00 P.M. September through May, and 8:00 A.M. to 6:00 P.M. June through August. The monument is closed on Christmas Day. Admission is $3.00 per person and includes admission to Sunset Crater.

For information call 520-556-7040.

CAMERON TRADING POST

One of the few remaining authentic trading posts in the Southwest, Cameron which was established in 1890, has remained a trade center where Indians exchange items for merchandise. There are handmade items for sale. The trading post is located fifty-two miles north of Flagstaff off Highway 89.

For information call 520-679-2231.

GRAND CANYON DEER FARM

Children of all ages have a great time being in close contact with deer, goats, llamas, buffalos, antelopes, peacocks, and many other animals, which they can hand-feed and pet.

Grand Canyon Deer Farm was opened to the public in 1969 and currently has about 44,000 visitors each year. The farm is designed to allow people to mingle with these friendly animals. In June and July when fawns are born, the frisky deer babies are

Llama snow games at Flagstaff Winter Festival,
courtesy of Flagstaff Convention and Visitors Bureau

seen throughout the park. You may even see one being born.

The privately owned and very well-maintained park provides a fun-filled time for the family. For many people a visit to the Deer Farm is the high point of their trip. The park, is open from 10:00 A.M. to 5:00 P.M. in winter, 8:00 A.M. to 7:00 P.M. in summer, and closed Thanksgiving and Christmas Day. It is located twenty-five miles west of Flagstaff off Interstate 40. Use exit 171 at Deer Farm Road. If you are coming from Williams, it is only eight miles east. Adult admission is $5.50.

For information call 520-635-4073.

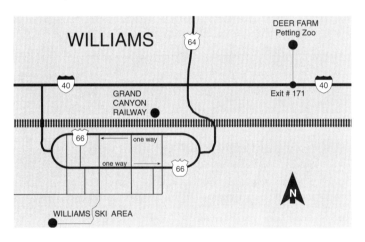

WILLIAMS

Located in the Kaibab National Forest, at an elevation of 6,780 feet, Williams attracts cross-country and downhill skiers and is still considered the gateway to the Grand Canyon.

Williams, founded in 1880 and named after a famous trapper, scout, and mountain man, became the last Route 66 town in America to be bypassed by Interstate 40. The main street in town, now Bill Williams Avenue, was the famous Route 66 and is still lined with buildings from that era. During the days when the Grand Canyon Line transported millions of passengers, including celebrities, presidents, and kings to the canyon, Williams was a prospering community, full of excitement and color. Today the city of Williams, with its population of a few thousand is listed on the National Register of Historic Places. It is also the starting point for outdoor activities such as skiing, and horseback riding.

For information call 520-635-4061.

SYCAMORE CANYON

When you are in Williams you may want to take advantage of horseback rides provided by Perkins Outfitters into nearby Sycamore Canyon. A veteran of Arizona's trails, knowledgeable of Arizona history, and fun-to-be-with professional guide, will take you to remote areas of unforgettable beauty. One mile wide and two thousand feet deep, the canyon surprises viewers with its awesome gamut of colors and rugged maze of unusual rock formations. The canyon is remarkably beautiful and accessible only to hikers and horseback riders. There are a variety of tours from which to choose depending on your capability and the time you have to spare.

For information call 520-635-9349.

GRAND CANYON RAILWAY

A large, black steam locomotive pulling old-fashioned passenger cars filled with a happy crowd, huffs and puffs its way for a sixty-four mile trip to the Grand Canyon. This passenger line began service in 1901 and functioned until 1968. Recently restored and reopened, the Grand Canyon Railway serves as a popular attraction among Arizona residents as well as tourists. Uniformed train conductors and the brick platform add to the nostalgia. Memories come flooding back when the older folk

Boarding the Grand Canyon train,
courtesy of Flagstaff Convention and Visitors Bureau

board the train. It is a wonderful opportunity for grandparents to pass on old family stories of train rides. The sightseeing is enjoyable for everyone as they are pulled along behind the hissing and chugging old engine No. 18. There are several renovated passenger coaches, which provide an historic ambiance, and add to the comfort of the passengers. The Railway combines a taste of history with sightseeing and entertainment.

The day-long trip takes you through scenic arroyos, grassy plains, and ponderosa pines to the south rim of the Grand Canyon. When the train arrives at the canyon, one of the world's seven great natural wonders, you will be awed by a view that is two billion years old. Passengers have four hours to explore the south rim attractions before boarding the train for a relaxing trip back to Williams.

The Grand Canyon Railway Museum, located in the Williams Depot, offers a wonderful exhibit and information about early railway transportation through the Old West, as well as ranching, logging, and mining artifacts. There is also the Indian Room Gallery, snack bar, and gift shop.

It is suggested that you call for reservations to secure a seat. The train runs on Fridays, Saturdays, and Sundays. It pulls out of Williams at 9:30 A.M. and returns at 5:30 P.M. Williams is located just off Interstate 40, thirty-two miles west of Flagstaff at exit 163. The adult fare is $60.35, child fare is $27.15.

For reservations and information call 1-800-843-8724

Grand Canyon Railway's vintage steam train,
courtesy of Flagstaff Convention and Visitors Bureau

GRAND CANYON NATIONAL PARK

The Grand Canyon was unknown to European explorers until Indians led the Coronado Expedition there in 1540. What they saw was the results of the Colorado River having cut through the Colorado Plateau for millions of years. They saw an incredible mixture of colored layers of time embedded in rock. The rainbow-like appearance and incredible depth of the mile-deep canyon makes an unforgettable impression on any viewer. It took nature two billion years to carve the 273 mile-long and ten mile-wide spectacle.

Possession of the Grand Canyon by the white man passed from Spain to Mexico when Mexico won its independence in 1821, and then to the United States in 1848 at the end of the Mexican War. Exploration was accomplished in bits and pieces by traders and fur trappers until in 1869, John Wesley Powell documented the whole canyon as he traveled its length by boat.

At first, entrepreneurs tried to exploit the canyon for mining purposes; but natural difficulties and increasing popularity of the site caused them to abandon the idea of mining, and become tourist hosts. In 1885 they developed a trail to the bottom of the canyon and built a primitive hotel.

Not much has changed since then except increased and improved facilities. Grand Canyon Village, off Highway 64, is the best place to begin your exploration of the canyon. The village is located at the south rim of the canyon, open year round, and visited each year by more than four million people from all over the world. Inside the village there are comfortable accommodations and the Visitor Center with a museum and ranger programs detailing every aspect of the Grand Canyon.

Bright Angel Trail originates here and leads you to Phantom Ranch at the bottom of the canyon. Hiking into and out of the canyon is physically demanding; however, mules can be rented to ride or to carry your backpack.

There are many other attractions and ways to view the canyon. You can rent a plane and view it from the air or join a white-water rafting excursion. These activities and lodging require advance reservations. If you visit for just a few hours, you can see the canyon from several vantage points and take photographs along short trails at the rim of the canyon. For an

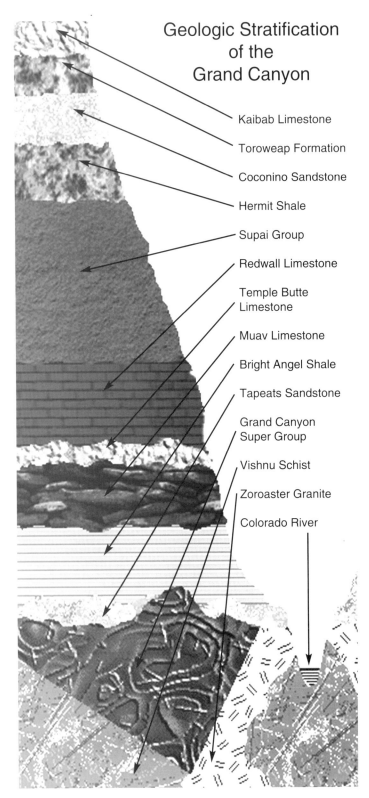

Geologic Stratification of the Grand Canyon

Kaibab Limestone

Toroweap Formation

Coconino Sandstone

Hermit Shale

Supai Group

Redwall Limestone

Temple Butte Limestone

Muav Limestone

Bright Angel Shale

Tapeats Sandstone

Grand Canyon Super Group

Vishnu Schist

Zoroaster Granite

Colorado River

Preceding pages: Oil painting, "Moran Point" by Charles Pabst

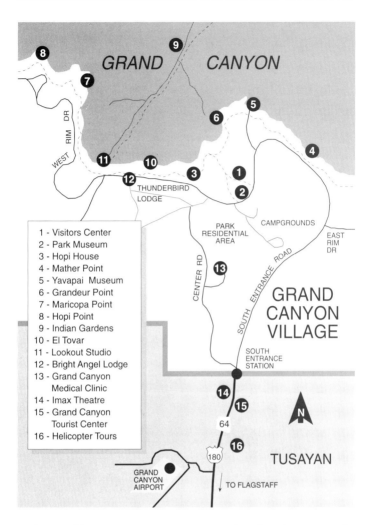

1 - Visitors Center
2 - Park Museum
3 - Hopi House
4 - Mather Point
5 - Yavapai Museum
6 - Grandeur Point
7 - Maricopa Point
8 - Hopi Point
9 - Indian Gardens
10 - El Tovar
11 - Lookout Studio
12 - Bright Angel Lodge
13 - Grand Canyon
       Medical Clinic
14 - Imax Theatre
15 - Grand Canyon
       Tourist Center
16 - Helicopter Tours

unforgettable experience we recommend seeing the canyon in the sunset light which is spectacular as the light comes across the flat surface of the plateau with no obstructions.

The north rim, which you can see a few miles across the canyon, can be reached by driving two hundred miles on the National Scenic Byway which takes you through the northern part of the national forest. When you reach the north rim you are one thousand feet higher. The north rim Visitor Center is open from the middle of May to the first heavy snowfall. It offers visitors excellent camping facilities and hiking trails as well as many remarkable canyon views. Because of the higher elevation the park offers cross-country skiing.

Desert View and Watchtower can be reached by the twenty-six mile-long East Rim Drive originating from Grand Canyon Village on the south rim. At the upper end of the canyon the river is more visible because the canyon is not as deep. From the tower you can see in all directions and enjoy the colorful scenery of the desert as well as different views of the canyon. When you climb to the second level of the tower you will find unusual looking boxes called reflectoscopes which enable you see sections of the canyon reflected clearly on black mirrors.

If you are interested in nighttime accommodations, reserving an RV space, renting a mule or horse, or finding a kennel for your pet, call *520-638-2401*. If camping out is your interest, you must have a permit to camp over night. Call *520-638-2401*.

To reach the Grand Canyon, take Highway 64 near Williams or Highway 180 north out of Flagstaff.

For information call 520-638-2401.

GRAND CANYON IMAX THEATRE

The Grand Canyon IMAX Theatre, located off Highway 64 just south of the park entrance, offers you a truly memorable experience. *Grand Canyon - The Hidden Secrets* is shown 365 days a year, beginning at half-past the hour. Billed as the world's largest motion picture system, the film enables viewers to experience both the thunderous rapids of the mighty Colorado River, and the quiet solitude of Grand Canyon's most remote areas. See the ancient Indian inhabitants who were the first settlers in the canyon. See Don Garcia Lopez as he discovers this awesome vista in 1541, and join John Wesley Powell on his first exciting expedition through the Grand Canyon.

The IMAX film format used to create the spectacular saga, *Grand Canyon - The Hidden Secrets*, makes it possible for you to explore the inside of the canyon up close and in breathtaking detail from the comfort of your theatre seat. Hailed as one of the most innovative developments in film since its debut in 1970, the IMAX system uses state-of-the-art film technology to create an image of unsurpassed clarity and impact. The key is a seventy millimeter film frame that runs horizontally through the projector. This large film frame enhances the picture quality to a remarkable degree, allowing every detail to be savored. The pro-

Preceding pages: "Grand Canyon - The Hidden Secrets",
courtesy of IMAX Theatre

jection screen is eight times larger than conventional screens; a six-track sound system pinpoints the sound to its precise action area on the screen; fourteen speakers allow sound to move through and behind the audience. You will experience many awesome moments as you view the Grand Canyon through this spectacular film. We recommend you see the film before seeing the mighty canyon itself.

For information and reservations call 520-638-2468.

ADVENTURES AT THE GRAND CANYON

Papillon Grand Canyon Helicopters offers you that special opportunity to see down into the canyon and to reflect on man's relationship with nature. Every year more than 100,000 canyon visitors enjoy this breathtaking experience. Large flat windows allow for great photographic moments to be effectively recorded through the glass. Your flight options range from a thirty-minute flight over the canyon to an overnight visit to the beautiful Havasupai Canyon. The Papillon Heliport is located three miles south of Grand Canyon's south entrance and one mile north of Grand Canyon National Airport off Highway 64.

For information call 520-638-2419 or 1-800-528-2418.

Kenai Helicopters fly you over gorges and red canyon walls of astonishing beauty. Hover near canyon walls that tell a story of history as you absorb the magic of the Grand Canyon.

For information call 1-800-541-4537.

Wilderness River Adventures. Try an easy twelve-mile floating trip, a five-day motorized raft adventure, or a rugged twelve-day oar-powered raft excursion down the Colorado River through the Grand Canyon. The trip combines water sport excitement with beautiful and memorable scenery.

For information call 1-800-992-8022.

Outdoor Adventure River Specialists (O.A.R.S.) offers a variety of river rafting trips on the Colorado River through the Grand Canyon. O.A.R.S. provides a great number of trips throughout the year which makes it convenient to fit one into your vacation schedule. Excursions vary in length from five days to two-and-a-half weeks and vary in degree of difficulty. For all trips it is necessary to be physically fit.

For information call 209-736-4677 or 736-2924.

Following pages: Oil painting, "Zoroaster Temple at Sunset" by Thomas Moran, courtesy of the Phoenix Art Museum

Windrock Aviation, Inc. Enjoy the Grand Canyon through a scenic airplane tour from Grand Canyon Airport or Bullhead City/Laughlin. The tour can be personalized for two or a group.
For information call 1-800-247-6259.

Airstar Helicopters Airlines. This owner-operated company specializing in personal service provides spectacular canyon flights. Located at Grand Canyon National Park Airport.
For information call 1-800-962-3869.

Air Grand Canyon provides guaranteed window seats, pilot narration, and video hook ups. Located at the main terminal of the Grand Canyon Airport.
For information call 520-638-2686

For information and phone numbers of other companies offering adventure opportunities call the Grand Canyon Chamber of Commerce at *520-638-2901* or the Arizona Office of Tourism at *602-542-8687.*

HAVASUPAI INDIAN RESERVATION

On the west end of the Grand Canyon, down a steep switch-back trail into Hualapai Canyon and then along the trail eight miles through the scenic gorge, you will come to Havasu Canyon. This is the only access to the reservation other than by helicopter. Follow the trail along Havasu Creek until you come to Supai Village, home of many of the Havasupai Indians. A short distance past the village, Havasu Creek forms four beautiful waterfalls as it flows on toward the Colorado River. Each waterfall is unique in its beauty. Navajo Falls drops seventy-five feet. Havasu Falls spills over the edge to a depth of one hundred feet, filling turquoise pools formed by travertine deposits. Mooney Falls thunders to a depth of one hundred and ninety-six feet and Beaver Falls, the smallest of the four, splashes down to a depth of thirty feet. This remote paradise is home to three hundred members of the Havasupai Indian tribe who are quite protective of their canyon oasis. They live in surroundings of unique beauty with fragrant peach trees, sheltered by the red walls of the canyon. The Havasupai Indians ("people of the blue-green water") are known for their beadwork and basketry.

Because access to the canyon is limited to a specific number of visitors, you need to make reservations for hiking and camping. The usual trip is a day hiking in, a day enjoying the canyon, and a day hiking out. It is possible to rent a horse to ride in and out or to rent space on a mule to carry your backpack up the steep switchback trail.

Camping costs $9.00 per night, per person. No campfires or alcoholic beverages are allowed. Staying in the lodge costs $80.00 per room, per night, during April through October. From November through March it drops to $50.00. There is also a $12.00 admittance fee to the village. Spring and fall are the best times to make the eight-mile hike to the village. The campground is an additional two-mile hike beyond the village. Call at least several weeks in advance for reservations. It is possible to arrange for helicopter or horseback rides if you are not a hiker. The trailhead begins at Hualapai Hilltop which can be reached by taking Highway 18 about sixty-one miles northeast, off Highway 66.

For information call 520-448-2021.

KINGMAN

Kingman, an important crossroad, small trading center, and old mining town, was once a railroad camp named for Lewis Kingman, the engineer in charge of building the Santa Fe Railroad. Downtown Kingman has an historic area which includes several eighteenth and early nineteenth-century buildings which range in style from Victorian to adobe. One of the most interesting is the Bonelli Mansion furnished with unique luxury items.

The Mohave Museum of History and Art, located at 400 W. Beale Street, has an exhibit about the construction of nearby Hoover Dam. You'll enjoy the exhibit of carved turquoise from the days when Kingman was internationally known for high quality turquoise. In the Kingman area there are several ghost towns you may want to visit.

Kingman, located at the junction of Interstate 40 and Highways 68 and 93, a city of over twelve-thousand residents, is a convenient stopping place for motorists on their way to California or Las Vegas.

For information call 520-753-6106.

Following pages: Burro caravan carries supplies to the village of Supai.

A busy day in Oatman

OATMAN

Oatman, a worn out gold mining town begun in 1906, is now kept alive by friendly and determined residents. They concentrate on attracting visitors with the charm of the town and its shops. Many visitors, tiring of gambling in Laughlin, make a trip to Oatman to enjoy the atmosphere of this little town nestled among the hills, almost like an Alpine village.

The Oatman Hotel is known for its museum which is spread through its upstairs rooms. Room number fifteen is said to be where Clark Gable and Carol Lombard spent their wedding night. There is even one of her dresses left lying on the bed.

Oatman, a different kind of town, with its own sleepy character is situated at the base of the Black Mountains which give the town its uniquely charming appearance.

On your way to visit Oatman as you drive around a curve you might come upon a group of wild burros ambling down the road on their way into Oatman for their daily petting and hand

Burros greeting tourists near Oatman.

outs of food. If you stop to pet and photograph them. You will enjoy their docile friendliness.

The town is located on both sides of the winding, picturesque stretch of Route 66 south of Kingman.

For information call 520-753-6106.

CHLORIDE

Northwest of Kingman, on the way to Las Vegas via Highway 93, four miles east of Grasshopper Junction is a little town called Chloride. This semi-ghost town is active with residents who are business people, retirees, artists, writers, craft persons and musicians, choosing a slower lifestyle. It's an old town with a young spirit which is visible in studios and shops of the local artisans.

The original town was born in 1860 when silver was discovered. There were once fifty mines operating near Chloride. The mines are dead now, but the town survives. For a look back in time, take a peek at the Chloride Post Office which began service in 1871, making it the oldest continuously operated post office in Arizona.

Once Chloride had a population of several thousand which decreased steadily to less than fifty in 1949, but has grown again to a charming community of four hundred. In spite of its small size, Chloride has an active historical society, located in an old miner's shack, which takes care of several local landmarks including the old jail, the Jim Fritz Museum, and the Silverbelle Playhouse, which the residents bring to life with their performances, making Chloride a friendly and fun place to visit.

People are moving here to avoid crime, noise, and expense of the big cities. Some of these people might show you surrounding sites of old tombstones and rusted mining equipment.

For information call 520-753-6106.

BULLHEAD CITY / LAUGHLIN

Facing each other across the Colorado River, these two cities are as different as day and night. Bullhead city provides tourists with daytime activities such as water sports, fishing, and boating. But when night falls, the air glows and the river sparkles with a million reflected lights, inviting tourists to participate in the excitement of pulsating casinos. Laughlin entertains crowds from both sides of the river. You can park your car on the Arizona side and enjoy the ferry ride to the night spots built along the river's shoreline, or you can drive over the new bridge and park in the crowded parking lots around each casino. Laughlin provides tourists with an opportunity to engage in gambling activities without going to Las Vegas, which saves several hours of driving time and provides a casual atmosphere.

Bullhead City, with a population of 22,000, is built mainly along Highway 95, next to the river. Begun in 1945 as a construction camp for Davis Dam, it was a relatively poor community until Laughlin attracted more tourists to the area. Nearby is Lake Mohave, formed by Davis Dam, with its wonderful opportunities for boating and fishing. Bullhead City is your headquarters for getting boats and bait.

There are motels and plenty of fast food establishments along the highway going through Bullhead City, which is located thirty miles west of Kingman and sixty miles north of Lake Havasu City. From Phoenix, take Highway 89 through Sun City to Kingman and then Highway 68 to Bullhead City.

For information call 520-754-4121 (Bullhead City)
or 1-800-227-5245 (Laughlin)

LAKE HAVASU CITY

London Bridge—the real London Bridge—is here in Arizona, purchased in 1964 by Robert McCulloch, founder of Lake Havasu City. The bridge was reassembled block-by-block and now spans an inlet of the Colorado River. This impressive structure is beautiful when bathed in evening lights. The bridge is an added attraction to an already popular city, a city known for its water sports, numerous hotels, motels, and English-themed shops. Forty-five miles of clear blue water provide a wonderful opportunity to boat and water ski. This is a recreational paradise for twenty-four thousand residents and thousands of visitors that come here each year. Enjoy a boat ride under the bridge and down the river. When you're not on the water you can be exploring nearby ghost towns, hiking in the surrounding desert or to Crosman Peak. If you're more adventuresome, you can take part

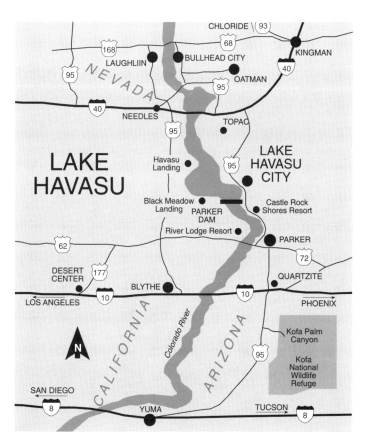

English Village near London Bridge

in a four-wheel-drive vehicle adventure tour conducted by a guide who will tell you about the flora, fauna, and history of the area. You will see places not accessible from the main roads. You may want to visit Parker Dam which forms Lake Havasu and hike in Buckskin Mountain State Park about twelve miles south of the city. North of the city lies the Havasu National Wildlife Refuge, a place to see bighorn sheep. If you are lucky, you will catch a glimpse of the giant tarantulas, desert tortoises, and red-tailed hawks found in this area during the spring and summer months. To reach Lake Havasu City travel Highway 95 along the western edge of Arizona.

For information call 1-800-242-8278.

Drawing of Anasazi art

HOOVER DAM

In the northwest corner of Arizona, separating two lakes, lies almost four-and-a-half million cubic yards of concrete formed into a majestic monument to human ingenuity, Hoover Dam, built between 1931 and 1936. The construction provided much needed employment for thousands of men during the great depression. Once known as Boulder Dam, it is the highest dam made of concrete in the Western Hemisphere, producing electricity for nearby Las Vegas and California. Its impressive size, 660 feet thick at the base and forty-five feet thick at the top, allows plenty of room for Highway 93. The dam stands 726 feet high and stretches 1,244 feet along its crest.

Most of the visitors are quite surprised at its architecture and artistic detail. The whole picture is a spectacular example of cooperation between man and nature. The massive structure was designed to last two thousand years, but the architects were unique in also caring about its outside appearance. When you're there, you will notice the Art Deco-style copper doors, fluted intake columns, ornate grill work, and sleek statues. Hoover Dam serves a double function by providing electricity to Las Vegas and Los Angeles and by being a one-of-a-kind tourist attraction.

Visitors can descend into the dam via elevators, be guided through its insides, and are allowed to see giant generator rooms where millions of kilowatts of hydroelectric power serve Nevada, Arizona, and southern California. For most of the visitors this is an extraordinary experience. Each year millions of people find it convenient to take the tour because the busy Highway 93 to Las Vegas runs right across the top of Hover Dam. On the Nevada side of the dam,recently constructed, is the world's largest and most costly Visitor Center. It will provide tourists with restaurants, plenty of parking, and most important, a spectacular view of the massive concrete wedge of the outlet side of the dam.

The dam is open for visitors daily from 8:00 A.M. to 5:45 P.M., except Thanksgiving and Christmas. The admission fee is $8.00 for adults. Children less than six are free. The extensive hard-hat tours are $25.00.

For information call 702-293-8367

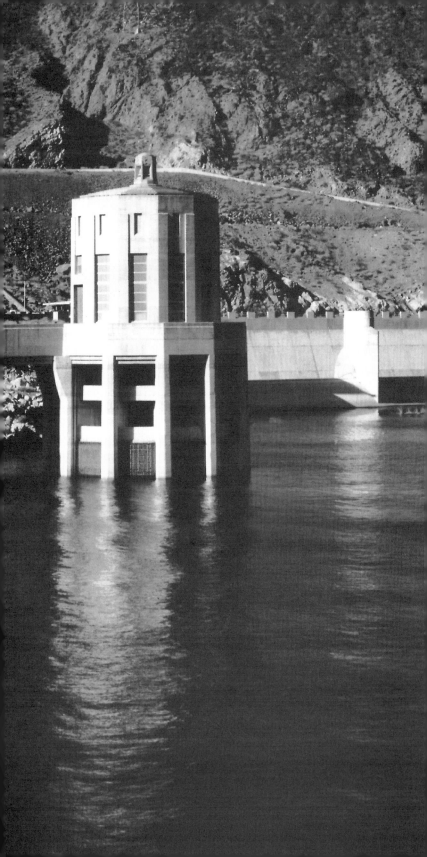

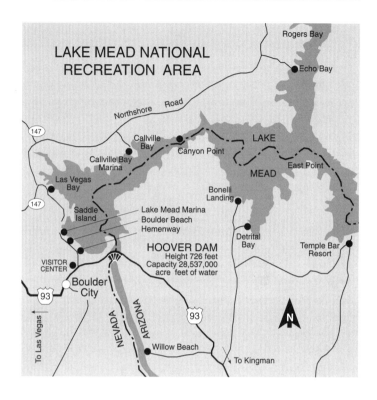

LAKE MEAD NATIONAL RECREATION AREA

Above Hoover Dam lies 110-mile long Lake Mead, the largest man-made reservoir in the U.S., and below is 67-mile long Lake Mohave. Together there are 822 miles of shoreline for boaters to explore. Water from Lake Mead irrigates rich farmland and helps cities as far away as Los Angeles and San Diego stay green and provide water for their people.

You will find nine developed recreational sites in addition to the sandy swimming beaches and picnic areas scattered along the shore. There are free launching ramps and marinas from which to rent boats. These lakes form a water playground in the middle of the desert for waterskiers, fishermen, sailors, and houseboaters. Lake Mead has an average depth of 280 feet of cool clear water which makes an ideal environment for scuba diving. The many coves and canyons provide uncrowded areas to explore. At night on a houseboat, away from the city lights, the stars appear larger and surprising in their number.

Fishing is excellent on both lakes. Fishermen on Lake Mead

Hoover Dam intake columns

catch largemouth bass, crappie, sunfish, and channel catfish. The heat of the sun brings striped bass to the top in summer and fall. Most fishermen also enjoy camping.

Temple Bar is one camping area on the Arizona side of the lake which offers 153 units for tent and trailer camping. Call *520-767-3401* for reservations. For RV camping at the resort at Temple Bar call *520-767-3400*. For camping with trailers and tents at Gregg's Hideout and Pierce Ferry call *520-564-2220*. There is camping with no facilities at Bonelli Landing. Call *520-767-3401*.

In addition to camping, fishing, and boating activities, the Lake Mead area is within easy reach of Las Vegas, Bullhead City, Laughlin, and Kingman. Camp or set up your RV near Lake Mead and then venture out to enjoy the top-rated entertainment, nightlife, and glitter of Las Vegas. The more informal atmosphere of Laughlin lets you enjoy glitter, gambling, and entertainment where the casino's are close together along the river's edge. Venture into Bullhead City for fast food dining and shopping for fishing tackle and bait. Nearby Kingman meets your needs for food, clothing, gasoline, and more. Take a break from your water activities to enjoy Kingman's historic sites and museum.

For information about recreation on Lake Mead and Lake Mohave, call Boulder City, NV at 702-293-8906.

Ferry on Lake Mead   *Banana Yucca blooming in the desert*

METEOR CRATER

An unusual site near Flagstaff, visited annually by hundreds of thousands of people from all over the world, is Meteor Crater.

Almost fifty thousand years ago, a giant meteoric mass plunged to Earth at the speed of 45,000 miles per hour, creating a crater almost a mile in diameter and 570 feet deep. The crater is wide enough at its base to accommodate twenty football fields. This gaping hole in the ground is the best preserved meteor site in the world.

You will look in wonder from the observation decks as you try to imagine this incredible force of nature, this giant mass of iron and nickel weighing millions of tons, crashing to Earth.It is thought that any living creatures in this area disappeared because of the impact and the gaseous cloud created by the explosion.

You will want to take advantage of the self-guided tour of exhibits and video presentations, detailing the role the crater plays in the study of space and earth sciences and the devastation that was caused by the impact. The crater's moon-like terrain was used by NASA as a training ground for the Apollo astronauts. The Museum of Astrogeology offers interesting material to satisfy your curiosity about this natural phenomenon. It is easily accessible from Interstate 40, just thirty-six miles east from Flagstaff. Open from 8:00 A.M. to 5:00 P.M. in the winter and from 6:00 A.M. to 6:00 P.M. in the summer. Adult admission is $8.00.

For information call 520-289-2362.

PETRIFIED FOREST NATIONAL PARK

The result of petrification, a fascinating process of nature, is observed in the incredible sights of trees turned to stone. Petrified Forest National Park is one of the few places on Earth that provides us with such a spectacle of time and nature. Beautiful layers of muted red, yellow, green, blue, and black make up the rings of these stone trees, once tall and pine-like, sheltering early dinosaurs.

Through years of climactic changes and the effects of minerals on the fallen trees, the wood turned to stone. First, the trees were buried under water, mud, and volcanic ash and later, they were pushed to the surface where they were exposed to wind and rain. The process is still occurring, as gradually more of the buried fossils and petrified wood are being exposed to nature's elements. You will see many long logs and many broken logs. You may touch and photograph them but may not remove any pieces from the grounds. You can buy petrified wood souvenirs from nearby shops.

Ancient Indians used this wood-turned-to-stone to make tools and arrowheads and as building material. An Indian legend tells the story of a giant monster, named Yietso, who was killed by their ancestors when they first migrated to this area. Yietso's bones turned into these magnificent stones. There are petroglyphs and Indian ruins which were built with petrified wood within easy walking distance from the main trail.

Petrified Forest can be reached from either Highway 180 or Interstate 40. Eastbound visitors should enter the park at the south entrance via Highway 180 from Holbrook, then travel north through the park, exiting eastbound on Interstate 40. Westbound visitors should use the north entrance off Interstate 40, proceed south through the park to Highway 180, to Holbrook

A magnificent piece of petrified wood lying by the side of the road

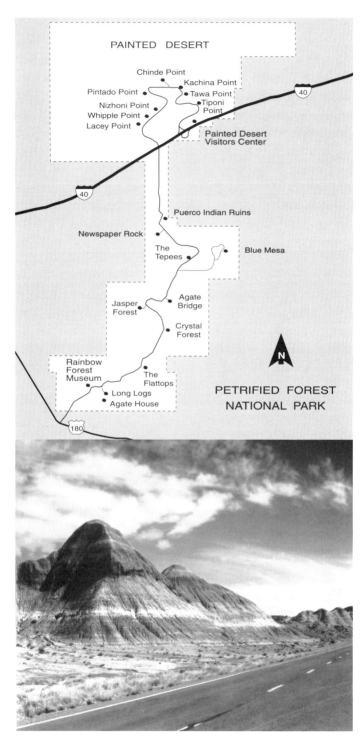

PAINTED DESERT

Chinde Point
Kachina Point
Pintado Point
Tawa Point
Nizhoni Point
Tiponi Point
Whipple Point
Lacey Point

Painted Desert Visitors Center

40

40

Puerco Indian Ruins

Newspaper Rock

Blue Mesa

The Tepees

Agate Bridge

Jasper Forest

Crystal Forest

N

Rainbow Forest Museum

The Flattops

PETRIFIED FOREST
NATIONAL PARK

Long Logs
Agate House

180

Driving through the Painted Desert

and Interstate 40. The park is open daily except Christmas from 8:00 A.M. to 6:00 P.M. There is an admission fee of $10.00 per vehicle. This is good for the Petrified Forest and.the Painted Desert. *For information call 520-524-6228.*

PAINTED DESERT

Another attraction in the same park is the intensely colored Painted Desert. Our curiosity was aroused by photographers directing their cameras toward the sky. When we looked, we noticed the rosy clouds which were beautifully colored by light reflected from the desert. We too used our cameras to record this unusual sight. This phenomenon appears above the Painted Desert because of the density and luminosity of its colors. The Painted Desert Visitors Center offers geologic explanations for the petrified logs and rainbow-colored land formations. The center also provides information about the dinosaurs unearthed in this area of Arizona. You can view this land of contrasts by driving the paved trail as it winds along the Painted Desert rim between Tawa Point and Kachina Point. The Painted Desert Park is open from 8:00 A.M. to 6:00 P.M. daily.

For information call 520-524-6228.

HIKING TRAILS IN THE
PETRIFIED FOREST AND PAINTED DESERT

Long Log Trail. Almost a mile long, this trail leads you to the largest conglomeration of petrified wood in the world. It is a relaxing and picturesque trail guiding you through colorful logs of stone, some of which are over 150 feet long.

Blue Mesa Trail. Unearthly-like surroundings of colorful clay hills make this an extraordinary hike through beauty caused by the process of erosion.

Agate House Trail. This short trail leads to the original petrified wood Indian dwellings. Two rooms have been restored and provide a unique example of Indian resourcefulness.

Painted Desert Hikes. You may choose one of several trails leading through beautiful uneven terrain with spires and pedestals silhouetted against the sky. You will be surprised to see so many people there with their cameras.

WINDOW ROCK

Window Rock, the Navajo Nation's tribal capital, was started as a Navajo administration center in 1934. It is near the Window Rock Monument sculpted by winds blowing against Kayenta sandstone for millions of years, creating a unique natural arch. The town sits at the crossroads of Highway 264 and Route 12.

The Navajo Tribal Museum has exhibits showing the evolution of inhabitants of this area from A.D. 50, including the development of silversmithing and contemporary life. The largest collection of Navajo arts and crafts on the reservation is offered at the Navajo Arts and Crafts Center. You will also enjoy the Zoological Park with a closeup view of rattlesnakes, tarantulas, scorpions, and some southwestern mammals.

A stop in Window Rock provides an excellent introduction to the Navajo Indian history and culture, before you go further into the reservation.

For information call 520-871-6436 or 871-7371.

GANADO
AND THE HUBBELL TRADING POST

On the way to Canyon de Chelly, stop at the town of Ganado and the currently active Hubbell Trading Post which was built in the 1870s by John Lorenzo Hubbell. The original building is still intact, and if you walk inside you will see things much as they were years ago. There are shelves full of canned goods, flour, candy, and sugar. You will see Indian baskets hanging from the

Tarantulas on the move,
courtesy of Willis Peterson

A step back in time -
Hubbell Trading Post barn

ceiling. Navajo rugs and blankets, traded for food and supplies, are displayed for sale. The whole scene is reminiscent of more active trading days. The trading post was the only connection between Indians and the white man's world.

If you peek inside the large doors of the next building you will catch a glimpse of history preserved by the rustic interior of the old barn with its relics untouched for many years. The small, sturdily built supply wagon on display outside the trading post was used to transport goods between Ganado and Hubbell's other smaller trading posts. The wagon's authenticity attracts curious sightseers who, while appreciating its historic quality, preserve the image with their cameras.

The trading post is open from 8:00 A.M. to 5:00 P.M. October through April and from 8:00 A.M. to 6:00 P.M. May through September. It is closed Thanksgiving, Christmas, and New Year's Day. The Navajo reservation does observe daylight savings time.

The town of Ganado and the Hubbell Trading Post are about thirty miles west of Window Rock off Highway 264. *For information call 520-755-3475.*

Original prisoner's wagon

PROTOCOL
FOR VISITING INDIAN RESERVATIONS

Indian communities, historically called reservations, are self-governed entities. The Native American Tourism Center requests that visitors remember they are guests on private land and that they observe the following rules of reservation protocol:

1. Respect the privacy and customs of native people.
2. Enter home areas only upon invitation.
3. Do not wander across residential areas or disturb property.
4. Do not wander on or into ceremonial areas.
5. Check with tribal officials before taking pictures and obtain permission before taking pictures of the people.
6. Do not disturb artifacts, rocks, plants, or animals. Tribal antiquity and federal laws are in effect.
7. Possession/consumption of alcoholic beverages or illegal drugs is prohibited.
8. A permit is required for fishing in any lakes or streams or hunting for game on lands under the jurisdiction of each reservation.
9. Reservation's Tribal Code prohibits the use of firearms or fireworks.
10. Stay on designated trails or established routes.
11. Off-road travel: dune buggies, jeeps, and motorcycles are prohibited on back-country roads, as well as travel off established roads and trails by four-wheel-drive vehicles.
12. Rock climbing and off-trail hiking are prohibited.
13. Fires are permitted only on grills, fireplaces, or similar controlled devices. No open ground fires in campgrounds.
14. Keep all areas clean; do not litter; do not bury trash.
15. Appropriate (conservative) dress is requested.

ARIZONA INDIAN RESERVATIONS

Fourteen Indian tribes, representing nearly 160,000 people, are found within Arizona. Although they are distinct tribes with unique characteristics, they are all proudly united by their Indian heritage. Twenty reservations, covering more than nineteen million acres, tell the story of the Indian people—a people and culture that withstood the trials of time and shaped American history. It is an honorable and spirited story, woven into tapestries

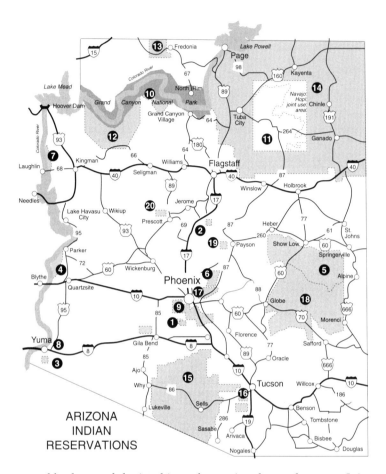

ARIZONA
INDIAN
RESERVATIONS

and baskets and depicted in sculpture, jewelry, and pottery. It is a story brought alive in Indian rodeos, ceremonies, and festivals.

Following is information about Arizona's Indian reservations, including location, attractions, addresses, and phone numbers for obtaining further information.

1. Ak-Chin Indian Community. Located fifty-six miles south of Phoenix, this reservation is home to almost 600 Native Americans. The tribally-owned farming enterprise is very successful. The tribe is noted for basketry. This community hosts Harrah's Ak-Chin Casino. *Ak-Chin Indian Community, 42507 Peters & Mall Rd., Maricopa, AZ 85239, 520-568-2618.*

2. Yavapai-Apache Nation. Approximately 1,400 Native Americans live here, ninety-four miles north of Phoenix. There are attractions, such as Indian ruins and the Yavapai-Apache Information Center which houses a tribal museum and arts and crafts. Other attractions are the well-known Montezuma Castle National Monument, Montezuma Well, hunting, hiking, fishing, and the Cliff Castle Casino. The tribe is noted for basketry. *Yavapai-Apache Indian Community, P.O. Box 1188, Camp Verde AZ 86322, 520-567-3649.*

3. *Cocopah Indian Tribes.* Twelve miles southwest of Yuma reside about 650 Cocopah Indians. A special attraction is the Heritage Art Museum with displays of cultural art including beadwork, traditional farming tools, hunting, recreational equipment, and mannequins in native dress. The tribe is noted for beadwork. They host the Cocopah Casino. *Cocopah Tribal Council, Bin "G", Somerton, AZ 85350, 520-627-2061*

4. *Colorado River Indian Tribes.* Almost 3,000 Native Americans live on this reservation, one hundred eighty-nine miles west of Phoenix. Attractions include one hundred miles of river frontage on both sides of the Colorado River. Lake Moovala is the home of famous speed boat races. There is an All-Indian Rodeo, Indian Day Celebration, Arts and Crafts Center and Museum, the Blue Water Casino, hunting, fishing, picnicking, and water sports. The tribe is noted for basketry and beadwork. *Colorado River Indian Tribes, Rt. 1, Box 23-B, Parker, AZ   85344, 520-669-9211.*

5. *White Mountain Apache Tribe.* Almost 10,000 people of Apache heritage reside one hundred ninety-four miles northeast of Phoenix. There are numerous attractions such as the tribally-owned and operated Apache Sunrise Resort, Hon Dah Casino, annual rodeo and fair on Labor Day weekend, ceremonials, camping, fishing, skiing, horseback riding, and hiking. The tribe is noted for basketry, burden baskets, and beadwork. *White Mountain Apache Tribe, P.O. Box 700, Whiteriver, AZ 85941, 520-338-4346.*

6. *Fort McDowell, Mohave- Apache Community of Arizona.* Located thirty-six miles northeast of Phoenix, the Fort McDowell reservation is home to about 700 Native Americans. Attractions include the Fort McDowell Gaming Center, camping, fishing, and inner tubing. The tribe manufactures jojoba bean oil for retail. They are noted for basketry. *Mohave-Apache Tribal Council, P.O. Box 17779, Fountain Hills, AZ 85268, 602-837-5121.*

7. *Fort Mohave Indian Tribe.* Located northwest of Bullhead City, the Fort Mohave Reservation is home to 850 Mohave

Indians. Visitor attractions include fishing, hunting, picnicking, camping, water sports, and the Spirit Mountain Casino. A tribal enterprise is the Smoke Shop. The tribe is noted for basketry and beadwork. (The reservation borders Arizona, Nevada and California, Tribal Headquarters are located in California.) *Fort Mohave Tribal Council, 500 Merriman Ave., Needles, CA 92363, 619-326-4591*

8. Quechan Indian Tribe. Located just north of Yuma boasts attractions that include Colorado River fishing, picnicking, water sports, and camping facilities. The tribe of almost 2,300 is noted for beadwork. They also host the Paradise Casino. (The Reservation borders Arizona and California, Tribal Headquarters are located in California.) *Quechan Tribal Council, P.O. Box 11352, Yuma, AZ 85366-9352, 619-572-0213.*

9. Gila River Indian Community. Located forty miles south of Phoenix is home to nearly 12,000 Pimas and Maricopas. Attractions are the popular Gila River Arts and Crafts Center, Gila Heritage Village & Museum, Firebird Lake & Water Sports Marina, Mul-Cha-Tha "The Gathering of the People", Wild Horse Pass Casino, Vee Quive Casino, Rodeo and Miss Gila River Pageant in April and the St. John's Mission Fair in March. The Reservation is noted for Pima basketry and Maricopa pottery. *Gila River Indian Community, P.O. Box 97, Sacaton, AZ 85247, 520-562-3311.*

10. Havasupai Reservation. Three hundred ten miles northwest of Phoenix. The "people of the blue-green waters" are located at the bottom of Havasupai Canyon, a tributary of the Grand Canyon. To reach the village of Supai you must take an eight-mile trail from Hilltop to Supai, either on mules or by hiking. Campgrounds among the beautiful scenic areas are limited; therefore, you must make reservations. The Annual Peach Festival is in August. The Havasupai tribe of 586 members is noted for basketry and beadwork. *Havasupai Tribal Council, P.O. Box 10, Supai, AZ 86435, 520-448-2021.*

11. Hopi Reservation. Two hundred fifty miles northeast of Phoenix live more than 9,000 Hopis. Attractions on the reservation include the Cultural Center and ceremonials which are held all year. Snake dances are now open to the general public. The tribe is noted for kachina dolls, basketry, plaques, pottery making, and silver crafts. Hopi silver overlay jewelry is popular with

Arizona residents and visitors. *Hopi Tribal Council, P.O. Box 123. Kyakotsmovi, AZ 86039, 520-734-2441.*

12. *Hualapai Tribe.* Two hundred fifty-two miles northwest of Phoenix, the western one hundred miles of the Grand Canyon are included within the boundaries of the Hualapai reservation. Attractions are camping, hiking, hunting, fishing, and white-water Colorado River trips. The tribe of eighteen hundred people is noted for basketry and the manufacturing of dolls. *Hualapai Tribal Council, P.O. Box 168, Peach Springs, AZ 86434, 520-769-2216.*

13. *Kaibab Band of Paiute Indians.* Located three hundred fifty miles northeast of Phoenix, the Kaibab-Paiute reservation is home to more than 200 Native Americans. Attractions are Pipe Springs National Monument, a fort built in 1870, the Kaibab-Paiute Camper & Trailer Park consisting of a museum, store and laundromat, and campsites with forty-eight complete hook-ups. The tribe is noted for coiled shallow baskets known as "wedding baskets". *Kaibab-Paiute Tribal Council, Tribal Affairs Bldg., Pipe Springs Rt., Fredonia, AZ 86022, 520-643-7245.*

14. *Navajo Nation.* More than 90,000 Navajos live on the reservation, two hundred sixty miles northeast of Phoenix. Attractions are Monument Valley, Canyon de Chelly, Little Colorado River Gorge, Grand Falls, Rainbow Bridge, Betatakin and Window Rock—"Seven Wonders of the Navajo Nation". There is the famous Four Corners, the only place in the United States where four states—Arizona, New Mexico, Utah, and Colorado—come together at one point. The Navajos have ceremonials, rodeo and fair, arts and crafts shops, and provide camping, hunting, fishing, and hiking opportunities. The tribe is noted for blanket and tapestry weaving, silver and turquoise jewelry, and some basketry. *Cultural Resources Dept., Visitor Services, P.O. Box 308, Window Rock, AZ 86515, 520-871-4941.*

15. *Tohono O'odham Nation.* (formerly Papago). Located one hundred and thirty-six miles south of Phoenix, this reservation is home to more than 17,000 Tohono O'odham. Attractions include Kitt Peak National Observatory, rodeo and fair, Papago Village Solar Power Project at Schuchuli—the world's first totally electric village, Ventana Cave, Forteleza Ruins, Desert Diamond Casino, and Mission San Xavier del Bac known as the "White Dove of the Desert". The tribe is noted for its beautiful basketry and pottery.

Tohono O'odham Tribal Council, P.O. Box 837, Sells, AZ 85634, 520-383-2221.

16. *Pascua-Yaqui Tribe.* Located one hundred thirty-five miles southwest of Phoenix, the main attractions are the Easter Ceremonial and the September Recognition Ceremonial. Tribal enterprises include a landscape nursery, charcoal packing center, and the Casino of the Sun. Business development is important to this tribe of more 6,500 Indians. *Pascua-Yaqui Tribal Council, 7474 S. Camino de Oeste, Tucson, AZ 85746, 520-883-2838.*

17. *Salt River, Pima-Maricopa Indian Community.* More than 4,600 Pimas and Maricopas live fifteen miles northeast of Phoenix adjacent to Scottsdale. Attractions include the Salt River which provides tubing, camping, and picnicking opportunities. The tribe is noted for basketry and pottery. *Salt River Pima-Maricopa Tribal Council, Rt. 1, Box 216, Scottsdale, AZ 85256, 602-850-8000*

18. *San Carlos Apache Tribe.* One hundred fifteen miles northeast of Phoenix live more than 10,000 Apaches. Main attraction of the reservation are the San Carlos Lake which provides fishing, camping, and hunting and the apache Gold Casino. These San Carlos Native Americans mine peridot and manufacture jojoba bean oil. The tribe is noted for basketry, beadwork, and peridot jewelry. *San Carlos Apache Tribal Council, P.O. Box O, San Carlos, AZ 85550, 520-475-2361.*

19. *Tonto-Apache Tribe.* On a small reservation, ninety-four miles northeast of Phoenix, live 97 Apaches. The attractions are hiking and picnicking in the beautiful scenic area. and the Mazatzal Casino. The tribe is noted for basketry and beadwork. *Tonto-Apache Tribal Council, Payson, AZ 85541, 520-474-5000.*

20. *Yavapai-Prescott Indian Tribe.* Located one hundred three miles northwest of Phoenix, the attractions are picnicking, hiking, and Bucky's Casino. This tribe of 120 Yavapai is noted for basketry. *Yavapai-Prescott Tribal Council, P.O. Box 348, Prescott AZ 86302, 520-445-8790.*

Drawing of a Papago design

INDIAN ART

For many centuries, American Indians created functional items such as baskets, pottery, and cloth to meet their daily needs for survival. They wore jewelry around their necks for pleasure and religious significance; they told stories and described the purpose of ancestral spirits through ceremonies, dances, or Kachina dolls.

In the late 1800s, when tourists began to travel west by train, fascination with Indian artifacts grew rapidly. Traders who saw a potential market, were responsible for encouraging Indians to produce more pots, baskets, jewelry, and rugs to satisfy the outside world's demand. The American and European tourists, captivated by the exotic culture of the Indians, searched for meanings and symbolism in the traditional designs and patterns. Often the traders made up stories and interpretations for these designs to please the buyer and even suggested new more-marketable designs to the Indians.

Today, many of the Indian people have developed their craft to such a high artistic level that it is regarded as a fine art form, and a number of Indian artists are emerging as well-known professionals commanding high prices for their work. They draw inspiration for their designs from their heritage but are developing contemporary styles and are using new techniques which make their products desirable to art collectors. Many visitors to Arizona become fascinated with Indian artifacts and purchase them as souvenirs or to enlarge their collections. In the following paragraphs we will introduce you to a wide range of American Indian creations with the hope that it will enhance your understanding and appreciation of their artistry.

RUGS

According to Navajo myth, the people were taught how to make a loom from sunshine, lightning, and rain by Spider Man, one of the Navajo holy people. It was Spider Woman who taught them to weave. Navajo women, devoting a large amount of time to weaving instead of pottery and basket making, developed more creative rug designs than women of other southwestern tribes.

The people of the Southwest wove garments with cotton for many years before the Spanish conquistadors introduced them to long-haired sheep. The switch from cotton to wool and Spanish weaving techniques were strong influences on the Navajo weavers. With time, the Navajo people developed more diverse designs and improved their weaving techniques, while the Pueblo people, from whom the Navajo had first learned weaving, remained very traditional, because their clothing is part of their religious ceremonies and has to maintain specific designs.

Other Indians and Mexicans who had prized Navajo blankets and rugs for more than two hundred years considered them to be status symbols and preferred them to those made by Mexicans. Tourists began collecting Navajo rugs around 1850.

In the late–1800s, with the influx of tourists, traders saw a new market for Navajo rug weaving. Commercial dyes were used and large, bold patterns were developed. In the 1920s, traders with a sharp sense of business and collectors encouraged the return to earlier vegetal dye colors, original patterns, and finer quality. John Lorenzo Hubbell, who ran the Hubbell trading post, preferred that the weavers who traded with him design rugs using the traditional patterns which were of their own history. Today, more Navajo weavers express their distinct individual styles within certain design limitations and weave what they assume will be hung as tapestries rather than walked on as rugs.

If you think Navajo rugs are expensive, think about the long hours that go into making one. Begin with clipping the wool from the sheep, then cleaning, carding, spinning, washing,

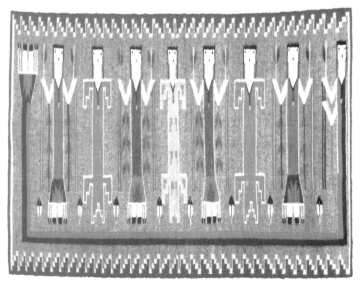

Navajo Rug,
courtesy of Gilbert Ortega Galleries

Navajo Textile,
courtesy of The Heard Museum

dyeing and again spinning it. The preparation of the yarn is often more time consuming than the actual weaving; therefore, the use of commercial yarn is becoming more common. Setting up a loom to prepare for the weaving often takes more than a solid working month. The weaving frequently takes as much as six months of eight-hour work days. Weaving these beautiful rugs has not been a livelihood for most weavers, because they often receive less than a dollar or two an hour for their labors. Fewer rugs are being made, but the quality is excellent. Many Navajo enjoy weaving for their own pleasure or when extra money is needed. Navajo weavers take pride in quality workmanship as they express beauty and harmony in their work. A few weavers are so well-known that they can make many thousands of dollars and possibly sell their rugs even before they are woven.

When buying Navajo textiles, buy from reputable dealers, Indian guilds, or cooperatives on the reservations, or special markets sponsored by museum shows. Indian-style rugs woven in Mexico should be labeled but sometimes are not.

POTTERY

For two thousand years pottery has been made in Arizona. Early pots were used for cooking, storage of grains and water, and for ceremonial purposes. To meet the new demand of collectors desiring to purchase pottery as objects of art, pottery making was increased and began to develop into an art form. Each tribe had its own style of designing and decorating pots, just as it does today. The uniqueness of each tribe's designs makes the pottery highly desirable to collectors.

Traditional methods of making pottery does not include the use of a potter's wheel. Most pots are made by either the coil, slab, or pinch method. Decorations are applied with mineral or vegetal dyes and a brush made of yucca, although some potters are now using ordinary paintbrushes.

The pots are fired over wood, dung, or coal fires. They are not glazed and are somewhat porous which allows seepage of water which evaporates, leaving the water inside cool.

Indian potters of today maintain traditional designs but are also being creative and innovative producing pottery of unique beauty. Of course, new techniques such as carving after firing the pot, use of the potter's wheel, and use of gas or electric kilns are beginning to be used and enable new possibilities for design.

A few Pueblo potters, located generally in the Colorado Plateau area of northeastern Arizona and northwestern New Mexico, are using a fairly new technique called *sgraffito* in which a design is scratched into the pot after firing. Navajo potters are now using applied clay designs of figures, animals, and designs borrowed from sand paintings.

Most Hopi (Pueblo) pottery is produced on First Mesa in the villages of Hano and Sichomovi to be used by the Hopi themselves. A small amount of decorative pottery is produced for sale. The Hopi villages of Walpi and Polacca also produce limited quantities of pottery.

Tohono O'odham and Pima pottery are similar. They both produce highly polished red ware with simple designs. The Tohono O'odham also produce pottery with black-on-white designs.

Maricopa Indians specialize in finely crafted long-necked jars with a very highly polished red finish.

Most potters ask a fair market price for their work because the process of creating a pot takes a long time—from finding the right clay and tempering material, through pot formation and firing, to decorating and finishing.

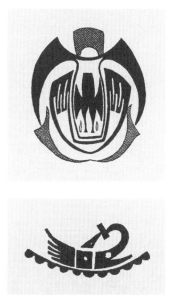

Drawings of Hopi pottery designs

To purchase Indian pottery it is best to visit the pueblos and villages where it is made. You can also purchase authentic pots at the Indian cooperatives, trading posts, museum shops, and special Indian markets. Prices range from ten to hundreds of dollars.

JEWELRY

The first tribe to learn silversmithing was the Zuni who then taught other southwest Indian tribes. The arrival of the railroad in the 1890s increased tourist travel to the Southwest and because many Easterners and Europeans began to desire the better pieces of silver jewelry, the 1920s silversmithing became a fine art.

Traditional jewelry that Indian people made for themselves included collar points for the collars of Navajo women's blouses, mother-in-law bells, tobacco canteens, and powder chargers. Although they continued to make a few unique things for themselves, such as the silver adjustable hatband, they began to respond to the market that was being built by traders. Silver

Contemporary Indian jewelry on display at Gilbert Ortega Galleries

cigarette boxes, napkin rings, salad spoons and forks, shoe horns, pillboxes, cuff links, money clips, and hip flasks, were designed to appeal to the non-Indian buyer. Many of the motifs used in the designs, such a thunderbirds and running horses, were given symbolic meanings by the traders to please the customers.

Until 1930 silver came from Mexican pesos, then from sheets and wire provided by anglo traders. The Indian people never mined their own silver. John Lorenzo Hubbell, owner of Hubbell trading post did much to provide the Navajo with materials and to help them learn the skills of jewelry making.

The Navajo and Zuni tribes developed their skills of jewelry making at the same time, often copying from each other. Navajo gradually became known for their silversmithing and Zuni for their lapidary skills. Today the Navajo and Zuni sometimes work together to produce some very striking pieces of jewelry. The Navajo designers create the silver frames for channelwork and the Zuni designers fill in the spaces with turquoise, mother-of-pearl, coral, or other semi-precious stones.

Most Navajo jewelry contains some turquoise, which has been mined in Arizona for more than fifteen hundred years. It was uncut and used in trade with other tribes as far south as the Aztecs in Mexico. Today the turquoise mines are privately owned by people other than Indians. Turquoise, which can range in color from a pale chalky blue to a very deep green, is often found along with copper. The value of a stone depends on its hardness, color, and markings. A deep blue stone with a fine matrix of black lines is a highly prized stone in the Southwest. Turquoise is most often used in jewelry but is sometimes crushed for use in sand paintings and may be used as an offering in certain ceremonies.

The Hopi are known for their overlay technique which has developed into an exquisite art form, sometimes copied by non-Hopi silversmiths. New materials and new techniques are stimulating finer silversmithing today than ever before. Indian artists who create beautiful jewelry today do so because they are expressing their individual artistic abilities as contemporary jewelry designers. The names of Begay, Gosh, Loloma, Monongye, and Yazzie, among others, have become known for their fine quality workmanship and their designs begun in tradition but finished as creative art.

The demand for Indian jewelry created a market for imitation Indian jewelry as early as the 1920s. Just because jewelry is said to be "made by Indians" does not mean that it is handcrafted with fine quality silver and real turquoise. Buy from reputable dealers, museum shops, or Indian guild fairs.

BASKETRY

Baskets have been used by Indian people in their homes and ceremonies from the time the first basket was woven, several thousand years ago. Baskets still play a strong role in the everyday life of the eight basket-weaving tribes of Arizona—the Havasupai, Hualapai, Chemehuevi, Hopi, Pima, Tohono O'odham, Apache, and Yavapai. The art of weaving baskets has been passed from generation to generation for hundreds of years.

The length of labor that goes into weaving a basket brings the weaver somewhere between twenty-five and fifty cents an hour. The preparation for weaving a basket can include traveling long distances to acquire the right plants during their optimum season and then bleaching, dyeing, soaking, stripping, and trimming them.

The people of each Hopi village are known for the types of baskets they produce, partly because the materials available dictate certain styles. Most baskets produced in the Hopi villages are used by them, leaving only the surplus for sale. Baskets are used for many purposes including healing ceremonies, sifting flour and grain, and as the awards for Hopi foot races.

Tohono O'odham people, who may have produced more baskets than any other tribe in the United States, weave from plants that produce their own colors; no dyes are used. Bear grass, yucca, devil's-claw seed pod, desert willow, green yucca leaf, and narrow-leafed yucca are examples of plants used by the Tohono O'odham to create naturally colored baskets of many shapes. The desire of tourists to purchase baskets for a small price has caused the Tohono O'odham to weave many baskets of yucca with simple designs.

The Pima weave a limited amount of baskets that are similar to those woven by the Tohono O'odham. Early Pima burden baskets were woven by the men and were designed to carry burdens on the shoulders. At one time the Pima wove very fine coil baskets with fine stitching and intricate patterns made from willow, cottontail, and devil's claw. These are now museum pieces. The geometric fret design is very common in Pima baskets. Less frequently seen are the squash blossom, turtle back, and whirlwind designs. A black circle is woven as the center starting point in most Pima baskets.

The Apache weave very fine quality burden baskets, once used for carrying heavy loads on the back, but the art of weaving burden baskets is declining. Apache baskets are also used at puberty rites for young Apache girls. The Apache baskets usually have multiple designs which are more tightly spaced than basket designs of other tribes.

The baskets of the Havasupai people, who live at the bottom of an arm of the Grand Canyon, are produced by the coil method. The Hualapai, closely related to the Havasupai, are known for their cradle boards and seedbeaters. Other tribes in Arizona also produce baskets but in limited quantities.

Some of the best places to view baskets representative of all Arizona tribes are at the Amerind Foundation in Dragoon, the

Drawings of Hopi Basket Designs

Drawing of Pima Basket Design   *Drawing of Papago Basket Design*

Two Hemis Kachina dolls, circa 1900
Left: Sio Hemis Katsina (Zuni)
Right: Niman Katsina (Hopi)

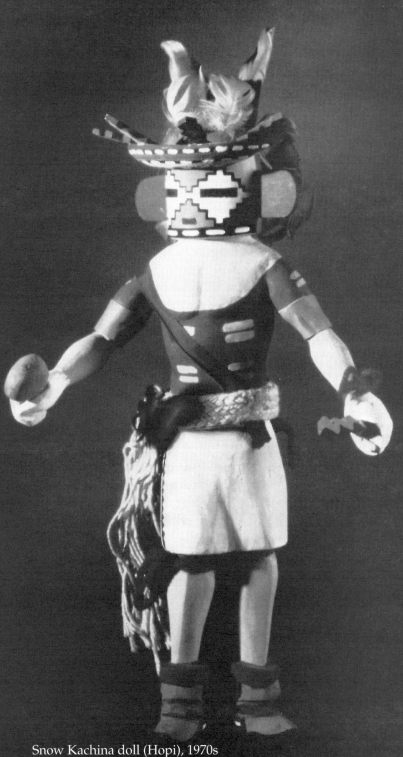

Snow Kachina doll (Hopi), 1970s
Because the Snow Kachina lives on top of the San Francisco
Peaks in Northern Arizona, he is thought to bring the cold
and essential winter moisture to the Hopi mesas.

Arizona State Museum in Tucson, the Heard Museum in Phoenix, and the Museum of Northern Arizona in Flagstaff.

When purchasing a basket you can judge its quality, probably reflected in the price, by the number of stitches per inch, the number of coils per inch, the fineness of the weave, the size of the basket, its symmetry, and complexity of its design.

KACHINAS

Kachina is the commonly known term for *Katsina,* the Hopi pronunciation for a religious supernatural being important to the Hopi people. The functions of Kachinas are similar to the functions of saints to Catholics. Carved Kachina dolls are representatives of Kachina spirits which represent things of nature and are given as gifts to babies, girls, and young women. Kachinas have specific roles in assisting with the prayers for rain, bountiful crops and harmony within the world for all life.

The San Francisco Peaks, north of Flagstaff, are believed to be a home of Kachina spirits who maintain the well-being and continuing life-cycle of the Hopi. There are more than three hundred Hopi Kachinas which are the spirits of animals, birds, places, natural forces, insects, objects, plants, and other things. Kachinas fall into groups based on functions such as clowns, disciplinary, women, hunters, and guards. The main purpose of Kachinas is to bring moisture, growth, and abundant crops.

The number of Kachinas varies because old ones are dropped and new ones are created as the need occurs. A few Kachinas are so secret that modern dolls are not made in their likeness. During the winter solstice it is believed that they leave their home in the San Francisco Peaks and assist in religious ceremonies within the Hopi villages. They live half of the year on the mountain peaks and half in the Hopi villages.

Cottonwood root is the preferred material used to create the Kachina dolls. Tools are used to remove bark, smooth the surface, and create details. Hopi men carve these figures, paint them with a white undercoating or cover them with a white clay and then paint them with acrylic paint. They were once painted with mineral and vegetal dyes. Originally the Kachina dolls were made as one piece. Today they are often made in a few pieces and then put together; however, many collectors prefer the dolls made from one solid piece of wood.

Objects often added to Kachina doll carvings include jewelry, clothing, bows and arrows, headdresses, etc. Placed in hands or worn as adornment, they are all very carefully made of shells, beads, painted wood, animal fur, or cloth. The most important part of the doll are the characteristics of its head by which each spirit can be correctly identified. Coloring is also important. The better quality dolls are intricately carved and decorated. Modern Kachina dolls are carved with more emphasis on anatomy, showing muscles and a more realistic figure.

Today, besides collectors who study kachina dolls and buy them to enrich their collections, tourists find these colorful figures to be a perfect reminder of a visit to the Indian land.

NAVAJO SANDPAINTING

As a simple definition, a sandpainting is a way of handling extremely powerful and incomprehensibly complex forces which affect the universe. There are good and evil forces which are connected by the concept of *hózhó*, creating harmony and a balance in the universe.

Until the mid–1950s, sandpaintings were known only in photographs and paintings of them. The actual sandpainting is created at sunrise and destroyed at sunset of each day during the healing ceremony. The failure to create a new sandpainting for each ceremony might result in serious consequences such as blindness or death to the sandpainter. The sandpainting is usually made inside the hogan. It is believed that when a Navajo becomes ill it is because he or she is out of harmony; therefore, a Navajo chantway is performed to restore this harmony. The ceremony consists of prayers, use of medicinal herbs, songs, and sandpaintings. During this ceremony, with the help of the medicine man, the ill person seeks to gain the strength of a supernatural being by identifying with it. Different illnesses are cured by identifying with different beings. The supernatural being is drawn to the sandpainting and inhabits it. The ill person sits on the sandpainting facing east, looking toward the dark doorway of the hogan. The holy spirits approach from the east to impart their powers into the painting. Sandpaintings are occasionally created to bring rain for good growth of crops. The five hundred recorded types of Navajo sandpaintings richly document images which have meanings of great spiritual significance.

Special sand used to create sandpaintings is the result of grinding and sifting sands from various Navajo locations. Colors are obtained from gypsum, red sandstone, and charcoal. For permanent sandpaintings a board is coated with glue, sprinkled with the background-color sand and allowed to dry for a few days. Glue is applied with a fine paintbrush to form the design for one color area. Then the sand is trickled out between the thumb and index finger in an even flow, falling onto the glue. When finished the whole design may be sprayed with a fine coating of shellac.

Sandpaintings can range in size from a foot to more than twenty feet across. A large sandpainting may require fifteen people to complete it in one day. Effectiveness is sometimes dependent on size and the number of repetitions of sacred symbols. Sandpaintings must not be exact copies of ceremonial sandpaintings. The Navajo sandpainter knows that the medicine man will disapprove when the sandpainting bears too strong a resemblance to an original. One must not step into a completed sandpainting, but walk around it in a clockwise direction. Sandpaintings are like prayers.

Currently the artists are making sandpaintings of non-religious subjects and are refining certain techniques. Visitors to the Southwest can find a great variety of sizes and shapes of colorful sandpaintings with different designs meant to please everyone's taste. This unique form of art represents Indian culture, beliefs, and artistry and is often affordable as a memento.

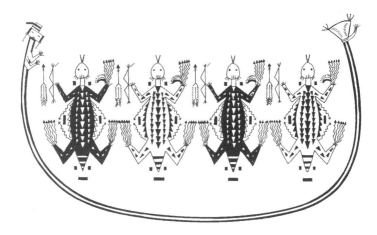

Drawing of Navajo sandpainting   *Navajo sandpainting*

CANYON DE CHELLY
NATIONAL MONUMENT

When you are on the Navajo Indian Reservation, one of the first monuments to see is Canyon de Chelly, formed by the Rio de Chelly and occupied by early hunters about two thousand years ago, and then by Anasazi civilizations. After the Anasazi left the area, Hopi Indians moved in followed by Navajos around the 1700s. The natural environment of the canyon allowed the Anasazi to build cliff dwellings which are preserved in large portions and can be studied by visitors today.

The 131 square-mile monument includes adjoining Canyon del Muerto (canyon of the dead). The name originated from U.S. cavalry findings of mummified bodies in one of the canyon caves. The colorful, seemingly sculpted walls of Canyon del Muerto shelter Anasazi ruins of dwellings and food storage structures. In several places you can clearly see petroglyphs depicting events in the lives of the early people who lived in this canyon.

For today's visitors, Canyon de Chelly offers many scenic trails leading to the popular points of interest, such as the 800 foot-tall Spider Rock.

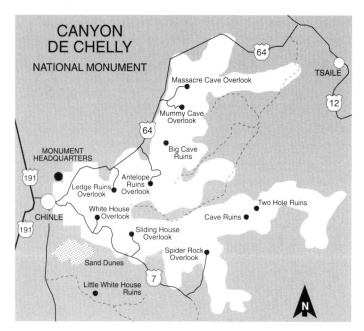

Canyon de Chelly, view of Spider Rock

White House Ruins Trail is the most popular trail and leads to one of the largest ruins in the monument. The picturesque ruin is named for its white walls, contains sixty rooms, and is located five hundred feet down into the canyon. This trail, the only one visitors can take without a guide, begins one mile northeast from the Visitor Center.

Canyon de Chelly is treated by the Indians as the center of the Navajo universe, and is home to many Navajo during the summer months. You will see hogans and small fields of crops. Remember that while you are in Canyon de Chelly you are a guest in a home of the Navajo people. Take pictures of the canyon and the ruins but not the people.

The Visitor Center offers a small museum, ranger programs, and arrangements for Navajo guides.

Canyon de Chelly is located near Chinle off Highway 191 and is open every day, October through April from 8:00 A.M. to 5:00 P.M. and May through September from 8:00 A.M. to 7:00 P.M.

For information call 520-674-5500.

ADVENTURE TOURS
AT CANYON DE CHELLY

There is much to do and enjoy at Canyon de Chelly within the following regulations :

You must have a permit and an authorized guide which you can arrange for at the Visitor Center. The exception to this rule is only the hiking trail to White House Ruin, for which you do not need a guide. You may not enter any ruin or archaeological site or remove or damage any natural or prehistoric objects. You may not drink alcoholic beverages or let pets roam free.

GUIDE SERVICE

At the Visitor Center you can hire a guide to hike with you or ride with you in your own four-wheel-drive vehicle through the canyons. You must get a free permit at the Visitor Center. The Navajo guide will cost about $10.00 per hour.

This was the way of touring the canyon that we chose. Our guide skillfully directed us, as we used the river for a road. Every stop we made was accompanied by his lectures about Navajo and canyon history. The sandstone walls of the canyon with

Canyon de Chelly, rock painting of Conquistadors

many cliff dwellings, petroglyphs, and sunlight playing tricks on them, create a fascinating experience. Make sure you have plenty of film because there is an infinite number of beautiful subjects you will want to photograph.

For information and reservations call 520-674-5500.

VEHICLE TOURS

A Navajo guide takes you into the canyons to see the ruins, petroglyphs, flora and fauna, and introduces you to the history of the canyon. The guide will tell you about Navajo homes, lifestyle, and legends. The tour is half-day or whole-day in four-wheel or six-wheel vehicles.

For information and reservations call 520-674-5841
or 520-674-5842.

HIKING TOURS

One way to hike the canyons is to hire a guide for a group of fifteen. Another way is to take the ranger-led morning hike for twenty-five people. In either case, you must be in good physical condition. Bring your own drinking water, snacks, insect repellent, a small towel, and sturdy shoes you don't mind getting wet, because you will be walking in water.

For information and reservations call 520-674-5500.

NATURE WALKS

Enjoy the late afternoon Archaeology/Nature Walks, which are less strenuous than the hikes. Walking enables you to take pleasure in the plant life and numerous birds that inhabit the canyon. Many Arizona animals make their home in the area. Learn about the flora, fauna, and geology of the canyon.

For information call 520-674-5500.

HORSEBACK RIDING

Riding a horse through the canyon for an hour, a day, or overnight, can be a truly exciting experience, enabling you to get close to the extreme beauty of this magnificent canyon. Either of those listed below is an authorized horse operator and will provide you with a suitable horse and guide.

Justin's Horse Rental, call 520-674-5678.
Twin Trail Tours, call 520-674-8425.

SELF-GUIDED TOURS

Drive along the north and south rims. Each drive takes about two hours. The South Rim Drive takes you to Spider Rock and past scenic overlooks. The North Rim Drive provides excellent views of the canyon floor and numerous Anasazi ruins built into the cliffs. It continues on as Navajo Route 62 to Tsaile. To make your trip more meaningful, pick up a guide book at the Visitor Center before you start.

Hike the moderate White House Ruin Trail which descends about six hundred feet down into Canyon de Chelly. You will hike two-and-a-half miles in about two hours round trip through this beautiful canyon. This is home to Navajo people. Please be courteous guests and photograph only ruins and the canyon, not the people.

For information call 520-674-5500.

SPECIAL PROGRAMS

Check at the Visitor Center for information about the nightly campfire programs and special events which include Navajo Day every Saturday with special cultural performances.

For information call 520-674-5500.

Indian Ruins in Canyon de Chelly

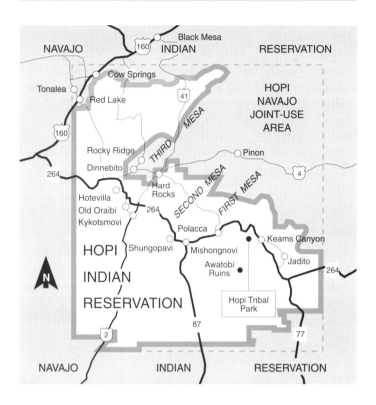

HOPI INDIANS

Descendants of the Anasazi people, the Hopi live on a reservation in the northeastern part of Arizona, totally surrounded by the Navajo reservation. They still live similar lives, to lives of their predecessors of the same village over 700 years ago.

The Hopi had become farmers and traded with other tribes. Their limited contact with Spanish explorers during the sixteenth and seventeenth centuries introduced them to horses, sheep, burros, and cattle. During the 1600s, the Spanish missionaries tried to convert the Hopi but failed. Most of the Spanish priests were driven out during the Pueblo Rebellion of 1680. Later there were more Spaniards and Navajo settlers to threaten Hopi lifestyle and control of their land. Only recently has federal legislation had some success in solving the land disputes between Hopi and Navajo tribes.

The simple lifestyle evolves around spiritual beliefs and family structure, which can be visible in their religious ceremonial observances. Most obvious evidence of this to the outside

Hopi Wedding Pot, courtesy of Northern Arizona Museum

world lies in their performances of Kachina dances. To the Hopi people a colorful Kachina dancer becomes the spirit of a super-natural being. Originally, little replicas of Kachina dancers carved by Indians from cottonwood roots were given to the children to help them understand their heritage and culture but now they are also prized by collectors.

The Hopi villages are located on the top or at the base of the three mesas.

First Mesa is fifteen miles west of Keams Canyon. At the foot of the mesa is a village called Polacca, on top of the mesa are three villages, Walpi, Sichomovi, and Hano/Tewa. The most spectacular of all the Hopi villages is Walpi, terraced into a narrow rock table, with cliff-edge houses and scenic views. It appears unchanged for centuries. You will need to register in Tewa Village and then be accompanied by a guide as you walk through the village.

Some Hopi homes have pottery, jewelry, or Kachina dolls for sale. The prices are fair and the Hopi people are friendly. All of First Mesa produces fine pottery, colorful kachina dolls, and attractive weavings.

Second Mesa is ten miles west of First Mesa. The mesa top villages are Shungopavi, Sipaulovi, and Mishongnovi. The tiny

Hopi wicker plaque, courtesy of The Heard Museum

settlement at the western foot of Mishongnovi is Toreva, the Hopi Cultural Center, having a museum, restaurant, motel, and several craft shops. A meal in the restaurant will enable you to enjoy unique Hopi cuisine. The Cultural Center is located off Highway 264 and is open from 8:00 A.M. to 5:00 P.M., Monday through Friday; 9:00 A.M. to 4:00 P.M. on Saturday and 9:00 A.M. to 2:00 P.M. Sunday, May through December. Second Mesa is known for its coiled baskets, as well as colorful Kachina dolls and silver overlay jewelry.

Third Mesa is ten miles further west of Second Mesa. The villages of Third Mesa are scattered throughout the western part of the Hopi reservation. They are Kykotsmovi, Old Oraibi, Hotevilla, Bacavi, and Moenkopi. Old Oraibi is the oldest continuously lived-in settlement in the U.S., having been lived in since A.D. 1150. Third Mesa villages are known for their wicker basketry, Kachina dolls, fine weavings, and silver overlay jewelry. Purchasing Native American arts and crafts on the reservation ensures authenticity.

Although Hopi are a private people, visitors are welcome to attend the public ceremonies and villages of the Hopi reservation. Please be reminded that while on the Hopi reservation, you are considered a guest. The Hopi ask you to be thoughtful while attending ceremonies. They ask for the same respect due any sacred event—neat attire and a respectful, quiet etiquette. Disruption of shrines or removal of artifacts are strictly prohibited. Photographing, recording, and sketching villages and ceremonies are strictly prohibited. Observe all rules and regulations established by the villages.

For information call 520-734-2441 or 520-734-2401.

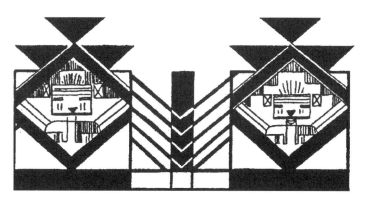

Drawing of Hopi Shawl Design

NAVAJO INDIANS

The largest Indian reservation in the United States, the Navajo Reservation, covers more than 25,000 square miles, occupying the northeast corner of Arizona and extending into Utah and New Mexico. Many think it possesses the most beautiful, breathtaking scenery in the world. Most recognizable is the magnificent Monument Valley with rock formations captivating millions of people—visitors, photographers, writers, and movie producers.

The Navajo, who call themselves "Dine' " (The People), believe the holy people of long ago taught Dine' respect for life, balance, and harmony between man and nature. Reverence for Mother Earth (Nihima Nahasdzaan) and Father Sky (Yadilhil) is the root of Navajo culture. They were a nomadic people who migrated from Canada's Northwest Territories and learned farming from the neighboring pueblo tribes such as the Hopi. Some Navajo people still prefer to live in east-facing hogans made of mud and logs rather than modern housing. Raising sheep, cattle, and crops are still important livelihoods for the Navajo people; however, many produce arts and crafts. Working outside the reservation is often a monetary necessity, but the need for spiritual renewal brings them back to the reservation.

Their colorful woven rugs are known around the world for beauty and unique designs. Squash blossom necklaces and concha belts made of silver and turquoise are popular items among shopping visitors. Navajo basketry made from aromatic sumac, is traditionally woven in white, black, and reddish brown, with the white center representing an escape hole for evil spirits. Sandpaintings are works of art with special meanings to the Navajo people. The Navajo language is still widely spoken and continues to be taught to the children. It was used by the Navajo code talkers as a totally secure cryptogram during World War II and was never deciphered by the enemy. Some of the older Navajo people speak no English, only Navajo. Currently the tribe is trying to balance the education of its children, to preserve Navajo culture while still preparing them for modern jobs.

When visiting Dine' Bi Keyah (Navajoland) abide by reservation laws and behave as a gracious guest. Do not photograph the Navajo people unless you ask their permission first.

For information call 520-871-4941.

Navajo Rugs, courtesy of The Heard Museum

MONUMENT VALLEY NAVAJO TRIBAL PARK

Famous Monument Valley, located on the Navajo Reservation, in the northern portion of Arizona, is a recognizable scene to moviegoers and television viewers. This home of the Navajo people is a land of mystery and intrigue to the visitor.

These lonely rock formations, created by wind and water erosion of sandstone tableland, will unfold with profound beauty, right before your eyes, when you pursue the scenic drives. Surrounding these giant geologic formations lies a rather arid valley which supports a few flocks of Navajo sheep, with sparse areas of grass, dotting the colorful reddish earth. Navajo families live here and raise their children, whom you may see tending the sheep and goats, that provide survival resources for these families. The family business is usually trading sheep wool and weaving beautifully designed rugs.

The mystical quality of your surroundings, as you explore the valley, begin to create an awareness of *hózhó*, the concept of harmony with the earth that Navajo people strive to maintain throughout life—unison and interdependence of all things.

Most of the guided sightseeing tours can be arranged for in Kayenta. You can be part of a large group tour or hire your own private tour guide who will take you to places that are not accessible to the general public. If you are a photography enthusiast, you can engage in specially designed photographic tours to cap-

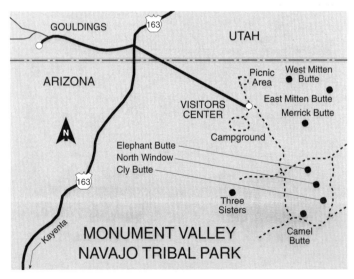

Preceding pages: Mitten Buttes in Monument Valley

ture the best that Monument Valley has to offer. To the photographer, the beauty of Monument Valley lies in its grandeur, colored by the changing light of sunrise and sunset. Monument Valley Tribal Park, open year-round, is where you can begin a self-guided seventeen-mile scenic drive .

When you arrive at the Monument Valley area, you will find pleasant accommodations for the night in Gouldings, Utah and Kayenta, Arizona or campground facilities just a quarter mile southwest from the Visitor Center. There is a camping fee of $10.00.

Monument Valley Tribal Park is open 7:00 A.M. to 7:00 P.M., May through September and 8:00 A.M. to 5:00 P.M., October through April. The park is closed Christmas, New Year's Day and the afternoon of Thanksgiving. General admission is $2.50 per person. To reach Monument Valley take Highway 163 north out of Kayenta for twenty miles.

For information call 801-727-3353 or 520-871-4941.

NAVAJO NATIONAL MONUMENT

These three ruins, over the years, have not been easily accessible and have been protected by the Navajo from pot hunters and vandals. As a result, they are the best preserved ruins in the state. Betatakin can be seen from an overlook a short distance from the Visitors Center or can be visited if you are part of a ranger-guided tour. It is a five-mile hike. Inscription House is so fragile that it is off limits for public viewing.

Eight miles away, Kiet Siel, a well preserved Anasazi ruin, is considered the most impressive of all Arizona Indian ruins. It can be visited only by special permit, applied for in advance. Hiking tours of no more than twenty people leave everyday to descend seven hundred feet into the canyon to view this ruin. It is a strenuous eight-mile hike. Tours are available from early spring to October. It is best to backpack and stay the night under the stars.

Navajo National Monument is open daily from 8:00 A.M. to 5:00 P.M. in winter and from 8:00 A.M. to 6:00 P.M. in summer. It is located off Highway 564, about nine miles from Highway 160, twenty miles southwest of Kayenta.

For information and reservations call 520-672-2366.

FOUR CORNERS NATIONAL MONUMENT

We have included this monument in our book because it is a novelty, and you will experience a special kind of feeling being in the only location in our country where you can be in four states at the same time. Try putting each of your hands and feet in the corners of Arizona, New Mexico, Utah, and Colorado. The scenery immediately around Four Corners is not spectacular but if you have seen Monument Valley or Canyon de Chelly on the way, the trip will have been worthwhile. Four Corners is located east of Monument Valley off Highway 160.

For information call 602-640-5250.

PAGE

Page grew out of the construction camp for Glen Canyon Dam. After the dam was finished in 1957, some of the residents stayed to form a town which is now an internationally known and popular vacation spot. The unique location of the town, on top of Manson Mesa, provides a spectacular view of Wahweap Bay and Glen Canyon Dam. You can choose from a limited number of accommodations, resorts, and marinas. While in Page, you will want to visit the John Wesley Powell Memorial Museum where you will find information, photographs and artifacts from his first expedition down the Colorado River. Right in front of the museum you will see a replica of the pine rowboat that Powell used on his expedition. Here at the museum you can make arrangements for exciting adventure tours.

Scenic Air Flights. Air Flights can take you to seven national parks, a national recreation area, a tribal park, numerous state parks, national forests, five Native American tribes, and four national monuments.

Colorado River rafting. You can choose either a short smooth water trip on the river or go to extremes and join the eight-day white water trip through the Grand Canyon.

Tour boating. Boating on Lake Powell is the only way to see its attractions. Because this way of enjoying the lake is so popular, we strongly suggest you make tour reservations in advance or at the John Wesley Powell Museum while you are in Page.

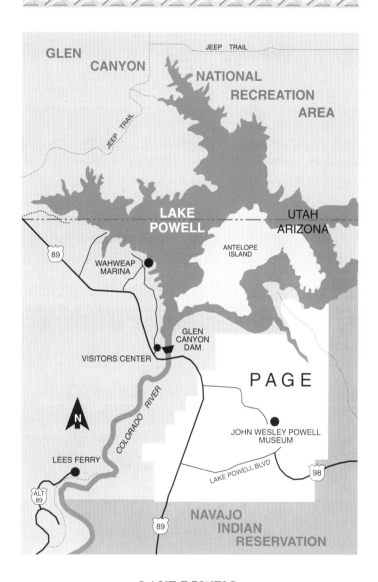

LAKE POWELL

Multi-colored canyons and soaring mid-lake peaks give Lake Powell unequaled grandeur. Lake Powell's sheer, twisting canyons intrigue and delight boaters. These indentures are interspersed with sandy beaches for sunbathing and swimming, and the opportunity to picnic or camp in the shadows of those multi-colored cliffs is a magnet to visitors. Many broad bays offer the space waterskiers are always seeking, and the entire lake is widely known for its large assortment of fish. A week, or only a few days spent on a houseboat with a small fishing boat tied behind, is one of the grandest ways to see this part of Arizona.

The flooding of Glen Canyon by the creation of Glen Canyon Dam, formed Lake Powell which buried history and natural beauty beneath its waters, but also produced an extremely beautiful lake surrounded by red rock formations, tall canyon walls, and a few impressive stone arches. Some Indian ruins are still visible, letting you feel a touch of history and triggering your imagination as to what life was like for those early Indian peoples who lived in Glen Canyon hundreds of years ago.

Currently, there are only a few roads that go through the sparsely inhabited areas near the lake, making it necessary to take a boat tour to see Lake Powell's attractions.

The Visitor Center at Glen Canyon Dam provides interesting displays and useful information. There are easily accessible elevators to take you down into the dam. Walking across the massive dam lets you have an excellent view of one end of this huge lake that extends for many miles into Utah.

Lake Powell is located on the Arizona/Utah border. Take Interstate 17 to Highway 89, northwest to the city of Page.

For information call 1-800-528-6154.

HOUSEBOATING ON LAKE POWELL

Houseboating seems to be made for Lake Powell, affording visitors the opportunity to live with all the conveniences of a floating motor home while exploring the beauty and intricacies of the many inlets of the lake. Waking up to the sunrise on the water is an experience you'll never forget. Houseboating season lasts from early spring to late fall. Even an experienced boater finds houseboating a bit of a challenge. One of the difficulties of piloting a houseboat on Lake Powell is anchoring it. The lake is so deep that you cannot drop anchor, making it necessary to drive the boat up on the beach just enough to secure it, while you camp on the beach or go hiking. The pleasure of the experience may make the difficulties seem worth it. To make the escapade truly relaxing, rent the houseboat from a company that provides an experienced operator to pilot the boat for you.

Houseboats can be rented at Wahweap Marina. They sleep from six to twelve people and can be rented year-round with the

Boating on Lake Powell, courtesy of Lake Powell Resorts & Marinas

least expensive rates being between November and March. You need to reserve a houseboat a year in advance or call periodically, hoping to pick up someone's cancellation.

For information call 1-800-528-6154 or call 602-278-8888.

RAINBOW BRIDGE NATIONAL MONUMENT

This well-known geological feature, fifty miles up-lake from Wahweap Marina, attracts a lot of attention now that it's easily accessible by boat. Almost three hundred feet tall, it is the world's largest natural stone arch, carved by the waters of the creek that flow through it. Before it was discovered by white people, Navajo people had already named it *"Nonne-Zoshi"* (rainbow turned to stone). The rainbow-shaped arch rises 290 feet above the stream bed. It is 275 feet wide. Lake Powell enables you to get near the arch but the lake does not flow through it. Boat tours to Rainbow Bridge and other attractions leave regularly from Lake Powell's Wahweap and Bullfrog marinas. Rainbow Bridge can be reached by two long and difficult hiking trails, recommended only for the very experienced hiker.

For information call 1-800-528-6154.

HIKING PARIA CANYON

Red sandstone formations have created a labyrinth-like pass of exceptional beauty which was used by Pueblo Indians and later, Mormon settlers, traveling from Arizona to Utah. The walls of the labyrinth of Buckskin Gulch are so close together in some places, that you will have to squeeze through two-foot wide spaces on your way to Paria Canyon. The colorful formation of the canyon walls and the light penetrating the space between them, create a magnificent scene that is worth the effort of getting there. At moments there is darkness, and then the glow of light from the sun bouncing from one wall to the next.

Another approach to Paria Canyon is to enter at White House Ruins about twenty-eight miles west of Page. You can park at Lees Ferry. There are shuttle services for Paria Canyon hikers. This photographer's paradise can be entered at four different trailheads—Lees Ferry in Arizona, Wire Pass, Buckskin, and White House in Utah. The canyon is located northwest of Page off Highway 89.

For information call 520-645-2741.

FISHING ON LAKE POWELL

Bring your own boat or rent one for the least crowded fishing you've ever experienced. The 186 mile-long lake enables you to have a really solitary fishing experience. Lake Powell offers great diversity in its fish which include largemouth bass, sunfish, trout, channel catfish, crappie, northern pike, and walleye. Largemouth bass fishing is very popular and most successful in the spring, when the fish come up to spawn. The incredibly clear water keeps the bass happy in deeper waters the rest of the year. Striped bass are plentiful in the summer.

You can fish any day of the year, day or night, from your boat or from shore, with or without lights. There are no size limits on any game fish caught in the Arizona part of Lake Powell. Of the five marinas on Lake Powell, four are land accessible and one can be reached only by water. There are numerous boat launching areas at the land-based marinas, which make Lake Powell convenient for anglers. Facilities for camping and RV sites are available at all of the land-based marinas. National Park Rangers are ready to help you at each marina.

For information call 520-608-6405.

PIPE SPRING NATIONAL MONUMENT

In 1870, Mormon colonists, headed toward their destinations in the west, resettled an abandoned ranch site established in 1863 along the trail known as Honeymoon Trail. The Mormon people were efficient in settling in isolated areas and surviving. They built a fortified ranch house over the spring. The high stone walls extended the house around the courtyard. Some think it was to prevent the Indians from having access to the water.

The first telegraph office in Arizona was set up here in 1871. Visiting Pipe Spring gives you an idea of the desolation of the area and isolation of the lives of those early settlers.

Today, the ranch house is restored and there are demonstrations of pioneer crafts and a Visitor Center showing the history of Pipe Spring. There is an admission charge of $2.00.

Pipe Spring is open daily from 8:00 A.M. to 4:00 P.M. and is located along the northern edge of Arizona, fourteen miles west of Fredonia, off Highway 389.

For information call 520-643-7105.

CENTRAL
ARIZONA

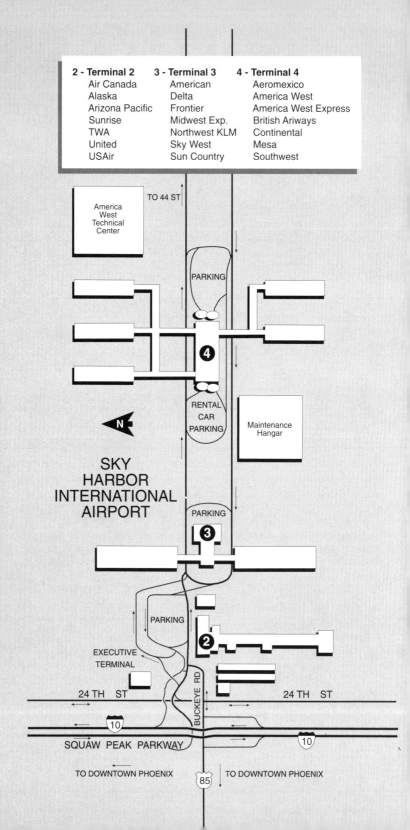

SKY HARBOR
INTERNATIONAL AIRPORT

Main Switchboard	273-3300
Airport Paging	273-3455
Emergency	273-3311
Lost and Found	273-3307
Information Center	392-0020
Ground Transportation	273-3383
Parking	273-0954

AIRLINES RESERVATIONS

Aeromexico	1-800-237-6639
Air Canada	1-800-776-3000
Alaska	1-800-426-0333
America West	1-800-235-9292
America West Exp.	1-800-247-5692
American	1-800-433-7300
British Airways	1-800-247-9297
Continental	1-800-523-3273
Delta	1-800-221-1212
Frontier	1-800-432-1359
Mesa	1-800-637-2247
Northwest	1-800-225-2525
Skywest	1-800-453-9417
Southwest	1-800-435-9792
TWA	1-800-221-2000
United	1-800-241-6522
USAir	1-800-428-4322

VISITORS SERVICES

AZ Office of Tourism	230-7733
Convention/Visitors Bureau	254-6500
Passport Information	506-3369
U.S. Customs	379-3514
Visitors Hotline	252-5588
Weather	265-5550
Doctor Referral	230-CARE
Arizona Shuttle Service	1-800-888-2749
Super Shuttle	244-9000 or 1-800-332-3565
Yellow Cab Company	252-5071

DESTINATION	MILES	FLIGHT TIME
Albuquerque	1350	3:30
Atlanta	1827	3:45
Boston	2350	5:00
Calgary, Canada	1517	3:40
Chicago	1742	3:35
Dallas/Forth Worth	1002	2:15
Denver	812	1:45
Frankfurt, Germany	5178	10:54
Las Vegas	287	0:55
London, England	4892	10:18
Los Angeles	376	1:05
New York	2445	5:20
Salt Lake City	1250	2:24
St. Louis	1481	3:10
San Diego	353	1:00
San Francisco	762	1:50
Seattle	1465	3:40
Tokyo, Japan	5520	11:35
Washington D.C.	2300	4:55

MAJOR HOTEL AND MOTEL CHAINS

Arizona Assoc. of Bed and Breakfast Inns	277-0775
Best Western International	1-800-528-1234
Comfort Inn	1-800-228-5150
Courtyard by Marriott	1-800-321-2211
Days Inn	1-800-325-2525
Doubletree Inn	1-800-528-0444
Econo Lodges of America	1-800-446-6900
Embassy Suites	1-800-362-2779
Fairfield Inn	1-800-228-2800
Hampton Inn	1-800-426-7866
Hilton Hotel	1-800-445-8667
Holiday Inn	1-800-465-4329
Howard Johnson	1-800-654-2000
Hyatt Hotel	1-800-233-1234
La Quinta Motel Inn	1-800-531-5900
Marriott Hotel	1-800-228-9290
Quality Inn	1-800-228-5151
Radisson Hotel	1-800-333-3333

Ramada Inn	1-800-228-2828
Red Roof Inn	1-800-843-7663
Regent International Hotel	1-800-545-4000
Residence Inn by Marriott	1-800-331-3131
Roadway Inn	1-800-228-2000
Sheraton Hotel	1-800-325-3535
Super 8 Motel	1-800-843-1991
Travelodge & Viscount Hotel	1-800-255-3050
Wyndham Hotel	1-800-822-4200

RENT-A-CAR AGENCIES

Advantage	244-0470 or 1-800-777-5500
Agency	242-0200
Alamo	225-5074 or 1-800-327-9633
Avis	273-3222 or 1-800-831-2847
Budget	267-1717 or 1-800-527-0700
Courtesy	273-7503 or 1-800-368-5145
Discount	437-4088
Dollar	275-7588 or 1-800-800-4000
Enterprise	225-0588 or 1-800-325-8007
Hertz	267-8822 or 1-800-654-3131
National	275-4771 or 1-800-227-7368
Thrifty	244-0311 or 1-800-367-2277
U-Save	276-9505
Value	273-0190 or 1-800-468-2583

Drawing of Hohokam art

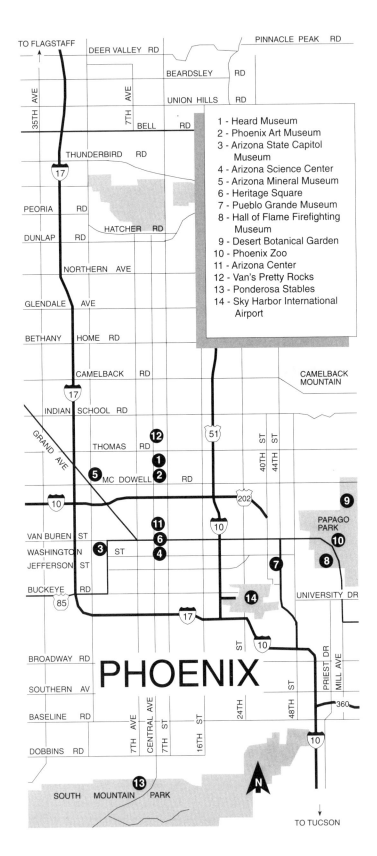

PHOENIX

From about two hundred B.C., the central part of Arizona was inhabited by Native Americans who farmed the area by building irrigation canals to direct water from the Salt River. According to archaeological findings the tribe of 100,000 people disappeared around A.D. 1450. Sometime after they left, the Pima Indians moved into the area and discovered the canals. They named the vanished people who had built the canals, Hohokam (those who have gone). Pima, and later Maricopa Indians, occupied the area and lived peacefully with the early settlers. The same source of water allowed that part of Arizona to grow in population and become what it is today.

Phoenix, named for the mythical bird that rose from its own ashes, seemed to rise from the Hohokam ruins to become Arizona's capital and the largest city in the state. The city that has something for everyone, from golfer's paradise to art collector's haven, is flooded with visitors year-round.

A major international airport provides comfortable access to the Valley of the Sun. Phoenix, ninth largest city in the nation with its population of approximately one million, is becoming a city of the young and young in spirit. With high-tech industry and several universities in the metropolitan area, Phoenix is very competitive in attracting new residents and new industries. Service industries are the largest employers in the Phoenix area and manufacturing is one of the strongest elements of the metropolitan economy. Some of the surrounding cities that make up the metropolitan area are Glendale, Peoria, Tempe, Scottsdale, Chandler, Gilbert and Mesa. The location, climate, vibrant southwestern lifestyle and modern facilities attract many conventions and professional sports events as well as a multitude of tourists.

A walking tour of downtown Phoenix reveals the renovated historical buildings that date from 1895 and the early 1900s. The uniqueness of Phoenix lies in its capability of balancing the past with the present. Evidence of this can be seen in new architecture, decorative motifs, outdoor sculptures and cultural festivities. Millions of visitors enjoy the revitalized downtown area with its modern Civic Plaza, theatre and symphony facilities, sports arena, restaurants, museums, and shops carrying a wide range of fine quality art and hand crafted items. Vacationers delight in the beautiful climate, magnificent scenery, unique flora, and warm hospitality.

The surrounding communities enrich a visitor's stay in the valley by providing a variety of cultural and outdoor activities, which range from hiking, sightseeing, touring an old gold mine to festivals, art shows, and pow wows.

We suggest you begin your exploration of this city of diversity with a visit to the Heard Museum which will set the stage and enhance your understanding of Arizona's heritage.

HEARD MUSEUM

The extensive thirty-thousand item collection of Native American artifacts and fine art fills the exhibit halls and showcases of this charming newly- expanded building.

As you enter the courtyard you may be attracted by an American Indian creating jewelry, weaving a rug, or playing a musical instrument. The museum believes in preserving and sustaining the peoples from which its art objects have come.

It is suggested that you begin your museum visit by viewing the interesting multimedia presentation about the history of Southwestern Indians. It will awaken your feelings of empathy for Arizona's first inhabitants. You will then begin to absorb the information in the award-winning exhibit, *Native Peoples of the Southwest,* and learn about their history. The high quality exhibits of basketry, pottery, and clothing are striking as are the cases of silver jewelry. The outstanding Kachina doll collection will occupy a large portion of your time as you examine the quantity and variation in style and colors. You will share his love of Arizona as you gaze at the collection of photographs of the Grand Canyon and American Indians taken by Barry Goldwater.

Hands-on activities thrill visitors of all ages in the *Old Ways, New Ways* family exhibit where you can design an Indian rug, make small animal figures, and through the use of video technology, play drums along with a Native American music group. There is an ongoing variety of fascinating events throughout the year, such as holiday festivals, Indian dances and Mexican celebrations as well as Native American music and Indian and Mexican food events. If you're here in March you'll want to attend the Annual Guild Indian Fair and Market. On weekends performances of native music and dance enchant the audiences.

The Heard Museum is internationally known for its superior collections, special programs, candlelight processions, lectures, special exhibits, and 45,000-volume library and archives.

A visit to Arizona would not be complete without a visit to the Heard. Make time to enjoy it and become one of the 250,000 people who visit the museum each year.

The excellent Museum Shop offers a beautiful selection of fine arts and crafts by Native Americans. Expand your library with your choice from their comprehensive array of books.

Museum hours are from 9:30 A.M. to 5:00 P.M. Monday through Saturday and until 9:00 P.M. on Wednesday. Sunday, the museum is open from noon to 5:00 P.M. It is closed on all major holidays. From 5:00 P.M. to 9:00 P.M. on Wednesdays the admission is free. At other times adult admission is $5.00. The museum is two blocks north of the Phoenix Art Museum at 2301 North Central Avenue. There is free parking and barrier free access.

For Heard Museum information call 602-252-88480
For Museum Shop call 602-252-8344.

PHOENIX ART MUSEUM

The largest visual arts institution between Denver and Los Angeles, the Phoenix Art Museum is visited frequently by residents and tourists who appreciate the fine quality permanent collections and the variety of changing exhibits. The museum has

Native American baskets from The Heard Museum collection

a permanent collection of over eighteen thousand paintings, sculptures, costumes, and other works of art dating as far back as the fifteenth century.

The *Asian Collection* is one of the best in the world, with specialties in porcelain and cloisonne. The *Western Collection* fills a large room with paintings and sculptures of superb quality, depicting Indian life and western settlement. If you are here in October you will want to attend the annual exhibition of paintings done by the *Cowboy Artists of America*, a popular event. The extensive *Costume Collection* display gives the viewer a glimpse of lifestyles in years past, and the *Thorne Miniature Rooms* delight people of all ages. A fine contemporary exhibit of powerful pieces of art will stir your emotions. There are frequent special exhibits which help build the museum's excellent reputation.

You will enjoy the gift shop full of novel and colorful items. The museum is open Tuesday through Saturday from 10:00 A.M. to 5:00 P.M., Wednesday from 10:00 A.M. to 9:00 P.M. and Sunday from noon to 5:00 P.M. It is closed on Monday and major holidays. The adult admission charge is $4.00. The museum is located at 1625 N. Central Ave. and has barrier free access.

For information call 602-257-1880 or 602-257-1222.

ARIZONA STATE CAPITOL MUSEUM

If you're a history buff, you'll want to visit the Arizona State Capitol Museum which provides detailed information about how life was in 1912, the year Arizona became the 48th state.

Restored to its original look, the museum offers exhibit areas which include *Government Offices, Territorial Library, Gifts to the Governors, Arizona Women in Government,* and *The USS Arizona.* The museum enriches visitors' knowledge of Arizona government and history through exhibits of photographs, documents, and memorabilia.

The copper-domed State Capitol is located at 1700 W. Washington. DASH bus service gives you easy transportation from the downtown area.

The museum is open from 8:00 A.M. to 5:00 P.M., Monday through Friday, is accessible to the physically challenged, and is admission free.

For information call 602-542-4581.

"Fancy Dancer" by John Nieto, courtesy of The Heard Museum

ARIZONA SCIENCE CENTER

Appealing to all ages, this museum offers interactive exhibits ranging from dinosaurs to present-day ecology and world hunger solutions. Experience the exciting world of athletics and discover the scientific secrets of sports with hands-on exhibits that measure the speed of your fastball, allow you to spin like an ice skater, and let you lift three hundred pounds. The halls of the museum are filled with laughter and exclamations of children and teenagers touching, pushing, and pulling exhibits especially designed for this purpose. Young visitors, through hands-on experiences, absorb the interesting museum content. Enjoy the Iwerks theater and state-of-the-art planetarium.

The variation of displays makes this museum an interesting and educational stop for tourists exploring the Phoenix area and is highly recommended for young people. The museum is open from 10:00 A.M. to 5:00 P.M. daily except Thanksgiving and Christmas. Basic adult admission is $8.00. The museum is located at 600 E. Washington in downtown Phoenix.

For information call 602-716-2000.

HERITAGE SQUARE

The only group of residential buildings from the original site of Phoenix is Heritage Square. One of the eight houses contained in Heritage Square is the charming Rosson House, an outstanding example of Victorian Eastlake architecture. It has been well pre-served, renovated, furnished, and decorated according to the times in which it was built. You'll enjoy the kitchen and other unique features of the house. Tours are conducted daily by knowledgeable and enthusiastic guides.

The seven other homes and carriage houses are currently occupied by the delightful Arizona Doll and Toy Museum and the Silva House Museum which contains exhibits about the history of electricity and water usage, and an interesting photographic display of the valley history. The Doll and Toy Museum features rare collections and it is open Tuesday through Saturday from 10:00 A.M. to 4:00 P.M., Sunday from noon to 4:00 P.M., closed Monday. Adult admission is $2.00.

Rosson House is open 10:00 A.M. to 4:00 P.M. Wednesday through Saturday, noon to 4:00 P.M. on Sunday, and closed

Monday and Tuesday. Adult admission is $3.00. Silva House is open 10:00 A.M. through 4:00 P.M. Tuesday through Saturday and noon to 4:00 P.M. on Sunday. Admission is free.

Heritage Square, located at 7th street and Monroe, is within walking distance of other downtown attractions.

For information call 602-262-5071 or 262-5029.

ARIZONA MINING AND MINERAL MUSEUM

The geology of Arizona, easily observed in massive rock formations or gemstones and minerals, is part of what makes Arizona one of the most beautiful states in the nation. Visiting old ghost towns and mines and even panning for gold yourself may be the start of your fascination with rocks and minerals, but a visit to the Arizona Mining and Mineral Museum will certainly make a rockhound out of you.

You will find mining tools, core samples from the mines, and samples of minerals lit to show off their remarkable beauty. There are extensive lapidary exhibits from Arizona and around the world to intrigue you.

The museum is located at 1502 W. Washington. It is open from 8:00 A.M. to 5:00 P.M., Monday through Friday and 1:00 P.M. to 5:00 P.M., Saturday. Admission is free.

For information call 602-255-3791.

PUEBLO GRANDE MUSEUM

The Hohokam lived in central and southern Arizona long before the time of written history. They settled at the place we now call Pueblo Grande around the time of Christ. This village was large and included homes and storage rooms. In the outside areas there were cemeteries, ballcourts, activity and cooking areas, and a platform mound. There were actually more than twenty villages along the Salt River in what is now the Phoenix area. Pueblo Grande was one of the larger villages. It was this group of Hohokam who constructed several hundred miles of irrigation canals to bring water to their crops of corn, beans, squash, cotton, and tobacco. Around A.D. 1450, they vanished from Pueblo Grande and the other villages. Some archaeologists believe it was because of drought, others think that social conditions or invading tribes caused their emigration. The real reason

is still a mystery. Pueblo Grande Park, a national historic land-mark, encompasses ruins of the Hohokam village and houses the museum that features permanent exhibits describing the Hohokam lifestyle. Exceptionally creative interactive exhibits for children make this museum a great family experience. There are a variety of workshops, lectures, and a Native American crafts gift shop. The second weekend in December, the annual Indian Market attracts thousands of visitors from all over the country.

Open hours are 9:00 A.M. to 4:45 P.M., Monday through Saturday and 1:00 to 4:45 P.M. on Sunday. The museum is closed on major holidays. Adult admission is $2.00. Admission is free to all on Sunday. Pueblo Grande Museum is located at 4619 E. Washington Street.

For information call 602-495-0900.

HALL OF FLAME FIREFIGHTING MUSEUM

Although fire engines are not unique to Arizona, this collection, the largest collection of firefighting equipment in the world, is displayed at the Hall of Flame Firefighting Museum for your perusal and delight. People of all ages thrill to the excitement of brilliant flashing lights, loud sirens, and the roar of strong engines heroically speeding to put out a fire. Years ago the noise wasn't as loud and the lights not as bright, but the thrill was just the same.

The museum is divided into four galleries—one for horse-drawn fire apparatus and three for engine powered vehicles. You can find a fire engine reminiscent of your childhood from among the one hundred restored fire engines on display. There is even one from England—a hand pumper from the year 1725. This is a collection and bit of history you won't want to miss. Try on fire-fighting helmets and climb aboard a fire truck. You'll be fascinat-ed by the exhibits of old and not-so-old equipment used to help fight fires. This is a fun place for children and adults.

There is an admission charge of $5.00. The museum is open from 9:00 A.M. to 5:00 P.M. Monday through Saturday and from noon to 4:00 P.M. on Sunday. It is closed, Thanksgiving, Christmas, and New Year's Day. It is located at 6101 E. Van Buren Street.

For information call 602-275-3473.

Valley of the Sun depicted in the modern architecture of Phoenix City Hall

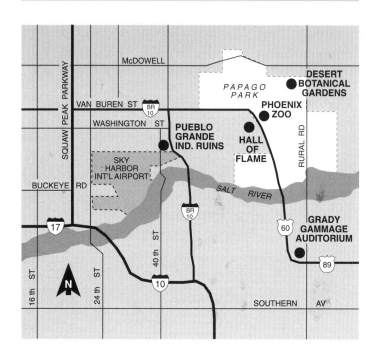

PAPAGO PARK

Adjacent to Phoenix and Tempe, Papago Park has many picnic grounds and hiking trails with abundant wildlife. It is also home to the Phoenix Zoo and the Desert Botanical Gardens.

Small rounded red-rock mountains of Papago Park, protruding picturesquely from the middle of the metropolitan area, are a landmark for the surrounding cities. Its closeness to Phoenix, Tempe, and Mesa makes the park a convenient spot to relax and enjoy the southwestern environment.
It is located at East Van Buren St. and Galvin Parkway.

For information call 602-256-3220.

DESERT BOTANICAL GARDENS

More than fifteen thousand desert plants from all over the world grow in a magnificent setting at the Desert Botanical Gardens. Each species of plant is labeled for easy identification. The prospect of seeing birds, jackrabbits, squirrels, desert tortoises and other creatures among the exotic plant life makes this a delightful adventure for all ages. Enjoy a self-guided tour along the winding paths through three acres of saguaro forest,

Agave at The Desert Botanical Gardens

mesquite thicket, desert oasis, and upland chaparral. The Gardens is one of the favorite places of Phoenix residents and draws more than 100,000 visitors each year. Arizona's early springtime allows plenty of time to enjoy the gorgeous display of wildflowers at the Desert Botanical Gardens, as well as out in the desert. The Gardens offers a weekly update on wildflower displays in the desert areas of Arizona by providing the Wildflower Hotline. Call *602-481-8134*, from March 1 through April 30.

Annual events, which could be happening while you are in town, are *Spring's Desert Fest* which includes a cactus sale, *Spring and Fall Landscape Plant Sales,* and *Noche de las Luminarias,* a December holiday event. The gift shop offers an excellent selection of desert gardening related items, books, cactus candy, and other unique desert souvenirs. The Sales Greenhouse offers unusual cacti and succulent plants.

The Desert Botanical Gardens is accessible to the physically challenged and is open every day except Christmas from 8:00 A.M. to 8:00 P.M. It is located at 1201 N. Galvin Parkway, near the Phoenix Zoo. Adult admission charge is $7.50.

For information call 480-941-1225.

Arizona Office of Tourism

THE EVANS HOUSE
(THE ARIZONA OFFICE OF TOURISM)

A beautifully restored example of Queen Anne-Victorian archi-tecture, popular in this country between 1880 and 1910, the Evans House stands by itself at 1100 West Washington. Over the years many people have passed through its doors for various reasons. It was built in 1893 by Dr. Evans and his wife, Jennie. Many patients climbed the stairs to his second floor office in the "Onion House", so called because of its unique onion-shaped dome .

In 1908, the house was owned by Drs. Oscar and Virginia Mahoney. He headed the mental hospital and she was one of four women licensed to practice medicine in the territory. Over the years it became a rundown boarding house and finally was purchased by the state and renovated.

Today many people from all over the world visit Evans House seeking information about Arizona, as it has become the location for the Arizona Office of Tourism. Stop in to browse

Teddy Bear Cholla, common to the Arizona desert

through a wealth of travel information, chat with the friendly staff, and enjoy this beautiful house. The Evans House is open from 8:00 A.M. to 5:00 P.M., Monday through Friday.

For information call 602-542-8687 or 1-800-842-8257.

THE ARIZONA CENTER

Arizona's visitors, sports fans, theater goers, and residents of all ages enjoy the variety of shops, cultural-cuisine restaurants, and activities at The Arizona Center, one of Phoenix's successful efforts to bring "life" back to downtown Phoenix. This is a great place to buy western wear, Mexican attire, gift items, decorator, items, souvenirs, and to visit the Arizona Highways store, where you can find a comprehensive collection of Arizona books for adults and children. You will also find brochures about Arizona places to visit and explore.

The Arizona Center is a short walk to the Herberger Theater, the Civic Center, and the sports arena. It is located in downtown Phoenix at 3rd Street and Van Buren and is open Monday through Saturday from 10:00 A.M. to 9:00 P.M. and from 11:00 A.M. to 5:00 P.M. on Sunday. Restaurants and night spots may be open until late evening hours.

For information call 602-271-4000.

BEYOND PRETTY ROCKS

As you travel through Arizona, you will be amazed by so many colorful and intriguing rock formations. To satisfy your curiosity and answer many of your questions about nature's phenomena you might want to visit one of the best rock shops in the state, Beyond Pretty Rocks.

The rock shop is educational and full of wonderful surprises that range from petrified dinosaur dung to a six-foot tall amethyst from Brazil. You'll find various forms of rocks and minerals from all over the world that can serve as decorative items, gifts, jewelry etc. Many rocks are from privately owned caves in Arizona. This is an excellent place for rockhounds and people looking for the unusual gift.

Beyond Pretty Rocks is located at 302 E. Flower St. and is open Tuesday through Saturday from 10:00 A.M. to 5:00 P.M.

For information call 602-241-1302.

Renaissance Plaza in downtown Phoenix

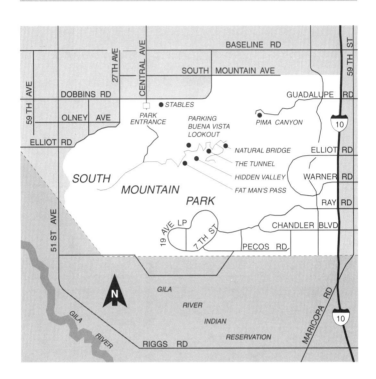

SOUTH MOUNTAIN PARK

Standing protectively at the southern edge of Phoenix, South Mountain forms part of the boundary of the Valley of the Sun. South Mountain Park, the largest municipal park in the world covers seventeen thousand acres of natural landscape criss-crossed with hiking and horseback riding trails.

A narrow, paved winding road guides your automobile or bicycle all the way to the top for a spectacular view of Phoenix and the valley. This is a very popular place from which to view the city at night. By day, the park is enjoyed by people of all ages who hike and picnic. The more active people find challenges in mountain biking, rock climbing and horseback riding. Trails are well marked and park rangers are attentive to your safety. As with all outdoor adventures in Arizona, wear appropriate shoes, carry water and protect yourself from the sun.

The main entrance to South Mountain Park is located at the southern end of Central Avenue. You can get a map and information about the park and hiking trails at the gate.

For information call 602-542-4174.

PONDEROSA STABLES

South Mountain Park is a wonderful place to enjoy horseback riding. At Ponderosa Stables you will be fitted with a horse suited to your size and riding level. Half and full-day rides are available. Try a special ride through the desert to a cheerful campfire, hot cowboy coffee, and a delicious grilled T-bone steak. Even the potatoes, beans, and garlic bread are cooked just the way the cowboys on the range did it. Then enjoy the moonlight ride back to the stables. If you're a morning person, make reservations for the 7:30 A.M. breakfast ride to a beautiful desert spot for pancakes, eggs, and coffee.

Ponderosa Stables, which is located at 10215 South Central Ave. at South Mountain Park, offers free transportation to and from your hotel.

For reservations and information call 602-268-1261.

ADVENTURE TOURS FROM PHOENIX

The best way to experience Arizona is to just get out there. Don't sit in your hotel. There are many tour companies offering their services to take you out into Arizona. For your convenience, we have included a few.

Open Road Tours. The guides of Open Road Tours share their favorite places with you as they escourt you around the most scenic and interesting parts of Arizona. To start your adventure you might try a tour around the Phoenix and Scottsdale area including a trip to the Heard Museum. A custom designed tour to please your whole family or any group of six or more can be arranged. Open Road Tours is experienced in conducting tours to Arizona's most beautiful spots or to any part of the western United Sates. Viewing the Grand Canyon can be a comfortable and memorable adventure. Enjoy other Arizona scenic spots such as Sedona, Monument Valley, Lake Powell, Canyon de Chelly, the Navajo and Hopi reservations, Jerome, Montezuma Castle and many more fascinating places by starting your tour from the Phoenix area. Check with your concierge, bell captain, or travel agent for information about Open Road Tours.

For information call 602-997-6474 or 1-800-766-7117.

Cloud Chasers Balloon Company. Take a balloon flight, not just a ride. Year-round flights depart at sunrise and land about an hour-and-a-half later. Refreshments are served during and after the flight. See the most beautiful desert in the world, the Sonoran Desert, by floating slowly over it—an experience you'll never forget. The Cloud Chasers office is located at 222 W. El Caminito Dr., Phoenix.

For information call 602-944-4080.

Gray Line Motor Coach Tours. Travel in the air conditioned comfort of a Gray Line motorcoach and leave the driving to your friendly bus driver/tour guide. Enjoy the companionship of others on the tour as you share experiences of sightseeing. There are a number of tours to choose from: Grand Canyon Express, Grand Canyon Overnight, Grand Canyon Railway Adventure, The Best of Northern Arizona, Canyon Lands, Sedona-Oak Creek Canyon, Nogales, Phoenix, and more. Not mentioned in the titles of these tours are stops such as Las Vegas, Lake Powell, and the Painted Desert. Each tour lets you enjoy the tremendous beauty of Arizona and takes you to the most spectacular sightseeing opportunities.

For information call 602-495-9100 or 1-800-732-0327.

Arizona Desert/Mountain Jeep Tours. Enjoy a half-day jeep tour through the desert and mountainous areas around Phoenix. By participating in one of these backcountry tours, you will be introduced to flora and fauna of the area while enjoying the spectacular views. Typically western cowboy cookouts can be arranged for groups of fifteen or more.

For information call 480-960-1777.

Western Excursions. The drivers of these four-wheel-drive vehicles are all police officers and firefighters. They are trained to safely take you out into the desert, into remote areas of the Superstition Mountains and the Sawtooth Mountains. They will also take you to Martinez Canyon and to Box Canyon on the Gila River. You are treated to a chicken or steak dinner with all the trimmings of a cowboy cookout. Western Excursions specializes in trips for seniors. They are based in Casa Grande.

For information call 520-421-9414.

Arrowhead Sonoran Desert Jeep Tours. Take a jeep tour through beautiful desert and foothills scenery to live the experiences of the Old West. Spend a half day gold panning on the Agua Fria and Verde rivers. Learn to throw a tomahawk and shoot a six-gun.
For information call 602-942-3361.

Arizona Bound Tours. Explore the mountains surrounding Phoenix and Scottsdale in a jeep. These exciting tours highlight nature walks, Hohokam ruins, six-gun shooting, cowboy competitions and more. Tours are one to five hours long.
For information call 480-994-0580

HIKING IN THE PHOENIX AREA

Squaw Peak. Squaw Peak trail is one of the most popular hiking trails in Arizona and is hiked by people of all ages and levels of experience. For more than a mile, the trail winds between southwestern flora and rock formations to the summit where there is a panoramic view of Phoenix and its surroundings. Its accessibility makes it an excellent place for family hikes. The trailhead is located off Squaw Peak Drive which turns north from Lincoln Drive (Glendale Ave.) near 16th Street.

Camelback Mountain. Hiking boots are a must. The four-mile trail has magnificent rock formations and great views. Unlike Squaw Peak, Camelback is not well maintained and in many places has a loose gravel surface. The beginning of the trail is south of the Tatum Boulevard and McDonald Drive intersection.

Christiansen Trail. An eleven-mile hike through the city of Phoenix can be surprisingly beautiful and certainly interesting. You'll enjoy the mixture of desert life with city dwellings, the tunnel under Cave Creek Road, Dreamy Draw Wash, and the pockets of peaceful desert surroundings as you hike through hilly terrain winding north of Squaw Peak. The trail can be entered at Cheryl Drive and Seventh Avenue in Mountain View Park, or on the east end, at 40th Street south of Shea Boule

South Mountain. Several trails winding through the park are of varying levels of difficulty. Most interesting is Hidden Valley

Trail beginning at Buena Vista lookout at the top of the mountain. Unlike the hikes up Squaw Peak and Camelback Mountain, the Hidden Valley trail leads hikers away from civilization. The three-mile-long trail leads you through interesting rock formations in a desert wilderness. The park is accessible at the southern end of Central Ave.

For more information call 602-262-6861

White Tank Mountains. Located twenty miles west of Phoenix off Olive Ave., White Tank Mountains Regional Park is an excellent place for families to spend the day hiking, picnicking, and searching for petroglyphs on the rocks.

Superstition Mountains. The Treasure Loop trail originates at Lost Dutchman State Park and gradually climbs around the base of the Superstition Mountains. This two-and-a-half-mile trail offers some of the best Sonoran Desert landscape and the mystique of the Lost Dutchman Mine. The park is located five miles northeast of Apache Junction off Highway 88.

Peralta Canyon Trail. The best and most popular trail in the Superstitions, is a two-and-a-quarter-mile trail which climbs fourteen hundred feet, providing hikers with a spectacular view of Weavers Needle. To get there take Highway 60, turn left on Peralta Canyon Road and drive eight miles to the trailhead.

Canyon Trail. If you're a mountain biker or enjoy riding horseback, you might want to try this trail which stretches for thirteen miles from Lake Pleasant Road to the Agua Fria riverbed. In this part of the Sonoran desert you may see mule deer, mountain lion, javelina, bobcat, coyote, golden eagles, roadrunners, and herons. You'll be among stands of saguaro cacti and paloverde trees as well as other desert flora which are strikingly beautiful in the spring. If you look carefully you may see desert tortoise, gila monsters and rattlesnakes. The best time to hike this trail is from October through May. To get to the trailhead take exit 232 off Interstate 17 and go southwest a little more than three miles on Lake Pleasant Road to the trailhead facilities.

Arizona's famous saguaro cactus

GILA RIVER ARTS AND CRAFTS CENTER

Just twenty minutes south of Phoenix you will find a museum of exhibits that interpret prehistoric to modern Indian culture. The well planned Gila River Arts and Crafts Center is owned and operated by the Gila River Indian Community.

Pima and Maricopa, who make up this community, still practice the ancient art of pottery and basket weaving. Instructed in these crafts from early youth, the Indian women are considered masters, and their beautifully decorated products are valued highly by art enthusiasts the world over.

On display are authentic tools used in the everyday life of early people of the Gila River. There is a Pima house made of mesquite beams, weeds, and earth. Authentic handmade pottery, once used by Indian families, are on display. A wide selection of baskets, primarily made by the Tohono O'odham, Pima, and Hopi Indians is for sale in the gift shop. There are also vases, bowls, figurines, and paintings done by noted Indian artists. The arts and crafts of twenty tribes are represented here.

Heritage Park, adjacent to the Gila River Arts and Crafts Center, offers an exhibit that tells a story of more than two thousand years of Indian life within the desert basin of the Gila River. To introduce the five cultures of the basin authentically, village

Early Indian wigwam

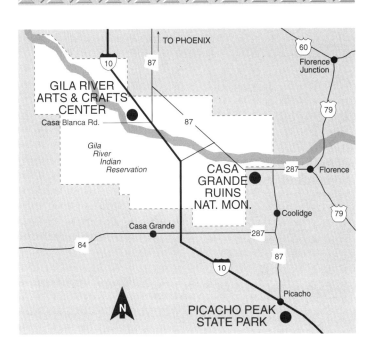

settings have been constructed to show the ancient and rich life of these early Native Americans. The cacti, grass, and trees growing in the villages are native to their time and altitude.

For information call 480-963-3981.

For RV Park information call 520-315-3534.

Wall mural at the Gila River Arts and Crafts Center

Four-story earthen main structure

CASA GRANDE RUINS
NATIONAL MONUMENT

The village around the Casa Grande, originally built by Hohokam Indians, was occupied until about 1450. The Hohokam farmed and traded with other southwestern tribes and peoples of Mexico. Their abundant crops included corn, beans, squash, tobacco, and cotton. Remains of their irrigation canals which brought water from the Gila River were used by the early settlers. The Casa Grande, the four-story, earthen main structure of the ruins, demonstrates the peak of Hohokam architectural development. It was built in the late 1200s and early 1300s and probably served several purposes including that of astronomical observatory and watchtower. The entire two-acre site including the Casa Grande and other buildings was surrounded by a seven-foot adobe wall. Pine and fir logs used for ceiling and floor supports were floated down the Gila River. The nearest forest may have been sixty miles away.

The Hohokam village was the leading trade and political center for all Hohokam villages of the Gila River Valley. The Hohokam vanished in the early 1400s but archaeologists believe the Pima and Tohono O'odham (Papago), who live nearby, are their descendants.

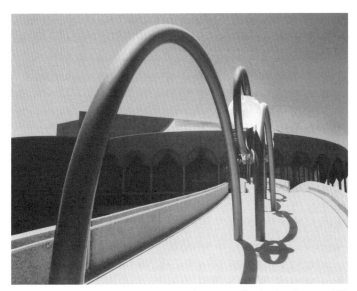

Grady Gammage Performing Arts Center at ASU

Father Kino gave Casa Grande (Spanish for "great house") its name when he visited the area in the late 1600s. Casa Grande Ruins was the first federally protected site in the nation. The monument is open daily except Christmas. October through May are the best months to visit, to avoid the hot summer sun. Admission is $4.00 per vehicle or $2.00 per person.

Entrance to Casa Grande Ruins National Monument is off State Route 87, about halfway between Phoenix and Tucson, a mile north of Coolidge and a short distance from the Pima Reservation. You can also take exit 185 off Highway 10.

For information call 520-723-3172.

TEMPE

Carl Hayden, owner of Hayden's Flour Mill and Hayden's Ferry, founded Tempe in 1872. The ferry was the only means of transportation across the Salt River at that time. The flour mill, very important to the development of Tempe, is the oldest industrial site in the Salt River Valley that is still in business.

Tempe grew into the present community of 150,000 people, retaining the color of its past which is enjoyed by visiting the many historic sites. The popular historic site is Old Town Tempe where tourists, residents, and Arizona State University students frequent the quaint shops, restaurants, and places of entertainment. The university, begun in 1885, is one of the largest state universities in the nation and contributes greatly to the cultural and educational offerings of Tempe. Enjoy a walk through the campus visiting the museums and looking at ASU's eclectic architecture. Grady Gammage Performing Arts Center on the southwest corner of the campus was designed by internationally-known architect, Frank Lloyd Wright. Catch a ride on the "turn-of-the-century" trollies to get to other places of interest in Tempe.

TEMPE HISTORICAL MUSEUM

The history of irrigation is demonstrated through a unique exhibit—a scale model of an irrigation system which allows you to let water into the ditches from a canal and to understand how the early Hohokam people created their irrigation canals. In addition, the museum displays memorabilia from early Tempe. The museum is located at 3500 S. Rural Road. Hours are from 10:00 A.M. to 5:00 P.M. Monday through Thursday and Saturday, 1:00 to 5:00 P.M. on Sunday.

Also enjoy the restored Queen Anne Victorian style Niels Petersen House located at 1414 W. Southern Ave.

For information call 480-350-5100.

MESA

Long before the founding of Mesa, prehistoric Hohokam Indians irrigated the tableland above the Salt River and proved it could be farmed. Canals they left behind were used as guides for new canals dug by Pimas, Maricopas and the settlers who chose to build communities on this tableland. The first English-speaking people to walk on this land were famous mountain men—Kit Carson, James Pattie and others. Later, the communities of Lehi and then Mesa (Spanish for "table") were settled by Mormon families moving westward to avoid religious persecution.

Founded in 1878 as a Mormon farming community, Mesa has grown to be the third largest city in the state and is home to the Champlin Fighter Museum, Arizona Museum for Youth and the Arizona Mormon Temple. The sports-minded will find Mesa to be a golfer's paradise.

For information call 480-969-1307

MESA SOUTHWEST MUSEUM

The museum provides a variety of southwestern experiences from ancient to modern times. Learn about the dinosaurs that inhabited the land we now call Arizona. Learn more about the Hohokam and other central Arizona Indians. Pan for gold and absorb bits of the rowdy territorial lifestyle of the early settlers.

This is a particularly good place for children. There are many hands-on experiences. Special events include the *Mesa Pow Wow*, a Native American arts and dance festival, and *Territorial Days*, an Old West celebration. The museum is open Tuesday through Saturday from 10:00 A.M. to 5:00 P.M. and Sunday from 1:00 to 5:00 P.M. Adult admission is $4.00. You will find the museum near downtown Mesa, at 53 N. MacDonald between University and Main St.

For information call 480-644-2230.

SCOTTSDALE

Currently considered the art mecca for the Valley of the Sun, Scottsdale began its existence around 1890 as a farming community. For many years it seemed to be an oasis in the desert because of its rich soil and abundance of citrus and olive trees. The town was named after civil war chaplin, Winfield Scott, who owned a ranch nearby and encouraged early settlement.

Located near Scott's original homestead site, historic Old Scottsdale will take you back into the town's history by presenting well-preserved historic buildings such as the first church, post office, blacksmith shop, and little red schoolhouse which is now occupied by the Scottsdale Chamber of Commerce.

Today's Scottsdale, with a population of 130,000 is considered a highly sophisticated community with a great assortment of specialty shops and art galleries. Scottsdale is known for having the largest selection of western art in the world. Many of these galleries and shops are located along colorful Fifth Avenue, Marshall Way, and West Main, where you can enjoy the Thursday evening Art Walks, October through May from 7:00 to 9:00 P.M. *Call 480-990-3939* for Art Walk information.

The town's offering of many western activities to its visitors once earned it the title of the "West's most Western Town". To experience the area's western attitude firsthand, we suggest you

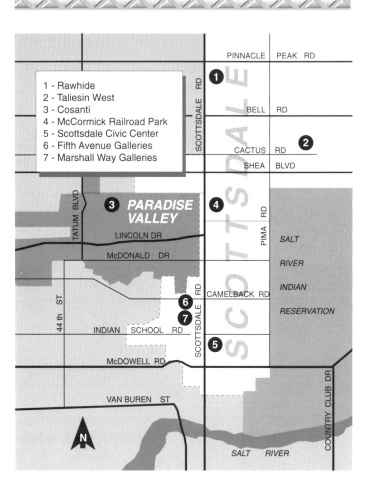

visit nearby Rawhide. Scottsdale borders Phoenix and stretches from Tempe north to Carefree.

For information call 480-945-8481.

THE OVERLAND GALLERY

The Overland Gallery is among the many fine galleries along Scottsdale's Main Street. It is an excellent place to view Western Art depicting the lives of Indian people, Hispanics, cowboys, and early settlers. These works of art are created by well-know western artists and are purchased by businesses, collectors, and individuals from all over the world.

The gallery is located at 7155 Main Street and is open Monday through Saturday from 10:00 A.M. to 5:00 P.M.

For more information call 480-947-1934.

THE LEGACY GALLERY

The Legacy Gallery features a large selection of original representational art with emphasis on Western, figurative landscape, still-life, sporting and wildlife paintings as well as many sculptures of children, cowboys, Native Americans, sports figures and wildlife. Located in the heart of the Main Street Art District in Scottsdale, the gallery represents more than 40 nationally recognized artists. Open daily January through April and Monday through Saturday, May through December. The gallery is open Thursday evenings year round as are most galleries in the art district.

For information call 840-945-1113.

"Warriors of the Raven People" by Frank McCarthy
courtesy of The Legacy Gallery

RAWHIDE

For those of you who came to Arizona to see, experience, and participate in movie-like Old West activities, Rawhide is the perfect place to go. Built on 160 acres of natural desert, this exact replica of an 1880s western town provides visitors with exciting experiences of that time.

This privately owned western theme attraction is the state's largest conglomeration of old time activities. Various amusements, live reenactments of history, live western music, and interesting shops, provide visitors with entertainment and souvenirs.

The management of Rawhide encourages visitors to enjoy participating in what is offered. You may test your skills in shooting, you may take a ride in a stagecoach, or you may try panning for gold. There is something for everyone. The children will love Kid's Territory, complete with the large Petting Ranch stocked with over one hundred animals, as well as Fort Apache and Ghost Town. Arts and crafts lovers visit the Pottery Shop, where you can watch as the potter turns his wheel to make a variety of southwestern items such as decorative pots, night lights, and wall hangings.

When you approach dinner time we strongly suggest you visit world-famous Rawhide Steakhouse which offers more than

Historical collection at Rawhide

great food. There is live country-western music, cowboy comedians, and a tableside magician to keep you entertained. Right next door is the Rawhide Saloon and Gambling Parlor where old time saloon girls serve your favorite libations. Try your luck against the crooked card dealers, or simply sit back and enjoy the music.

Rawhide, proud of its status as the signature attraction of "The West's Most Western Town", is open daily. Hours are from 11:00 A.M. to 10:00 P.M. Entrance into Rawhide is free but there is an admission charge to the Rawhide Museum.

To get there go north on Scottsdale Road, just four miles north of Bell Road.

For information call 480-563-5600.

TALIESIN WEST

Taliesin West, a national landmark, occupies six hundred acres of Sonoran Desert in the foothills of the McDowell Mountains, a landscape filled with cactus, ironwood and mesquite. Taliesin West, built of redwood and desert stone, was begun in 1937 as Frank Lloyd Wright's home and architectural studio. Twenty-three young apprentices made up the Fellowship that helped build Taliesin West.

It is today the winter home, studio, workshop, and office of more than seventy architects, staff members, and students associated with the Frank Lloyd Wright School of Architecture and Taliesin Associated Architects.

If you take the tour of Taliesin West you will cross courtyards and terraces, go down garden paths past a citrus grove and alongside the large drafting studio used by architects and apprentices of the Fellowship. You will enter a conference room, the Pavilion Theater and Cabaret Theater, where you can watch a continuous slide show illustrating Frank Lloyd Wright's architecture and Taliesin way of life. Gammage Auditorium, the beautiful performing arts facility at Arizona State University was Frank Lloyd Wright's last major conception.

There are special tours such as the *Early Morning-light Photographer's Tour*, *Behind-the-scenes Tour*, *Insights, and Panoramic Tour* which range in price from $14.00 to $35.00 for adult admission. The guided *Desert Walk Tour* of the Sonoran desert surrounding Frank Lloyd Wright's Taliesin home and studio is

$20.00. Taliesin West is located off Frank Lloyd Wright Blvd. between Bell Road and Shea Blvd.

For information call 480-860-8810.
For reservations call 480-860-2700 .

COSANTI

A visit to the Cosanti complex provides tourists with a totally unexpected experience. Instead of viewing dwellings of Arizona's early peoples you will be presented with visions of a futuristic self-sufficient city. The Cosanti complex houses the studios, offices, gallery, foundry, and windbell shop of architectural innovator Paolo Soleri, the creator of Arcosanti, city of the future, located at Cordes Junction. Here at Cosanti, Soleri experiments with the design of energy efficient cities.

Tours through the complex are conducted for groups of five or more and are concluded with pouring of bronze to form windbells. If you do not take the tour you are welcome to browse and enjoy the lush desert landscape. Open 9:00 A.M. to 5:00 P.M. daily except holidays. Adult admission for tours is $5.00. Cosanti is located at 6433 Doubletree Ranch Road, Scottsdale.

To arrange a tour please call 480-948-6145.

McCORMICK RAILROAD PARK

This unique park stays open seven days a week, except Thanksgiving and Christmas, and caters to children, but adults love to come here, too. It features an old steam engine and a Pullman car used by three presidents of the United States. The smaller scale Paradise & Pacific Railroad train is available for rides, taking you through a tunnel and over trestles. Even smaller scale models are on display.

On weekends you can see miniature locomotives being run by the Live Steamers Club. On Sunday afternoon you may find a model railroad enthusiast setting up his railroad display for the public to view. You get an additional historic treat when you ride the restored 1950s carousel. The railroad museum housed in a baggage car, vintage 1914, contains working telegraph equipment and other railroad memorabilia.

Come here during the week to avoid the weekend crowd. Enjoy the playgrounds, and picnic under the trees. Admission to

the park is free, but there is a $1.00 charge for rides on the carousel and the train. The park is open from 10:00 A.M. to 6:30 P.M. and is located at 7301 E. Indian Bend Road, Scottsdale.
For information call 480-312-2312

ADVENTURE TOURS FROM SCOTTSDALE

West Wind. Flights depart from either the Scottsdale or Deer Valley Airport and provide you with wonderful aerial views of Lake Powell, Monument Valley, Navajo and Hopi Reservations, Rainbow Bridge, Painted Desert, Meteor Crater, Sedona, Oak Creek Canyon, Montezuma Castle, Flagstaff, and the Grand Canyon. On-the-ground tours include Monument Valley, Canyon de Chelly, Grand Canyon, and Lake Powell. The West Wind office is located at 732 W. Deer Valley Road.
For information and reservations call 480-991-5557
or 1-888-869-0866

Hot Air Expeditions. Float high over the Arizona desert and experience a different viewpoint of the Valley of the Sun. Morning and afternoon flights are available during the winter. Sunrise flights are year-round and are subject to favorable winds and weather. Each flight is about one to one-and-a-half hours in duration. The exact course and landing site cannot be predicted, so you should plan about three hours for the total excursion. Enjoy the champagne breakfast. The Hot Air Expedition office is located at 4901 E. Bloomfield Road, Scottsdale.
For information and reservations call 1-800-831-7610

Unicorn Balloon Company. Take a fantasy flight over the spectacular Arizona-Sonoran Desert in a hot air balloon. You will look down on the beautiful scenery of the north Scottsdale and Carefree areas, and experience a unique panorama filled with interesting flora and fauna. Drifting slowly over the valley in an open basket is a breathtaking experience. It's romantic. It's a journey you will never forget. During the winter, morning and afternoon flights are available. In the fall and spring, flights depart at sunrise. Flights are between one and two hours long.
    The Unicorn Balloon Company office is located at 15001 N. 74th St., Scottsdale Airport.
For information call 480-991-3666 or 1-800-HOT-AIR-8.

Apache Trails Tour. Take a jeep tour with professional guides into the beautiful Sonoran Desert and the Superstition Mountains. See two-hundred-year-old saguaro cacti, hear stories of mines and miners, and learn to pan for gold. If you find gold you can keep it. There are rugged 4-wheel drive tours into Box Canyon and the beautiful Four Peaks area. Be sure to wear a hat and closed-toe shoes.

For information and reservations call 480-982-7661.

Wayward Wind Tours. Professional cowboy guides take you on a 4-wheeler or a horseback tour. Target shooting, nature walks, and beverages are included in all four-hour trips. Ask about fishing, hunting, camping, river rafting, or cookouts. Wayward Wind Tours will pick you up at your hotel.

For information call 602-867-7825.

PIONEER ARIZONA
LIVING HISTORY MUSEUM

Situated about twenty-five miles north of downtown Phoenix, Pioneer Arizona Living History Museum brings to life the everyday existence of the early settlers, struggling to survive and to carve out a living.

The museum employees, wearing historical clothing are actually working at printing on 19th-century presses, cooking a meal on an old wood stove, and spinning yarn on an old spinning wheel. The structures, well furnished with items from the turn-of-the-century, create the atmosphere of an old town including a working blacksmith, the old bank and The Stagecoach Restaurant where you can eat some tasty food for a reasonable price. It's a great place for the whole family to study the lifestyle of early Arizona settlers.

Open hours are Wednesday through Sunday from 9:00 A.M. to 5:00 P.M., October through May. The museum is closed on Tuesdays and on Christmas Day. There is an admission charge of $5.75 for adults and $4.00 for children . To get there take Pioneer Road, exit 225, west from Interstate 17.

For information call 623-993-0212.

CAREFREE AND CAVE CREEK

These comfortable scenic towns, adjacent to each other about twenty-five miles north of Phoenix and Scottsdale, are set next to the Tonto National Forest and are frequented by the fauna of the area. The sunsets are a photographer's passion. Horseback riding, biking, and hiking are good ways to get out into the surrounding scenery to enjoy the essence of Arizona.

Carefree is a modern planned community but Cave Creek grew out of the old Butterfield stage coach stop of the 1880s. It was also a gold and silver mining town. You'll enjoy the quiet lifestyle and the abundance of shops and leisure activities.

For information call 480-488-3381.

GLENDALE

Construction of the forty-four-mile long Arizona Canal, carrying water from the Salt River to the Agua Fria River, opened the land for farming and the subsequent establishment of Glendale and its neighboring city, Peoria.

Glendale, began in 1892 as a God-fearing agricultural town, a contrast to the many gambling, alcohol-sipping, gun-toting mining towns so widespread in Arizona in the late 1800s. The first settlers were farmers from the eastern and midwestern

Prickly pear cactus

states, followed by Hispanic, Japanese, Chinese and Russian settlers, giving Glendale a multicultural reputation from its beginning. This diversity helped Glendale to develop into a thriving family community. The "family community" image is what Glendale boasts today as it continues to be a rapidly growing, modern city of more than 150,000 residents.

Glendale enjoys the presence of The American Graduate School of International Management (built on the grounds of the old Thunderbird airfield) and Glendale Community College, known worldwide for its High Tech Complex providing easy access to education with the use of computers. The community college was built on part of the land that was once an elegant homestead and fruit farm. Eighty acres of the rest of the land and its buildings have become a National Historic site called Sahuaro Ranch Park.

SAHUARO RANCH PARK

Sahuaro Ranch, once the valley's showplace, is now a busy park with restored buildings from the 1890s containing exhibits and a few furnished rooms. You'll enjoy looking at the farm machinery from the early 1900s. You'll marvel at the one thousand rose bushes in the palm-shaded garden, home to many peacocks that roam freely frequently displaying their colored tail feathers. It's a beautiful park for the whole family to enjoy. There are ball courts, playgrounds, several picnic areas, and ramadas with

Saguaro cactus in bloom   *Preparing for the Thunderbird Balloon Race*

kitchens. Sahuaro Ranch Park is located off 59th Avenue at Mountain View Road.

For information call 623-937-4754.

CATLIN COURT HISTORIC SHOPS DISTRICT

An intriguing area of small older homes turned into antique and craft shops, Catlin Court attracts many tourists as well as residents with its brick sidewalks, gaslight-style street lamps, and more than thirty antique and specialty shops that stay open every third Thursday evening of the month for the self-guided Antique Walk. A meal at the Spicery, a turn-of-the-century home converted into a restaurant, is truly a delight. Enjoy viewing the antiques and nicknacks as you eat lunch at Aunt Pitty Pat's Pantry. Catlin Court is located between 57th and 59th Avenues, bordered by Myrtle and Palmaire Drive in Glendale.

For information call 623-937-4754.

CERRETA CHOCOLATE FACTORY

Although not part of Glendale's history, the family-run chocolate factory is very much a tourist attraction in today's Glendale. Enjoy a tour of the factory that produces an average of almost five thousand pounds of candy daily, and satisfy your sweet tooth with delicious samples. Monday through Thursday starting at 10:00 A.M. is open house when you can watch the candy being made. Factory are located at Glendale Ave. and 54th Drive.

For information call 623-930-1000.

THE BEAD MUSEUM

Recently moved from Prescott to Glendale, the Bead Museum is the only museum of its kind in the United States. There are ancient Indian tribal beads, beaded tapestries, beads used as a medium of exchange, and other oddities. This is the most extensive collection of ancient and contemorary beads in the world. This is also a great place to find beads to make the perfect necklace to complete an outfit. The Bead Museum is located at 5754 W. Glenn Drive.

For information call 623-930-7395.

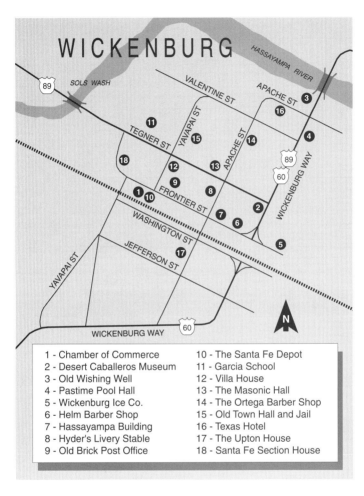

1 - Chamber of Commerce
2 - Desert Caballeros Museum
3 - Old Wishing Well
4 - Pastime Pool Hall
5 - Wickenburg Ice Co.
6 - Helm Barber Shop
7 - Hassayampa Building
8 - Hyder's Livery Stable
9 - Old Brick Post Office
10 - The Santa Fe Depot
11 - Garcia School
12 - Villa House
13 - The Masonic Hall
14 - The Ortega Barber Shop
15 - Old Town Hall and Jail
16 - Texas Hotel
17 - The Upton House
18 - Santa Fe Section House

WICKENBURG

Wickenburg, begun in 1863 when the Vulture Mine was established, was the first Arizona town built north of Tucson. It is filled with pioneer adobe and wood-frame buildings that are still used as stores and homes. Wickenburg is a town where the excitement and romance of the West are still alive.

The Hassayampa River runs nearby, and its waters are said to be responsible for many of the tall tales told by the early miners. The miners are gone, but the mine remains and is open to the public. In addition, there is a wonderful self-guided walking tour of the historic area of the town. Pick up your copy of the tour guide at the old Santa Fe railroad depot and proceed at your leisure along the one-mile walking tour.

Wickenburg today has several top-rated resorts, numerous art galleries, antique shops, and facilities for a luxurious and leisurely way of life. It also boasts one of the most outstanding western art museums in the country. Not far from the town you will find several ghost towns remaining from the gold mining days. When driving from Phoenix to Wickenburg you will pass through the well-known retirement community of Sun City.

Wickenburg is located fifty-eight miles northwest of Phoenix off Highway 93/60.

For information call 520-684-5479.

DESERT CABALLEROS WESTERN MUSEUM

The Desert Caballeros Western Museum is one of the outstanding western art museums in the country, with a collection of paintings, bronzes, Indian artifacts, and memorabilia that are the envy of many big city museums. The museum's art collection features works by Catlin, Moran, Bierstadt, Dixon, Russell, Remington, and several members of the Cowboy Artists of America Association. There are also artifacts of Anasazi, Hopi and Navajo Indians. You will enjoy the very popular black light exhibit of gems and minerals. On the lower level, the furnished turn-of-the-century rooms and general store delight visitors of all age groups. The museum is located at 21 N. Frontier Street in Wickenburg and is open Monday through Saturday, 10:00 A.M. to 5:00 P.M. and Sundays from 1:00 to 4:00 P.M. It is closed on major holidays.

For information call 520-684-2272 .

THE WICKENBURG GALLERY

Among the several fine galleries, in this historic and artistically sophisticated town, is The Wickenburg Gallery which emits a warm and welcome style. The gallery displays a fine representation of Americana, Cowboy, Southwestern, and Wildlife Art. In addition, The Wickenburg Gallery offers a beautiful collection of traditional Indian weavings, cowboy trappings, distinctive pottery, handmade leather goods, limited edition lithographs and prints. While touring Wickenburg, enjoy a visit to The Wickenburg Gallery located at 67 North Tegner St.

For information call 520-684-7047.

"The Vaquero" by Frederic Remington,
courtesy of the Desert Caballeros Western Museum

HASSAYAMPA RIVER PRESERVE

The word "Hassayampa" is Apache for "river that runs upside down", so called because the river usually runs underground, except for a four-mile stretch around Wickenburg, where it flows above ground providing water for the area's lush vegetation. The preserve, which stretches along the banks of the river, supports one of Arizona's last and finest Sonoran Desert streamside habitats. An extensive woodland has evolved along the Hassayampa flood plain. Several types of Sonoran Desert habitats are protected by the Conservancy and include river and lake communities, cottonwood-willow forest, mesquite scrub, and upland Sonoran Desert scrub community.

The riparian area (on the bank of a watercourse) at the Hassayampa includes a cottonwood-willow forest and several rare animals and birds. The preserve's riparian area is an impor-

"Thanks for the Rain" by Joe Beeler,
courtesy of the Desert Caballeros Western Museum

tant migration corridor for over 220 species of birds. Drawn to the water's edge are mule deer, bobcat, mountain lion, javelina, and ring-tailed cats.

Spring-fed Palm Lake is a unique four-acre pond and marsh habitat. The pond attracts an impressive number of water birds, such as the great blue heron, snowy egret, white-faced ibis, pied-billed grebe and a host of migrating waterfowl. Palm Lake shelters endangered fish species.

The preserve is located about three miles southeast of Wickenburg on the west side of Highway 60 near mile marker 114. It is open Wednesday through Sunday. Hours from September 16 to May 14 are from 8:00 A.M. to 5:00 P.M. and during the summer are from 6:00 A.M. to noon. Please stop at the Visitor Center when you arrive.

For information call 520-684-2772.

VULTURE MINE GHOST TOWN

Vulture was begun in 1863, when Henry Wickenburg discovered a ledge of gold while searching for quartz. Being an inexperienced miner, he let individuals mine their own ore and charged them fifteen dollars a ton. For a while in the late 1800s, Vulture was the third largest town in the territory.

Seeing it today is a real treat, because it is a ghost town that has not been renovated or changed into a tourist trap. Vulture is just as it was when its inhabitants left after the mine shut down. A few minor efforts have been made to stabilize structures but the town continues to age and deteriorate with time and weather conditions. One of the finest territorial school houses, built in 1887, still stands next to one built in 1936. Mining continued to some degree in Vulture until 1942. Just a few years ago effort was made to find gold in the old tailings. It is thought that there is still gold in the mine but the price of gold is not high enough to make renovating the mine and working it profitable.

Taking the walking tour of Vulture gives you a wonderful opportunity to shoot interesting photographs of old mining equipment, dilapidated houses, blacksmith shop, emptied ball mill, and the power house with its great diesel engine. You will also see the old Wickenburg house, the mess hall, and the hanging tree. There are many artifacts and antiques in Vulture, but

Following pages: "Eatin Dust" by W.H. Ford,
courtesy of the Wickenburg Gallery

Hank Ford

they are not for sale and are left pretty much as they were many years ago.

Vulture is an easy ghost town to get to. Head west out of Wickenburg on Wickenburg Way, turn left on Vulture Mine Road and follow it for thirteen miles. You can visit the mine from mid–September to mid–May daily from, 9:00 A.M. to 5:00 P.M. and from mid–May through mid–July, Saturday and Sunday from 8:00 A.M. to 4:00 P.M. There is an admission charge of $5:00. It is advisable to call to confirm the seasonal schedule.

For information call 520-684-5479.

PRESCOTT

While the Civil War was being fought in the eastern United States, Prescott was being settled in the west, among the pine covered Bradshaw Mountains, great granite boulders, and open grasslands. Prescott became the first Territorial Capitol in 1863, but a few years later, relinquished that honor to Tucson. As a result, the growth of Prescott was temporarily stunted until mining became important in the area. The capitol was again moved back to Prescott for about twelve years and then was moved permanently to Phoenix.

During this time a young girl named Sharlot Mabrith Hall moved to Prescott, grew into adulthood and in 1909 became Arizona's first Territorial Historian. You will appreciate her efforts to preserve history when you visit the Sharlot Hall Museum complex. Another aspect of Prescott's history took place on Whiskey Row, across the street from the old and beautiful Yavapai County stone courthouse. The row of twenty-six saloons provided activity and entertainment for cowboys trying to outdrink each other.

These saloons are now shops, museums, and restaurants catering to tourists as well as the folks who live in the early American and Victorian style houses lining the tree-shaded walks. Prescott, a tranquil, agreeable community of about 26,000 people was rated the number one retirement city in the United States, by Money magazine. This mile-high city is a lovely community any season of the year.

To enjoy the walking tour of the historic sights in downtown Prescott, pick up a tour guide at the Chamber of Commerce. If you are in Arizona on the fourth of July, you will enjoy *Prescott*

"Bend of the River" by W. H. Ford,
courtesy of The Wickenburg Gallery

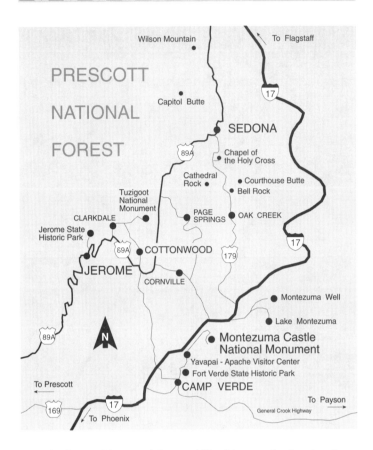

Frontier Days with one of the world's oldest professional rodeos, as well as the festival and parade down Whiskey Row, location of the famous Palace Bar.

Prescott is located southwest of Sedona and north of Wickenburg off Highway 89. It is about ninety miles north of Phoenix.

For information call 520-445-2000 or 1-800-266-7534.

SHARLOT HALL MUSEUM

Sharlot Hall, a remarkable woman, poet, and dedicated historian, spent much of her life gathering artifacts to preserve the history of Prescott. While she was living in two of the early houses that are part of the museum complex, she was building many of the collections which are housed there. More has been added, including the John C. Fremont House, moved to the complex and restored to present a comprehensive picture of the times. Fort

Misery, built in 1864 as the general store, became the courthouse where "misery" was dispersed in the form of justice.

Eight other buildings complete the museum complex to give a fairly good picture of life in Prescott about a hundred years ago. Take several hours to wend your way through the buildings, absorbing history and viewing fascinating collections. The museum is located at 415 W. Gurley Street and is open 10:00 A.M. to 5:00 P.M., April through October and 10:00 A.M. to 4:00 P.M. November through March. Sunday hours are 1:00 to 5:00 P.M. Recommended donation is $4.00 for adults.

For information call 520-445-3122.

PRESCOTT'S PHIPPEN MUSEUM OF WESTERN ART

Named for George Phippen, one of the founders and first president of Cowboy Artists of America, the museum will impress you with its collection of sketches, paintings, ceramics, and bronze sculptural pieces done by western artists. Some of this work is for sale in the gift shop. The museum is located just north of the junction of Highways 89 and 89A.

For more information call 520-778-1385.

YAVAPAI COUNTY COURTHOUSE

Imposing because of its beauty and age, the courthouse reflects history through its architectural style, impressive sculptures, and unique timeline painted in the concrete walk. The courthouse is located at Gurley and Montezuma streets.

Drawing of Hohokam art

SMOKI MUSEUM

To expand your knowledge of Indian artifacts and lifestyle visit the Smoki Museum with its excellent collection of Indian basketry, pottery, and stone tools excavated from the area. There is a fine reproduction of a kiva, a round structure used for Indian ceremonies. The museum is located at 147North Arizona Street.
   For information call 520-445-1230.

HOTEL ST. MICHAEL

Hotel St. Michael on the corner of Gurley and Montezuma streets is almost one hundred years old. Step inside to see and hear its history. Notice the gargoyles on the outside. Stay awhile.
For information call 520-687-3757

HIKING AROUND PRESCOTT

Thumb Butte Trail is the shorter and easier of the two trails in the Prescott National Forest. The trail is well-maintained, well-marked, and also has signs identifying some of the vegetation. The six-hundred-foot climb during the first mile gets you to the saddle of the mountain where the view is spectacular. This two-and-a-half-mile trail is a good one to acquaint you with the Prescott area. The trailhead is located three miles down Thumb Butte Road which begins at the west end of Gurley street.
   Granite Mountain Wilderness is popular with serious rock climbers and offers trails for hikers of all ages. Trail 261 is best for hikers and campers. Carry your water, wear appropriate shoes and be aware that the area is home to mountain lions. To reach Granite Mountain Wilderness go three miles west of Prescott on Iron Springs Road to the Granite Basin Lake turnoff (Forest Service Road 374), turn right, go five miles to the trailhead.
   Spruce Mountain provides excellent forest hiking on either of two trails. The trailheads are six miles south of Prescott off Senator Highway at the first Groom Creek Loop sign.
   Mingus Mountain Woodchute Trail offers a magnificent view of red rocks, Verde Valley, Sycamore Canyon, and the San Francisco Peaks as a reward for your hike. The trailhead is located off Forest Service Road 107 leading out of Potato Patch Campground on Mingus Mountain.

ARIZONA'S GHOST TOWNS

We assume that many of our readers are adventurers with a strong curiosity about the history of the Old West and its old mining towns. If you are traveling in a strong and dependable vehicle, you may want to sidetrack from main roads to find yourself alone with the ghosts of early prospectors while you walk through the empty, hot and dusty remains of a once-booming town. Do not expect comforts of civilization. You are on your own, experiencing the uneasy feelings of being back in time, surrounded by uninviting remains, listening to the winds blowing dust through the dilapidated buildings. In your explorations of ghost towns you may find old mining equipment, abandoned grave sites, partially standing structures, and the essence of those who have gone before. The experience of the ghost town cannot be predicted. This individual experience depends on the viewer's personality, knowledge of history, and taste for adventure. Each visitor is affected differently, sees and feels different things, and has different memories of the visit.

It is advisable to be cautious when exploring ghost towns. Stay away from mine shafts because of the danger of falling several hundred feet into the old pit. Watch where you walk to avoid hidden mine shafts. To assure that there will always be ghost towns, please do not remove any objects for souvenirs; instead, use your camera to preserve the memory.

Below is a brief description of the most interesting ghost towns in Arizona, according to the Arizona Office of Tourism, and a map showing their locations.

1. Bisbee. Ninety-five miles southeast of Tucson. "Queen of the Mining Camps." The brawling mining days of the 1880s blend with the modern city of today. Famous for its underground Queen Mine tours, Brewery Gulch, Queen Hotel, and Lavender Pit Mine. Today it is populated with artists, writers, and retirees.

2. Cochran. Sixteen miles east of Florence on Kelvin Highway, north on a dirt road to Gila River. Once the site of the railroad depot, now only a few buildings remain. Coke ovens are directly across the river. Pick-up or high-clearance vehicles are recommended.

3. Congress. Two miles from Congress Junction. Site of the rich Congress gold mine. You will find ruins of old cabins, rubble-strewn flats, and an old cemetery. (The mine and adjacent buildings are closed to the public.)

4. Dos Cabezas. Off Highway 186, fifteen miles southeast of Willcox. Semi-ghost town where a few residents still support a small post office. Formerly an active supply center for surrounding mines and cattle ranches. It was a Wells Fargo station in 1885. Now there are vacant, crumbling adobes and a stage station.

5. Duquesne. Nineteen miles east of Nogales. Established around the turn-of-the-century, this former mining center had a peak population of 1000 residents, including Westinghouse of Westinghouse Electric, who lived here while taking $4,000,000 in

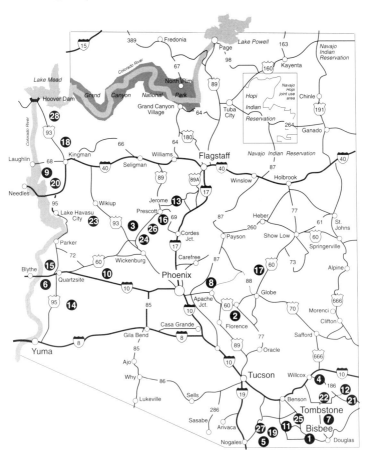

Retired mining equipment

ore from his nearby mine. It is in a state of ruins now with Washington Camp 3/4 mile beyond.

6. *Ehrenberg.* Now a growing community, the only things of original Ehrenberg to be seen are a few old adobe buildings and a cemetery which was also used by its neighbor across the river, Blythe, California.

7. *Gleeson.* Sixteen miles east of Tombstone. Even before the arrival of Spaniards in this area, Indians were mining turquoise near the present site of Gleeson. John Gleeson prospected the area in the 1880s. Later Tiffany's mined the same blue gem while other interests mined copper, lead, and zinc. You will see picturesque ruins and a cemetery.

8. *Goldfield.* Five miles from Apache Junction off Highway 88. There is visible evidence of mining during the middle of the 1890s. Four of the original mine shafts, slopes, and timbers can be seen.

9. *Goldroad.* Twenty-three miles southwest of Kingman. Gold was discovered here by John Moss and party around 1864. A new strike was made by Joe Jerez in 1902. In 1949, most of the remaining mining operations and buildings were razed to escape taxes. Now there are mostly diggings and minor ruins.

10. *Harrisburg.* Eight miles south of Wenden. Harrisburg was the first town in this part of the desert. Gold was discovered near the town site by Bill Bear around 1886. The town was started by Captain Charles Harris on the site of the old Centennial State Station.

11. *Harshaw.* Ten miles southeast of Patagonia. Settled about 1875, this place soon boasted a newspaper, "The Bullion", saloons, numerous stores, and a hundred working mines nearby. Today you will find stone and adobe ruins and a cemetery.

12. *Hilltop.* Thirty-six miles southeast from Willcox off Highway 186. The mine was established by Frank and John Hands. The town of Hilltop was first started under the west side of the

mountain, then a tunnel was built through to the east side where an even larger town was established.

13. Jerome. Off Highway 89A, thirty-three miles northeast of Prescott. Established in 1876, this famous copper camp hit a peak population of 15,000 around 1929 and its main mine produced $500,000,000 in ore before closing in 1952. There are many picturesque buildings, ruins, museum, and other points of interest. Because the population has grown to about 400, Jerome is now referred to as a restored mining town.

14. Kofa. Twenty-eight miles south of Quartzsite. Kofa is the site of the rich King of Arizona gold mine established in 1896 by Charles Eichelberger. During its thirteen years of prime activity, ending in 1910, the King mine produced close to $14,000,000. Today it is mostly ruins.

15. La Paz. Eight miles north of Ehrenberg. La Paz flourished for seven years as a gold center and river port. Between 1862 and 1873 the town had over 5,000 residents. The central portion of the town is being reconstructed, and the public may view the excavations.

16. McCabe. Two-and-a-half miles west of Humbolt. McCabe was a mining and milling town, dating from the late nineteenth century. Remains of old cabins, cemetery, ruins of large mill, mine dumps, and rubble can be seen.

17. McMillen. Ten miles northeast of Globe. The mine was established in 1876 and supported by celebrated Stonewall Jackson, mine. The mine is believed to have produced close to $3,000,000. Today it is ruins.

18. Mineral Park. Fifteen miles northwest of Kingman near Duval Copper Mine. This was one of the county's important early towns and the county seat. It is still populated.

19. Mowry. Fifteen miles southeast of Patagonia. Mowry was a small town that grew up around old silver, lead, and zinc mines. It was purchased in the late 1850s by Sylvester Mowry. United

States Army Lt. Mowry's operations were cut short in 1862 when Mowry was charged with supplying lead for confederate bullets, jailed at Fort Yuma, and his mine confiscated by the government. Today you can see extensive ruins.

20. *Oatman.* Thirty-two miles southwest of Kingman. This gold-mining town was active from 1900 to 1942. It is situated at the foot of Black Mountain. Many empty buildings and picturesque ruins remain. There are small places of business operated by hardy group of "Never say die" citizens. The town has become a popular tourist attraction.

21. *Paradise.* Six miles northwest of Portal. Briefly active mining town dating from the early 1900s. Paradise is still "home" to a few oldtimers who are glad to point out the old town jail and ruins of various businesses. Part of the town is privately owned.

22. *Pearce.* Twenty-nine miles south of Willcox. This old gold camp once had a population of two thousand, all of them well supported by the wealth of the Commonwealth Mine. It was discovered by Johnny Pearce in 1894, and in its heyday the old Commonwealth was the richest gold digging in southern Arizona. It has an operating store and post office, with many vacant adobes and ruins of mines and mills.

23. *Signal.* Twelve miles west of Wikieup. Signal was established late in the 1870s as the mining town for the people who extracted ore from McCrackin and Signal mines. In its heyday, it had stores, shops, hotels, saloons, and a brewery to supply beer to the thirsty miners. Freight was shipped from San Francisco to Yuma then to Aubrey Landing. From there it was hauled by mule thirty-five miles uphill to Signal, which was prosperous for many years. There are mill ruins, one old saloon, foundations, rubble, and cemetery.

24. *Stanton.* Forty-two miles southwest of Prescott. In 1875 the town was named for Charles B. Stanton who kept a store and stage station and was also postmaster. Later the town became an active mining camp. Remaining buildings are in fair-to-good condition, all are privately owned.

Scorpion enjoying the solitude of a ghost town,
courtesy of Willis Peterson

25. Tombstone. Sixty-nine miles southeast of Tucson. "The town too tough to die." One of the Old West's most famous towns where silver was king. Most of its notorious landmarks remain—OK Corral, Boot Hill, Tombstone Epitaph. It is an active town and a popular tourist attraction.

26. Walker. Four miles east of Prescott. Captain Joseph Walker, in 1863, led a gold prospecting expedition into Yavapai County. As a result of his success the town of Walker came into being. Walker has a few winter and many summer residents. There are mill and mine ruins.

27. Washington Camp. Twenty miles south of Patagonia. It once was the major service community for Duquesne, Mowry, and Harshaw. At its peak, in 1905, it had a population of 5,200 miners and their families. Today there are ruins. Check road conditions before going. Rains sometimes wash away parts of roads.

28. White Hills. Fifty miles north of Kingman. In the 1890s it was the rowdiest silver camp between Globe and Virginia City. In a brief six years, the fifteen now forgotten mines, which surrounded it, gave up $12,000,000 in silver bullion. There are mostly old diggings now.

Old mining train cars at Bisbee

JEROME

Jerome is alive again with its five hundred residents who live an active arty lifestyle in the renovated ghost-town homes on the side of Mingus Mountain. Once a wild and wicked town full of saloons, Jerome, at its peak (somewhere between World War I and the stock market crash of 1929), had a population of fifteen thousand people, hoping to get rich from the mines giving forth their gold, silver, zinc, and copper. The mining began in 1883 and lasted until 1953 with the closing of the last copper mine.

A few hardy souls stayed on, forming the Jerome Historical Society and gradually turned the town into the tourist attraction it is today. Much of Jerome slid down the hill over the years, but some buildings have been stabilized and preserved, others torn down and some renovated and lived in today. There are buckled sidewalks, and the old jail that slid 225 feet down the hill rests in a vacant lot.

Many resident artisans enjoy the rebuilding of a community and hope to sell their wares. There are art galleries and shops along the old main street and a couple of restaurants housed in the old bordellos. You'll enjoy visiting the twenty-four-studio art center housed in the old Mingus Union High School and wonder

Powder Box Church

at the Powder Box Church which was built from wooden dyna-mite crates, and is now a private residence. There's a lot of good mining history and a few bawdy stories to be heard. To reach Jerome you can take Highway 89A out of Sedona or Highway 89 from Prescott.

For information call 520-634-2900.

JEROME STATE HISTORICAL PARK

In 1912, Jimmy "Rawhide" Douglas bought the Little Daisy Mine at the foot of Cleopatra Hill and had his fortune secured when he discovered a five foot thick vein of copper.

A visit to the Douglas Mansion, built in 1916, now the Visitors Center and State Historical Park, will bring alive the his-tory of this very realistic, once colorful and ribald town. The Mansion, located on Douglas Road, has a magnificent view of the surrounding valley and contains a few restored rooms and unique mining memorabilia.

For information call 520-634-5381.

JEROME HISTORICAL
SOCIETY MINE MUSEUM

The gift shop in front of the museum offers a good assortment of crafts and souvenirs. The museum although small, offers old photos of mining days, household objects, stock certificates and much more to recall the early days of underground mining. The museum is located at 200 Main Street.

For information call 520-634-5477.

GOLD KING MINE MUSEUM

Along with your visit to Jerome you may want to stop at the Gold King Mine Museum where you will be entertained by a petting zoo and a blacksmith, hammering out metal objects. There is an odd collection of mining equipment and other relics, in addition to a gift shop containing unique hand-painted sou-venirs and other mining related collectibles.

The museum is located about a mile east of Jerome on the site of the Hayes mining camp.

TUZIGOOT

An impressive hilltop Sinaguan village, Tuzigoot, with its well-preserved rooms laid out down the hillside, commands a grand view of the Verde Valley. It once contained about one hundred rooms and probably housed 250 people during its busiest era. As drought and famine during the 13th century began to effect out-lying groups of Indians, they may have moved to Tuzigoot for survival, swelling its population.

Archaeologists excavated 450 graves and through careful examination were able to determine that the life expectancy was somewhere in the mid–forties and that almost two-thirds of the Sinagua never lived past twenty-one. The fact they were a small people with the tallest men being about 5'6" helps us to understand their small rooms and doorways.

The strange barren dirt patterns at the foot of the hill that look like some unique farming technique are a result of slurry dumped from the mines and have nothing to do with the lifestyle of the early Indians. Tuzigoot lies between Cottonwood and Clarkdale off Highway 89A.

For information call 520-634-5564.

Tuzigoot Indian ruins

VERDE RIVER CANYON RAIL EXCURSION

Verde River Canyon Rail Excursion (Arizona Central Railroad) is a four-hour round trip train ride beginning at 300 N. Broadway in Clarkdale. The train travels forty miles around the edge of scenic Sycamore Canyon and through Verde Valley at a leisurely pace of twelve miles per hour. There are no roads through this rugged country, so the rail trip offers an opportunity to view beautiful scenery and Arizona wildlife seen only by horseback riders, hikers, or train passengers. As the train passes through the river canyon with its seven hundred-foot high sandstone walls, passengers can stand out on the gondolas to observe the geology of the canyon up close and maybe catch a glimpse of one of the seventy-five bald eagles that live in Verde Valley Canyon. In these days of fast transportation, a ride on an old train is quaint and nostalgic way to watch this scenic world slowly pass by. Verde River Canyon Rail Excursion is an experience well worth including in your vacation plans. Rates range from $20.95 for children in coach to $59.95 for adults in first class.

For reservations and information call 1-800-293-7245.

DEAD HORSE RANCH STATE PARK

Along the Verde River, near Tuzigoot National Monument, sits Dead Horse Ranch State Park, a place for picnicking, camping, and hiking. Fishing is a year-round sport in the lagoon, stocked with thousands of catfish and bass. In winter there is an abundance of trout. In the park there are 132 species of birds, making this a very popular place for bird watchers. The riparian vegetation along the Verde River is accessible to explorers because it borders the park. Campsites have good facilities and hiking trails winding down to the river. Enjoy the wildlife and cool off with a swim in the river. An Arizona fishing license is required to fish in the lagoon.

For information call 520-634-5283.

Drawing of Hohokam art

SEDONA

One hundred twenty miles north of Phoenix and thirty miles south of Flagstaff, sits Sedona which was settled by farming families in the late 1800s. Because of its remoteness, the community lived without electricity until 1936. It is now a thriving and popular community surrounded by towering red rocks.

The best tip we can give our readers is to approach Sedona from the north by driving down from Flagstaff on Highway 89A. This downhill curving drive, which drops three thousand feet in fifteen miles, is considered one of the most scenic in the nation. The grandeur of Oak Creek Canyon unfolds at every turn. The fresh air and year-round moderate climate attract writers, artists, entrepreneurs, retirees, and visitors who bask in the beauty of the surrounding Coconino National Forest. The brilliantly colored sandstone cliffs, bluffs, and spires are favorite subjects for a photographer. Sedona was popularized by the western author Zane Grey, as the setting for many of his novels. The Association of Cowboy Artists of America was founded in a little Sedona tavern in 1965. Well-known artists also live and work here. You can view some of their works in local galleries.

The 4,400-foot elevation makes Sedona warmer than Flagstaff and cooler than Phoenix which is an ideal climate for horseback riding, fishing, hiking, and exploring throughout the year. The town, itself, boasts many exciting shops and galleries.

Sedona offers a year-round calendar of impressive art events and the opportunity to enjoy nature at its most spectacular.
For information call 520-282-7722.

CHAPEL OF THE HOLY CROSS

A remarkable intertwining of the work of humans with the work of nature is the smooth geometric form of Chapel of the Holy Cross built into the rugged red rocks of Sedona. If you want to gain everything the chapel has to offer, you need to be there at early morning when the sunrise highlights the interior through the glass windows. The natural lighting of the chapel changes dramatically as the day progresses.

The Chapel of the Holy Cross provides a restful place for quiet reflection and enjoyment of its soft lights and music. The only regular service is a Monday evening prayer service at 5:00.

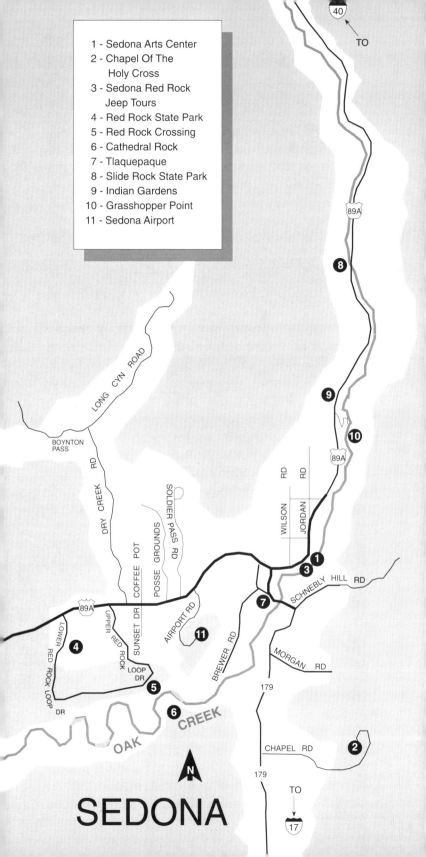

1 - Sedona Arts Center
2 - Chapel Of The
    Holy Cross
3 - Sedona Red Rock
    Jeep Tours
4 - Red Rock State Park
5 - Red Rock Crossing
6 - Cathedral Rock
7 - Tlaquepaque
8 - Slide Rock State Park
9 - Indian Gardens
10 - Grasshopper Point
11 - Sedona Airport

SEDONA

The imposing cross on its facade is strikingly simple against the complex geologic formations. the chapel was designed by Marguerite Brunswig Staude, a disciple of Frank Lloyd Wright and is one of Sedona's best known landmarks. It is located above Chapel Road off Highway 179, two miles south of Sedona.

For information call 520-282-4069.

SEDONA ARTS CENTER

There are numerous art galleries in Sedona now, but The Sedona Arts Center, sometimes called the "Barn", has been operating for more than thirty years, offering residents and visitors theater, musical performances, monthly exhibits, and classes in the performing and visual arts. The gallery, free and open to the public, is an excellent place to view work of local artists as well as others. You might want to check with them when you arrive in Sedona to see what is currently happening in the Sedona art world. The "Barn" is located at the juncture of Highway 89A and Art Barn Road in uptown Sedona.

For information call 520-282-3809.

SLIDE ROCK STATE PARK

Camping, picnicking, and fishing are all part of a relaxing day at Slide Rock State Park. However, the main attraction, Slide Rock, draws many people to the Oak Creek Canyon area. The water of Oak Creek flows quickly over the smooth surface of the red sandstone rock, carrying the seated bathers over the rock and tumbling them into a pool of cool, clear water. On a hot summer weekend, Slide Rock can be uncomfortably crowded with people of all ages. It seems to be most popular with young people, ages twelve to thirty. Wear a sturdy old bathing suit or some rugged cut-offs. Parking is at a premium along the roadside but is available for a small fee in the State Park parking lot nearby.

To reach Slide Rock State Park take Highway 89A north from Sedona about six-and-a-half miles.

For information call 520-282-4119 or 520-282-3034.

Escaping the summer heat in Oak Creek Canyon

ADVENTURE SIGHTSEEING
AROUND SEDONA

Get out into Arizona one way or another! There are a variety of ways to make your visit to Sedona exciting and memorable. The sampling of many fine sightseeing companies listed below represent the most popular ways of sightseeing around Sedona.

Sedona Pink Jeep Tours. One of the best ways to see the back country among the red rocks is by jeep. Your guide will drive you over rocks and into places you never would drive yourself. You can even be driven to the magnetic vortex, which is believed to give people new energy.
For information call 520-282-5000 or 1-800-873-3662

Sedona Adventures. Let Sedona Adventures guide you in experiencing the peace and magic of Sedona's enchanting red-rock country. They provide many different kinds of jeep tours that can fit your schedule and interests. You can engage in a group tour or arrange for a private one.
For information call 520-282-4114.

Sedona Red Rock Jeep Tours. Sedona's Cowboy Tour Company offers you typically western excitement, as their jeeps take you through rugged red-rock back country of Sedona. *For information call 1-800-848-7728.*

Kachina Stable. The stables offers you every thing from simple two-hour rides to customized pack trips that last from two to six days into beautiful Sycamore Canyon. *For information call 520-282-7252.*

Northern Light Balloon Flights. A company vehicle picks you up at your hotel about a half hour before sunrise to take you on a scenic hot-air balloon flight over the red rock country. The flight usually lasts three to four hours and includes a champagne picnic on the ground. *For information call 520-282-2274.*

Arizona Helicopter Adventures. AHA offers helicopter flights over Boynton Canyon, the city of Sedona, Verde Valley, Oak Creek Canyon, as well as the Grand Canyon. A unique experience is being dropped off for a picnic on the top of a mesa. You let the pilot know, by two-way radio, when to pick you up. Located at Sedona Airport. *For information call 602-282-0904 or 1-800-282-5141.*

Time Expeditions. This company takes you on archaeological and geological tours, exploring a twelfth-century cliff dwelling. This is Sedona's only ancient ruin tour. *For information call 520-282-2137.*

DRIVING SCENIC ROADS AROUND SEDONA

Verde Valley School Road. This road turns west off Highway 179, two miles south of the Village of Oak Creek, and takes you to the base of Cathedral Rock and then on to Red Rock Crossing.

Red Rock Loop. On this scenic drive you will come to the most popular photographic spot in Sedona—Cathedral Rock reflected in the waters of Oak Creek. Red Rock Loop takes you through fifteen miles of beautiful panoramas. To begin the drive, turn left off 89A, about four miles south of West Sedona. After

two miles turn left onto Chavez Road and follow it to Red Rock Crossing. When you have seen enough of Cathedral Rock, go back the way you came to continue the Red Rock Loop.

Schnebly Hill Road. This road connecting Sedona to Interstate 17 at Munds Park, is part dirt and part paved, very bumpy and very scenic. Stopping at one of several vista points will give you a pleasant break from the rough road and a chance to experience and photograph some of the best views of the Sedona area. Don't take this road in bad weather.

Dry Creek Road. It turns north off Highway 89A out of West Sedona, and takes you through some of the more striking scenery. It is also a good road for mountain bikers.

HIKING AROUND SEDONA

West Fork Trail. Categorized as one of the best, this trail in Oak Creek Canyon surprises its hikers with a variety of hiking difficulties and natural beauty. Hikers can choose, according to their capabilities, either a short, few-hour hike or a longer, more difficult adventure. People from all over the world come to explore this mixture of red rock and green lush flora interrupted unexpectedly with crystal clear rivulets of water. In the fall, Oak Creek Canyon is flooded with photographers taking advantage of the incredible explosion of color. During the summer rainy season, people are often surprised by dangerous flash floods. We recommend you check the weather report before hiking. If you are carrying a walking stick, it is customary to leave it at the trailhead as you depart so someone else can use it. The West Fork trailhead is eleven miles north of Sedona off Highway 89A.

Boynton Canyon Trail. This five-mile long, heavily used trail is best hiked during the week. It takes you gradually up through typically pleasant scenery into a red-rock walled box canyon of such outstanding beauty that you will enjoy staying for a while to eat your picnic lunch, take photographs, and absorb this distinct environment.

The trailhead is located just before the John Gardiner Resort on Boynton Pass Road which turns right, off Dry Creek Road which turns north from Highway 89A just west of West Sedona.

Following pages: Oak Creek

Vulte Arch Trail. This trail is also found off Dry Creek Road, five miles down Forest Road 152 which may be best traveled in a four-wheel-dive vehicle. The trail is a round trip hike of three-and-a-half miles and takes you through uniquely beautiful red-rock scenery to a natural arch.

Doe Mountain. The awe inspiring view from the top of the mesa, Doe Mountain, is worth every step of the two to three-hour hike. Actual climbing time is about one-and-a-half hours but you will want to spend extra time appreciating the view. You will be able to see the uninterrupted 360 degree horizon and get a different perspective of Sedona, Jerome, and the Verde Valley. The trail is not as steep as it first looks because it crisscrosses the side of the mountain. You do not need to be an experienced hiker for this trek, but as always, wear hiking shoes and carry water and sun protection.

To get to the Doe Mountain trailhead take Dry Creek Road off Highway 89A. Head toward the Enchantment Resort, pass over a low-water crossing, turn left and continue on to Forest Road 152C which turns left. Go past a parking area at the entrance to Fay Canyon until you come to another parking area from which trail #60 leads you up Doe Mountain.

MONTEZUMA CASTLE
NATIONAL MONUMENT

Looking upward one hundred feet to the sun bathed limestone-block dwelling, built into the cliff side, one wonders how many of the ancient inhabitants climbed up and down the cliff each day gathering food, weaving materials, and water from Beaver Creek and the surrounding area. The peaceful Sinagua who resided here in the twelfth and thirteenth centuries probably had emigrated from Wupatki or Walnut Canyon during a time of drought. The Sinagua were farmers who depended on rainfall to water their crops; however, as they moved into areas previously inhabited by Hohokam, they began to use the abandoned irrigation canals.

They also changed their building habits from pithouses to above-ground masonry in cliffs or on hilltops. The Verde Valley was home to the Sinagua until they left in the early 1400s, either

Montezuma Castle Indian ruins

because of poor farming conditions or conflicts with the Yavapai Indians who had begun to move into the valley. The Sinagua are thought to have been absorbed into the Pueblo culture to the north.

Exploration of Montezuma Castle National Monument begins at the museum-like Visitor Center where you can view the displays of original Sinagua pottery and tools, and be introduced to their lifestyle.

In addition to the original Sinagua artifacts you are also introduced to local insects and reptiles on display in a large showcase. From the Visitor Center you proceed along a paved walk in a park-like setting to the base of the cliff in which the ruins remain. The sudden appearance of the large and impressive structure is startling. Visitors walk back and forth trying to find the best angle for their perfect photograph. The well-maintained monument is a pleasure to visit.

The monument is open from 8:00 A.M. to 5:00 P.M. daily during the winter months and from 8:00 A.M. to 7:00 P.M. daily during the summer months. Adult admission charge is $2.00. You can reach Montezuma Castle National Monument by taking Interstate 17 north from Phoenix or south from Flagstaff.
For information call 520-567-3322.

MONTEZUMA WELL

Once the home of the Hohokam and then the Sinagua, this distinctive dwelling place seems like a resort. The water surface sits fifty-five feet below the rim and has a 470 foot diameter. The dwellings are built into the wall above the water and also near the water's edge. This oasis in the desert is a spring-fed sink hole created when an underground cavern collapsed many years ago.

There is a long paved walk to the rim of the well. Stay on the walkway to avoid any desert reptiles or insects that inhabit the area. On the way up, enjoy the well identified desert plants, the view, and peacefulness of the environment. The more curious visitors follow the trail down into the well to explore the numerous ruins cleverly built into the walls of this large natural well. The monument is located eleven miles northeast of Montezuma Castle off Interstate 17.
For information call 520-567-3322.

CAMP VERDE

At one time in Arizona's history, fifteen hundred Indians from several tribes were forced by the U. S. cavalry to walk for ten days in cold weather to newly established reservations. Some, not being used to confinement, became renegades.

Camp Verde, the oldest community in the Verde Valley was established as a cavalry outpost to protect settlers along the Verde River from renegade Indian raids on their fields of corn. When the raids ceased in 1882, the fort became unnecessary and was abandoned in 1891. The fort had no walls and never was invaded.

Fort Verde State Historical Park, built around the old outpost in the middle of town, commemorates the U.S. Army garrison that opened the Central Territory for settlement in the 1870s. Here you will get a real feel for how the military personnel of this time lived. In the three buildings that make up the complex you will see the hospital and doctor's quarters which are furnished rather well, including a piano and fireplace.

The commanding officer's quarters is furnished comfortably with household items of the times and provide a picture of what life was like during those years; but the quarters of the bachelor officer displays relics of a less than luxurious existence.

The Fort Verde State Historic Park is located on Lane Street which turns off Main Street. Camp Verde is eighty-six miles north of Phoenix off Interstate 17.

For information call 520-567-9294.

ARCOSANTI

Understand first, the term "arcology", a term coined by Paolo Soleri to describe the concept of architecture and ecology working as one integral process to produce new urban habitats. Arcosanti is a prototype arcology for five thousand people, combining compact urban structure with large scale solar greenhouses on fifteen acres of a four thousand-acre preserve. Still in the early stages of construction, Arcosanti rises dramatically from basalt cliffs near Cordes Junction, sixty miles north of Phoenix. Since 1970 thousands of students and professionals have come to Arcosanti to participate in seminars, conferences, and workshops conducted by Soleri and his staff. You may be interested in tours

of the foundry and living quarters. There are Elderhostel programs, overnight accommodations, and outstanding musical events at Arcosanti. To reach Arcosanti, exit from Interstate 17 at Cordes Junction and follow the signs.

For information call 520-632-7135.

TONTO NATURAL BRIDGE STATE PARK

Up along the Mogollon Rim where it is cool all summer, near the towns of Pine and Strawberry, you will find the monumental arch of Tonto Natural Bridge. This natural arch stands 183 feet tall and towers over hikers who have hiked the quarter mile to see it. It is thought to be the longest natural travertine arch in the world and spans a 150-foot wide canyon. This part of Arizona is worth several days of your time. Enjoy the forests and small quaint towns that welcome tourists and provide them with accommodations necessary to make their stay comfortable.

You'll find delicious strawberry pie in the town of Strawberry and you'll have a chance to visit Arizona's oldest standing schoolhouse. There are cozy bed and breakfast hotels in several of the small towns. Campgrounds abound but fill up quickly on the weekends with people escaping from the desert valley's summer heat. To assure a camp site, call ahead for reservations, especially before holiday weekends.

The turnoff to Tonto Natural Bridge State Park is approximately five miles past the community of Pine. The park is open from 8:00 A.M. to 6:00 P.M. The admission fee is $5.00 per vehicle.

For information call 520-476-4202 or 520-476-3547.

Drawing of Anasazi art   *Bronze Soleri bells*

APACHE JUNCTION

The area around Apache Junction has been frequented by a variety of people over the years. The ancient Hohokam lived in the area from 300 B.C. to approximately A.D. 1425 and were later followed by miners, prospectors, settlers, farmers, and ranchers. In 1923 the Apache Junction Inn was built at the crossroads to serve travelers; and in 1950, with a growing population, the crossroads officially became the town of Apache Junction.

Today, tourists will find a variety of activities, a retirement community or two, and a welcoming spirit toward winter visitors (Snowbirds). Many people pass through Apache Junction because it sits at the intersection of Highway 60 and the Apache Trail. The rural looking town, with a population of eighteen thousand, backed by the Superstition Mountains serves as the entrance to the Tonto National Forest and the Salt River Canyon.

For information call 602-982-3141.

GOLDFIELD GHOST TOWN

When Goldfield was in its prime it had three saloons, including the famous U-shaped bar, a hotel, and boarding house. It all began as a rich gold strike at the foot of the Superstition

Mountains. The founding of the Goldfield mining district of fifty working mines caused a boom town to be born in 1892. Millions of dollars worth of high-grade ore were mined over the next five years.

Be sure to take the underground mine tour of the Old Mammoth Mine, and enjoy one of the Southwest's finest collections of antique mining equipment. Visit the Superstition Mountain Museum for information on the Lost Dutchman's Mine and much more. There is a mineral collection and other memorabilia and artifacts representing the history of cowboys, Indians, military, folklore, mining, and archaeology. The museum also has multimedia presentations of historical events. At Goldfield they'll even let you pan for gold. Goldfield Ghost Town is located east of Phoenix, almost four miles north of Apache Junction off Arizona's Scenic Highway 88.

For information call 602-983-0333.

LOST DUTCHMAN MINE PARK

The mine may or may not really exist. It is said to be in the Superstition Mountains, east of Apache Junction. James Waltz, who either found or stole this mine, left only clues as to its whereabouts when he died in 1891. He said to look for a pointed peak and that it is located in a place no miner would ever think to look. He also said the mine is so rich you can remove the gold

Remains of old gold mining days—saloon at Goldfield

with a knife. There are several different legends about the Lost Dutchman Mine and many people have tried unsuccessfully to find the legendary treasure.

To get to the park, go east from Phoenix on the Superstition Freeway to Apache Junction and then north on Highway 88 to the Lost Dutchman Park.

TORTILLA FLAT

Tortilla Flat, with a current population of less than ten, is an old road camp located eighteen miles northeast of Apache Junction off Highway 88. Don't make Tortilla Flat your destination, but be sure to stop on your way through to the lakes or Roosevelt Dam. It's as good a place to stop today, as it was many years ago. In 1904 work crews began traveling through Tortilla Flat transporting materials to build Roosevelt Dam. For their convenience, a restaurant was built which serves travelers tasty food even today. When you stop there for a meal you might want to staple a dollar bill to the interior walls of the restaurant as your calling card, the way many others have done.

If you're planning to go farther east on Highway 88 to Roosevelt Dam, be prepared for a bumpy ride over twenty-two miles of dirt road. The road is often closed due to bad weather.

For information call 480-982-3141 or 602-984-1776.

View of Superstition Mountains   *Interior of the restaurant at Tortilla Flat*

ADVENTURE SIGHTSEEING
FROM APACHE JUNCTION

OK Corral Stables and Horseback Riding. Licensed by Tonto National Forest, these stables have become an historical pack station for Lost Dutchman Mine hunters. Join the owners on scenic desert rides and hear them describe the plants and animals of the area. Enjoy a trail ride and evening around the campfire. For information and tales of the Superstition, this is the place. The stables are located northeast of Apache Junction on Highway 88.
For information call 480-982-4040.

Don Donnelly Stables. The Don Donnelly Stables at Gold Canyon Ranch gives you a western riding experience you'll never forget, by providing you with some of the finest horses and wranglers available in the Southwest. Enjoy the fabulous Superstition Mountain Wilderness area by taking a short ride or a multiple-day pack trip on a horse suited to your ability. For a unique steak-fry dinner or breakfast, take a hay wagon ride to the outdoor cook site. Inquire about the very special, week-long trips to Monument Valley.

The stables are located at 6010 South King's Ranch Road about seven miles east of Apache Junction.
For information call 480-982-7822.

Trail Horse Adventures. Experience the essence of Arizona's Old West with adventurous horseback riding, pack trips, breakfast and steak cookout rides, horse-drawn hay wagon rides, and western theme parties. Have a cowboy adventure in authentic cowboy wilderness areas. Tour the high Sonoran Desert, the foothills of the mountains, and the lush valley. Ride the old Indian and cavalry trails to catch the thrill of yesterday and the beauty of today.

You'll be given a horse suited to your ability, guided through acres of beautiful Arizona country, and might even see coyotes, lizards and snakes. The breakfasts and dinners are fantastic and the hospitality is warm and genuine. It's like going back a hundred years to Arizona's Old West, where cavalry soldiers, Indians, and famous outlaws once roamed.

Trail Horse Adventures is located off Meridian Road in Apache Junction. They also have locations in Scottsdale, Prescott, and Sedona. *For information call 1-800-723-3538.*

DOLLY'S STEAMBOAT CRUISES

Enjoy the scenery around Arizona's most beautiful lakes. See magnificent canyons, wildlife, and unique desert plants in their natural habitat. Parts of these lakes can be seen only by boat.

Dolly's Steamboat on Canyon Lake

Take a relaxing ninety-minute tour on the one hundred-foot replica of a double-deck sternwheeler which will transport you on Canyon Lake, in riverboat fashion. Try the Nature Cruise at noon or 2:00 p.m. to enjoy the fresh air, sunshine, and sightseeing. Try the twilight Dinner Cruise for the romance and beauty of the lake in the evening. Nature Cruises are $14.00 plus tax per person and Dinner Cruises are $37.95 plus tax per per person. Dolly's Steamboat Cruises is open for business daily except for Thanksgiving and Christmas.

To cruise Canyon Lake on Dolly's Steamboat travel north out of Apache Junction on Highway 88 for sixteen miles. *For information call 480-827-9144.*

TUBING DOWN THE SALT RIVER

The most popular way to cool down during the hot summer days is tubing down the lower Salt River. About an hour northeast of Phoenix, people of all ages float down the river on innertubes, getting sunburned while trying to stay cool.

On weekends, in hot weather, the river seems to be covered with people. Often you will see a couple of tubes tied together, one holding a cooler full of soft drinks and snacks. It is not advisable to tie a group of tubes together because they can get caught on tree branches and rocks. Tubing can be dangerous because when the flow of water is heavy there can be rapids which might flip a tube, dunking the rider. Children should wear life jackets and everyone should wear tennis shoes and plenty of protection from the sun. If you go during mid–week, when it's not as crowded, you have a better chance to enjoy the scenery of the Tonto National Forest and might even see a bald eagle, javelina, or mule deer enjoying the river's edge.

Begin your adventure at the Salt River Recreation Area where you can park your car and rent a gigantic innertube, if you don't have your own. There is a shuttle bus which, for a few dollars, will take you to points along the river. The season for tubing is from April fifteenth to mid–September. To get to the Salt River Recreation Area take Highway 87 out of Fountain Hills, travel for ten miles to the Saguaro Lake turnoff and go another ten miles to the river. The Recreation Center is actually located where Bush Highway and Usery Pass Road cross.

For information call 602-984-3305 or 602-379-6446.

SALT RIVER CANYON
AND WHITE WATER RAFTING

The Salt River Canyon is often a beautiful surprise to travelers because it resembles the Grand Canyon, but on a smaller scale. The beautiful drive down into the canyon and up the other side, where you cross the Salt River Bridge and enter the Apache Indian Reservation, makes up for the canyon's smaller size. The Salt River, which originates in the peaks of the White Mountains, flows through the bottom of the canyon toward Phoenix. A good place to view the canyon is about thirty-five miles northeast of Globe off Highway 60.

While the lower Salt River is calm and ideal for people who just want to relax, the upper Salt River is an exciting place for the challenge of white water river rafting through Class III (quite powerful) rapids. Being part of this magnificent environment is truly memorable.

For information call one of the following licensed outfitters:
Far Flung Adventures 1-800-359-4138
MDX 1-800-833-6550
Salt River Rafting 1-800-964-RAFT
Sun Country Rafting 1-800-2PADDLE

ROOSEVELT DAM

The completion of Theodore Roosevelt Dam in 1911 assured Phoenix a steady supply of water. The 280-foot tall structure is the largest masonry dam in the world. It was built with stone blocks which were chiseled by imported Italian stonemasons. Everything had to be hauled up the Apache Trail, making this a very difficult project. Before the work began on the dam, there were often water disputes between California and Arizona, once escalating to near warfare.

Roosevelt Dam is visited by large numbers of people passing by on their way to other nearby tourist attractions. Because work crews are often working on the dam and the road is narrow, it is wise to drive cautiously. Perhaps in the near future, tourists will be provided with an easily accessible scenic view point. Both the dam and the surrounding view are worth seeing.

For information call 602-982-3141.

TONTO NATIONAL MONUMENT

The monument offers the opportunity to explore ruins of the prehistoric Salado Indians—farmers who had gradually moved up into alcoves in the side of rugged hills. They used rocks and mud to construct rooms. A few of the dwellings had second stories. The Salado lived in the Tonto Basin for about three hundred years but left the same time the Hohokam left, around A.D. 1450. The Salado people left us with pottery, remnants of fabric, handprints, and smoke stains from their cooking fires as proof they had lived there. Several of the ruins can be accessed only with special permission, granted in advance.

Ruins at Tonto National Monument

The well-maintained park provides paved trails winding through hillside vegetation which is labeled for your education. The walk up the hillside to the Lower Ruin is challenging if you are in poor shape, but the path is paved and there are many resting spots. Take your camera. The twenty-room ruins and the hillside forest of saguaro cacti with Roosevelt Lake in the background, are worth a few pictures. Tours of the Upper Ruins are at 9:30 A.M. on Wednesday, Saturday and Sunday

Tonto National Monument is open to the public every day from 8:00 A.M. to 5:00 P.M. except Christmas, and is located off Highway 88 eighty miles east of Phoenix and five miles east of Roosevelt Dam. The admission charge of $4.00 per vehicle.

For information call 520-467-2241.

GLOBE AND MIAMI

Often spoken of in the same breath because of location , these towns are about seven miles apart with silver and copper mining being their origin. The clearly visible mine tailings stretch from one town to the next, and although they are man made, have an uncanny beauty. Mining is still the major industry of Globe and Miami.

In Miami you can enjoy old houses built on hillsides, see a few other historic buildings including the old library, and follow

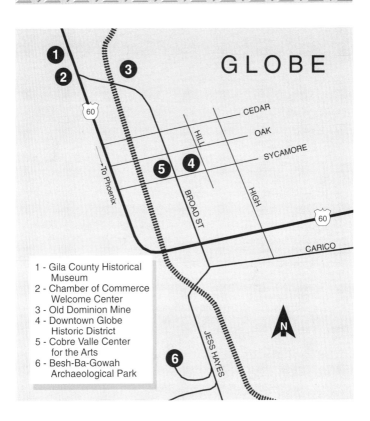

1 - Gila County Historical Museum
2 - Chamber of Commerce Welcome Center
3 - Old Dominion Mine
4 - Downtown Globe Historic District
5 - Cobre Valle Center for the Arts
6 - Besh-Ba-Gowah Archaeological Park

maps for self-guided driving tours of the mines in the vicinity.

For your pleasure in Globe, there is a walking tour of interesting relics such as an old Woolworth store, railroad Engine No. 1774, and solid old homes built by the same Italian stonemasons who built the Roosevelt Dam.

This whole area of Arizona has a rich history of heroic lawmen such as Bat Masterson and infamous outlaws like Pearl Hart, the first woman stage coach robber, and the Apache Kid, who was convicted of wounding an army scout. He later successfully escaped en route to the Yuma Territorial Prison. They all traveled the Old West Highway (highway 60), and it is believed they spent time in Miami and Globe. The famous Apache Indian, Geronimo, also frequented this area, sometimes viciously defending his homeland from encroaching settlements.

The city of Globe is located on Highway 70, near the San Carlos Indian Reservation, and the city of Miami is located on Highway 60, about seven miles west.

For information call 520-425-4495.

BESH-BA-GOWAH ARCHAEOLOGICAL PARK

Pottery produced by the Salado Indians was traded widely to other areas of the Southwest. The Salado were known for the painting of black and white on red clay. These people of the fourteenth century also wove mats, sandals, and baskets of yucca fibers and made fine cotton cloth. The shells they received in trade were made into necklaces, bracelets and rings.

The Besh-Ba-Gowah (place of metal) pueblo of three hundred rooms was built on a ridge overlooking Pinal Creek. The crops of corn, squash, beans, and cotton grew well along the creek until the supposed drought years arrived around A.D. 1400. It was then that the pueblo was slowly abandoned; there remains a loom, ladders, and grinding stones among the ruins of the buildings. Visitors can walk around in the ruins, climb ladders to the second floor, and peek in windows. It is thought the Salado went to New Mexico and they are ancestors of the Zuni Indians.

The park offers a museum with information about the life of these early people. Extensive research and continued excavations are going on to catalog artifacts and skeletal remains. Besh-Ba-Gowah Park is accessible to the physically challenged and open every day from 9:00 A.M. to 5:00 P.M., except Thanksgiving, Christmas and New Year's Day.

Besh-Ba-Gowah is located one-and-a-half miles from downtown Globe. To get there, go north on Broad St. and follow the signs to Jess Hayes Road.

For information call 520-425-0320.

BOYCE THOMPSON SOUTHWESTERN ARBORETUM

The world's greatest garden of desert plants sits on thirty-nine acres and includes a hidden canyon, a creek, and a lake. The Visitor Center offers educational displays, a cactus collection, and a demonstration garden. When you follow the natural trails you can view and learn about the labeled plants and trees from all over the world which make this a fascinating place to spend the day. Walk the shaded paths in summertime, see colored autumn leaves, fruits and berries, see wintertime blooms brought out by the warm winter sun, and be amazed at the profusion of

Preceding pages: Besh-Ba-Gowah artifacts,
courtesy of Besh-Ba-Gowah Archaeological Park

cacti and flowers blooming in the springtime.

The arboretum serves as a place of scientific study of plants for drought tolerance and usefulness to man. It is open daily except Christmas. Adult admission is $4.00. The arboretum is located three miles west of Superior off U.S. Highway 60.

For information call 520-689-2811.

APACHE INDIAN RESERVATIONS

Apache, the name which sounds so familiar, thanks to Hollywood's interpretation of history, is the tribe of Geronimo and Cochise. Many of their descendants live today on reservations. The two largest and best-known Arizona Apache Indian reservations are San Carlos and Fort Apache, located in the beautiful White Mountains.

San Carlos Apache Tribe. The Apaches on the San Carlos reservation are cowboys, ranchers, and farmers. Their cattle rank among the best in the state and are owned by individual members of the tribe. The San Carlos Apaches also mine peridot, create jewelry, and make jojoba bean oil. The reservation provides many attractions for its visitors including rodeos nearly every weekend and San Carlos Lake with its fishing, camping and hunting. You can purchase items you will treasure from a large selection of souvenirs, baskets, and jewelry. The San Carlos Apaches have developed their art of basket weaving.

For information call 520-474-5000.

White Mountain Apache Tribe. Unlike San Carlos Apaches, the Indians on adjacent Fort Apache Reservation build much of their economy around tourists who enjoy camping, fishing, and skiing in the White Mountains. There are a thousand campsites, twenty-six lakes or ponds, and four hundred miles of trout streams flowing among the pines. These pines provide a lumber industry that is a major financial resource to the tribe. In winter, the tribally owned and operated Sunrise Resort is popular among winter sports enthusiasts.

The annual *Labor Day Weekend Rodeo and Fair* attracts many local and out-of-state spectators for colorful fun and excitement. This tribe is noted for burden baskets and beadwork but is best known for their native ritual, the "*Coming out and Healing*" dance,

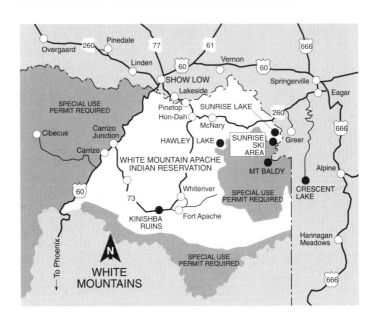

performed by the masked Mountain Spirit Dancers.

The Apache tribal headquarters is located at Whiteriver off Highway 73. You can get sports licenses and permits here and in the town of Hon Dah, which means "welcome" in Apache.

For information call 520-338-4346

GREER

At an elevation of 8,500 feet, summer daytime temperatures rarely reach 85 degrees. Greer's population of only six hundred residents depends on summer visitors for its economy, and truly enjoys making Greer a delightful and welcoming spot to visit. Two-hundred thousand people visit the town every summer, seeking the high altitude with its cool temperatures. Greer, southwest of Springerville, is nestled in the same mountains that give the Coronado Trail its great beauty. In summer, it provides beautiful hiking trails and nearby fishing lakes. In winter, there is downhill skiing, cross-country skiing, and horse drawn sleigh rides.

Settled by Mormon pioneers in 1879, Greer was forced to become very strict with law enforcement to control the actions of outlaws, thieves, and gangs. It was known for holding trials after the executions. Zane Grey, the western novelist, often stayed in the well known Molly Butler Lodge. Just outside of town, next to John Wayne's 26 Bar Ranch, is Winkie Crigler's ranch and the Little House Museum. Stop in and talk to Winkie, the grand-daughter of Molly Butler, to hear stories of the area's history.

Greer is located south of Highway 260 off Highway 373.

CASA MALPAIS

Sheepherders named these ruins Casa Malpais, (house of the badlands), in around 1890. The ruins actually were built as living units, burial chambers, and ceremonial rooms, by the Mogollon people, a tribe living at the same time as the Anasazi and the Hohokam during the thirteenth century. Archaeologists have unearthed nine rooms out of a sixty-room pueblo and guess that three hundred people lived there at any given time. It is believed that this was a ceremonial site and served people from nearby pueblos. The natural volcanic land formations created fissures and crevices that made this location ideal for burial grounds and dwellings. These burial grounds are sacred to the Hopi and Zuni who have been gracious in granting permission to archaeologists to explore and record history. The burial grounds are closed to tourists. This is a special archaeological site that is currently being excavated. As a tourist you may be walking near those

Casa Malpais excavation

working at the site and will climb down a ladder and up through a narrow crevice to the top of the pueblo, much the same as the Mogollon people did over six hundred years ago. Both Hopi and Zuni people, who believe the Mogollon to be their ancestors, are contributing their time and knowledge to make this a worthwhile and well-documented historical event. During the summer there are special programs which may be held in the Kiva. Call to find out about these programs.

The museum, located at 318 Main Street in Springerville, presents cultural history and displays of artifacts found at the site. At the museum you will find a well-stocked book store and have the opportunity to watch a video about the excavation. Guided tours of the excavation site leave the museum daily from May 15 to October 15 at 9:00 A.M., 11:00 A.M., and 2:30 P.M. From October 15 to May 15, they leave at 9:00 A.M. and 2:30 P.M. The fee for the tour is $3.00. Springerville, near the eastern border of the state, can be reached via Highway 60.

For information call 520-333-5375.

CORONADO TRAIL

Perhaps the best part of being in this part of Arizona is driving the Coronado Trail, Highway 666, which begins in Springerville and ends in Clifton. The views are more spectacular driving from north to south, especially in the fall, when the sumac and maples are red, and the aspens are yellow. The trail winds past the Morenci Mine and on through virgin ponderosa pine forests, surprising you with a variety of magnificent views and hiking opportunities. The scenery, today, is much the same as it was when the Spanish explorer, Coronado, made his way through these mountain ranges more than four hundred years ago.

The trail winds for more than a hundred miles through some of the most spectacular mountain and forest landscapes in Arizona. This eastern part of the state, sometimes called "high country", is full of fishing lakes and popular campgrounds such as Hannagan Meadows which, at an elevation of more than nine thousand feet, is considered one of the most beautiful campgrounds in Arizona.

During the winter months, Hannagan meadows is the starting point for cross-country skiers. You can rent ski packages at the lodge. During the rest of the year, the Coronado Trail can

Archaeological dig at Casa Malpais

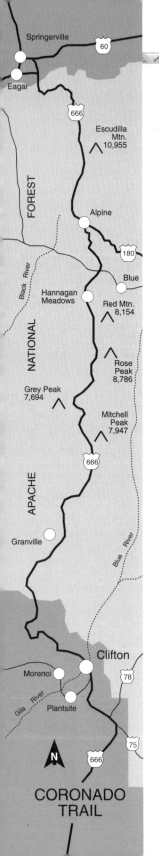

CORONADO
TRAIL

serve as a starting place for adventure, whether sightseeing in the local communities or fishing, hiking, or horseback riding along the trails that begin at the Coronado Trail. As you approach Morenci, you get a magnificent view of one of the largest open pit mines in the U. S. owned by Phelps-Dodge. Fill up your gas tank before starting down the trail because there are no gas stations between Alpine and Clifton. The winding Coronado Trail, very dangerous in bad weather, is often closed when snow and ice are present.

For winter road conditions
call 520-339-4384.

CLIFTON AND MORENCI

Clifton, located at the southern end of the scenic Coronado Trail, grew into a town after 1872, when a peace treaty with the Apaches was signed. Copper mining drew many people to Clifton, hoping to reap their livelihood from this precious metal. In 1895 Phelps-Dodge took over full control of the mining efforts and built the industry into one of Arizona's most productive copper operations. As a result, many people became wealthy and built handsome homes and businesses. Clifton has forty-seven of these turn-of-the-century buildings listed on the National Register of Historic Places. Most of them are along Chase Creek and can be enjoyed by going on a walking tour through the town. You'll want to stop at the Greenlee County Historical Museum to see memorabilia of the early days of Clifton and learn colorful stories of its citizenry. Nearby is Morenci, a relatively new town constructed to replace the old Morenci, built right on top of the rich copper deposits. As the open pit mine grew larger, it swallowed up old buildings until now nothing is left of the original Morenci. The mine is the second largest open pit mine in the world and is quite impressive when viewed from the overlooks.

Tours conducted by retired mine employees, last from two to three hours and are free. It is best to make reservations before going. To get to Clifton and Morenci take Highway 70 east from Phoenix to Highway 666 and then go north.

For information call 520-865-3313.

PETROGLYPHS

Petroglyphs, pecked out pictographs, appear in all except nine states, but in Alaska they are found only on Kodiak island. They also appear in Central and South America. Throughout Europe, Australia, Asia, and Africa there are pecked out and painted pictographs in caves and on rocks. The oldest petroglyphs on rock are located in northern Europe and are about 50,000 years old. The best known cave paintings date from about 20,000 years ago and are found in Europe. It is thought that the creation of painted and pecked rock art was for religious purposes and to increase the hunt. Many symbols, or pictographs appear in similar form among numerous groups of Native Americans. The North American petroglyphs may have been made as early as eight thousand years ago and according to archaeologists were magico-religious symbols to help secure a successful hunt rather than a form of communication.

Each petroglyph figure required hours and possibly days of a person's time to peck into the rock with a hard sharp stone. The lack of accurate information has made archaeologists cautious about interpreting the symbols. Although the information on these pages has been gleaned from a variety of credible sources, there is still much cause for speculation. The designs pecked into rocks and those found in basketry may or may not be meaningfully related. Many of the design elements are simple geometric forms that could be commonly created by anyone. Often the figures are explained as part of a story or legend, handed down as part of a culture. Somewhere else the same figure could be explained in a different way. Today, Native Americans seem to have little knowledge of meanings of the designs or who made them. In northern Arizona and New Mexico there are petroglyphs representing astronomical phenomena. Meanings for the following petroglyph symbols have been gathered from a number of bibliographic sources.

DEER VALLEY ROCK ART CENTER

The rock hills that protectively surround the Valley of the Sun sometimes hold surprises. The White Tank Mountains west of the valley, South Mountain to the south, and the Hedgepath Hills located toward the north, all reveal clues to their past visitors through petroglyphs. Many of these petroglyphs are thought to be made by Hohokam who came here to gather grinding stones.

The Rock Art Center in the Hedgepath Hills provides visitors with an excellent exhibit about petroglyphs created by the ancestors of several tribes, all of whom contributed to the identification and documentation of these petroglyphs. Hedgepath Hills are part of the original Yavapai land, and the Yavapai Indians that have studied these petroglyphs believe that they tell the myths and legends which are reality for the Yavapai.

You will enjoy the video and artistically presented exhibits in the center. The outdoor trail leads you past several petroglyphs that are close enough to see well. Those toward the top of the hills can best be seen with binoculars. The Rock Art Center in Phoenix is open from 9:00 A.M. to 2:00 P.M., Tuesday through Friday, from 9:00 A.M. to 5:00 P.M., Saturday and from noon to 5:00 P.M. on Sunday and is located at 3711 West Deer Valley Road, accessed only from 35th Avenue.

For information call 623-582-8007.

Petroglyphs at Gila Bend

Arrows piercing an animal or evil medicine man take away its power. The arrowhead by itself is thought to mean the power to kill a fierce animal. More contemporary thought suggests the arrowhead means protection. These arrows are found on Hopi mesas.

Badger image as a petroglyph represents the badger animal that digs out roots, and according to legend, taught the Hopi how to use these roots to cure illnesses.

Bear paw, a modern symbol of good luck, once represented the strength and courage it took for the great feat of killing a bear. The bear was very important in tribal mythology and rituals.

Bird-headed figure appears in numerous pictographs and petroglyphs in Canyon de Chelly and Canyon del Muerto. The figure might represent a medicine man whose soul could take flight in the form of a bird.

Butterfly appears in Hopi art as a symbol of fertility and life. It appears throughout the Southwest and into Mexico as a symbol of rebirth of eternal life. A series of stacked triangles on Hopi pottery often depicts the butterfly. This symbol is a petroglyph in the Hopi area.

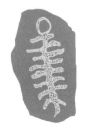

Centipede found as a petroglyph in Arizona's Santan mountains, may have several mythical or magical meanings. In some cultures it is associated with death or is an aid to a medicine man.

Concentric Circles can mean to the Hopi, the footsteps of Masau—God of Death. In other instances it may mean an area of habitation; or it can represent visual images that one sees in an altered state of consciousness. In a more universal sense it represents the ability of a medicine man to travel between the middle and lower worlds.

Cloud is commonly seen in petroglyphs and represents rain, fertility, and prosperity. This cloud is from a petroglyph near Willow Springs.

Coyotes appear in many stories passed from generation to generation. The coyote usually plays tricks, and the stories about it teach lessons of proper behavior and social customs. This coyote petroglyph was found in Springerville. It is assumed it was running ahead of the clan to find a place to settle.

Cross symbol appeared on pottery in the Southwest long before the Spaniards arrived wearing crosses. It is thought to be the symbol of the sky god. Here it appears on a shield pecked into rock by the Tusayan Pueblo people of northern Arizona.

Dragonfly, thought highly of by the Hopi and their ancestors, would fly ahead to reopen springs of water that had been closed. It is thought to have represented water and fertility to the ancient Native Americans. This symbol is found at the Hopi Mesas.

Feathers were very important to ancient Native Americans and are still important in ceremonial dress. Eagle and hawk feathers help in battle and the turkey feathers relate to rain and harvest.

Kokopelli, flute player, appears pecked into stone throughout the Western Hemisphere. He carries seeds in the hump on his back and creates warmth. These figures are pictographs in Canyon de Chelly, painted on walls of a cave. In the canyon, petroglyphs of similar figures without rainbows are found.

Nested Line or Maze has been found in Ireland, South America, Crete, and in Europe on an Etruscan vase dating from 600 B.C. Indian tribes believe it to mean emergence and the Creator's universal plan of the Road of Life that man must follow. This petroglyph is from Hopi mesas near Oraibi. It also appears inside the ruins at Casa Grande.

Sun symbols, often observed in various forms, represent creation, life, and happiness. This version is from the Kayenta area.

Spirals, which appear in numerous petroglyphs, are thought to have been used mostly by the Zuni to represent the solstice, comets, or other astronomical events. They also represent wind. The spirals at Oraibi (shown here) are said to represent travels to the four directions and the return.

Swastika, unfortunately adopted as the Nazi symbol, originated with the ancient Native American people as a symbol to represent migration. You can see it woven into a few older Navajo rugs. The spiral ended swastika means peace or friendship.

Woman is a figure not often found in petroglyphs. The one shown here is from a wall of Canyon del Muerto. The blocks at the sides of her head are representative of the hair style worn for many years by the Anasazi women.

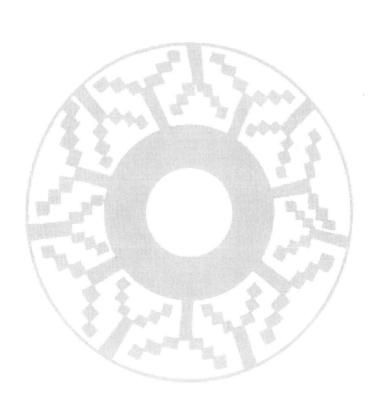

SOUTHERN
ARIZONA

TUCSON

Tucson is alive with its history, character, diversity, and pure charm. The city is located in a striking desert setting, surrounded by rugged mountains. This area of natural beauty, rolling hills, and clear skies was first occupied and farmed by native people called Hohokam (the vanished ones). They disappeared in the latter part of the first century, later to be replaced by Pima and Tohono O'odham tribes.

The original city of Tucson was established in 1775 by an Irishman, Hugh O'Connor, who built a walled presidio for residents and travelers as refuge from Indian attacks. Tucson was nicknamed the "Old Pueblo" because of the architectural style of the Presidio facilities. The name is still used occasionally among old-time residents. In 1821, Mexican independence ended Spanish influence in the region, but lengthy occupation left the southern section of Arizona rich in Spanish heritage.

Today's Tucson, because of its history, provides tourists with numerous museums and galleries of Spanish art and artifacts. This vibrant and progressive society of 400,000 residents cherishes and continues many cultural activities supporting their art and history. To help enrich your visit you will want to attend the various cultural festivals occurring throughout the year in Tucson and in locations nearby.

The pleasant climate and lush green valleys of the area south of Tucson have drawn many visitors and permanent dwellers who retire in the attractive retirement communities. For a good view of the Tucson metropolitan area and its surrounding mountains, you can make your way up Sentinel Peak which is located southwest of the downtown area. University of Arizona students have marked Sentinel Peak with a large White "A". Much outdoor activity takes place at the northeastern edge of Tucson where visitors and residents like to hike and picnic in the Catalina Mountains and Sabino Canyon. For interesting Saturday-night activity, enjoy the downtown Arts District which entertains visitors every first and third Saturday with open galleries, performance art, and music.

To gain appreciation and understanding of Tucson we suggest you start your exploration with the Presidio District.

EL PRESIDIO HISTORIC DISTRICT

The original neighborhood of Tucson, called "Old Pueblo", was established in 1775 and is currently bounded by city streets and downtown businesses, offering visitors the core of local history.

El Presidio District takes visitors into the past introducing them to the colorful lifestyle of early settlers. The southern half of the original Presidio forms today's El Presidio Park, which in the eighteenth century was known as Plaza de las Armas. The northern half, once known as Plaza Militar, now contains the Tucson Museum of Art.

The best introduction to this district, rich in architecture and history, is one of the popular walking tours guided by professionals who take you to the key places in the Presidio. Among them are Stanfield Mansion, site of Tucson's first bathtub with running water Edward Nye Fish House, and La Casa Cordova.

The Edward Nye Fish House was built in 1867 as the home of Mr. Fish and his first wife, Maria Wakefield. She played a major role in starting the first territorial university. The home has adobe walls that are 2 feet thick and the ceiling is lined with saguaro cactus ribs. The Fish House is at 120 N. Main Ave.

La Casa Cordova, now the home of the Mexican Heritage Museum, was built in 1848. and has been named for its last resident, Maria Navarette Cordova. You will enjoy the small-scale replica of the original Presidio and the seasonal display of nativity scenes. La Casa Cordova is located at 175 N. Myer Ave.

The Sosa-Carillo-Fremont House Museum, not in the Presidio district but south of it, near the Convention Center, is well worth the visit. It was built of adobe in 1858 and was lived in by the families whose names it bears. One of the most notable inhabitants was John C. Fremont, explorer and fifth territorial governor of Arizona. This house-museum is furnished in the style of the 1880s and offers exhibits of territorial life. One of its bedrooms has a cotton mantra spread across the ceiling to prevent bugs and mud from falling on the people below. It is located at 151 S. Granada Ave.

El Presidio District is roughly bounded by Granada Avenue, W. 6th Street, N. Church Avenue, and W. Pennington Street.

For information call Old Pueblo Walking Tours, 520-323-9290 and Freemont House Museum, 520-622-0956.

Tucson Museum of Art

TUCSON MUSEUM OF ART

The Tucson Museum of Art is located in El Presidio Historic District in the Plaza of the Pioneers. The museum shares this location with five of Tucson's oldest houses and maintains some of them for public viewing. The museum treats its visitors to five thousand exhibits of important Regional, Pre-Columbian, Spanish Colonial, Twentieth-Century American, and European works. The collections are outstanding in reflecting history and regional heritage. Its display of two hundred regional pieces of artwork provides an excellent representation of the spirit of the West. Many pieces of fine sculpture on the museum grounds will enhance your visit. The museum store offers art reproductions and local crafts. The museum is at 140 North Main Avenue.
For information call 520-624-2333.

ARIZONA HISTORICAL SOCIETY MUSEUM

Arizona's oldest historical museum celebrates Arizona's cultural heritage from the indigenous Indians and the early Spaniards. Many families enjoy tracing their genealogy back to these early Spanish-Colonial and Mexican-National people who explored and settled the Southwest. The land of Arizona became part of the United States in the mid–1800s as a result of the Mexican-American War and the Gadsden Purchase. After the completion of the transcontinental railroad in 1880, settlers came from all over the United States, Europe, and Asia to this beautiful warm climate to build a future.

The museum features exhibits that trace Arizona's multi-cultural heritage chronologically from the earliest days to the twentieth century,with original artifacts. You will particularly enjoy the Mining Hall with its full-scale underground tunnel and the transportation exhibit taking you from ox cart to automobile with a lot in between. This is a fine museum and well worth your time. It is located at 949 E. Second Street.

For information call 520-628-5774.

CENTER FOR CREATIVE PHOTOGRAPHY

Works of many great photographers, including Ansel Adams, Laura Adams Armor, Richard Avedon, Louise Dahl-Wolfe, W. Eugene Smith, Alfred Stieglitz, Paul Strand, Minor White, Marion Palfi, and Edward Weston are housed here in permanent collections. Videotaped lectures and interviews with leading photographers can be viewed in the library. The center contains one of the world's richest and most comprehensive collections of photographs to be researched for historical purposes. If you are at all interested in photography, treat yourself to a visit.

The gallery, with its ever-changing exhibits, is open from 10:00 A.M. to 5:00 P.M., Monday through Friday and from noon to 5:00 P.M. on Sunday. The library opens at 10:00 A.M. on weekdays. Admission is free. The gift shop contains unusual cards and interesting gift items.

The University of Arizona's Center for Creative Photography is located at Olive Street and Speedway Boulevard.

For information call 520-621-7567.

Example of Spanish Colonial Architecture—
Pima County Courthouse surrounded by modern Tucson

UNIVERSITY OF ARIZONA MINERAL MUSEUM

The structure and color of mineral formations fascinates everyone. This museum has about 1,900 mineral specimens on view in display cases and positioned throughout the room on pedestals where you can touch them. Attractive exhibits of gemstones and fluorescent mineral samples will grab your attention. The museum is open from 9:00 A.M. to 5:00 P.M., Monday through Friday and from 1:00 to 5:00 P.M., Saturday and Sunday and is closed major holidays. It is located off North Campus Drive in the old Geology Building.

For information call 520-621-4227.

ARIZONA STATE MUSEUM

The oldest museum in the state offers exhibits on Indian cliff dwellings, fossils found in Arizona, and Arizona Sonoran desert animals. Several excellent exhibits depict prehistoric Arizona. You'll enjoy the many artifacts of early Indian dwellers that are on display. Located at University Boulevard and N. Park Avenue, the museum belongs to the University of Arizona and is open from 10:00 A.M. to 5:00 P.M., Monday through Saturday and from 12:00 to 5:00 P.M., Sunday. It is closed major holidays. Admission is free.

For information call 520-621-6302.

FLANDRAU SCIENCE CENTER & PLANETARIUM

The University of Arizona houses the planetarium which offers a popular theatrical interpretation of the work performed at Arizona observatories. There are many participatory programs and exciting high-tech exhibits. There is a general admission charge of $2.00 and a charge of from $2.50 to $5.00 for the laser and planetarium shows which take place in the theater every day except Monday. Some of these shows are *Navajo Nights, The Violent Universe, Inside Lasers, Alternative Music Laser Show,* and *Pink Floyd–Dark Side of the Moon.* The public telescope is available from 8:00 to 10:00 P.M. on clear nights. The Flandrau Science Center and Planetarium is located at Cherry Avenue and University Boulevard. Call for hours and program descriptions.

For information call 520-621-7827.

REID PARK ZOO

Reid Park Zoo is located to the southeast of downtown Tucson. this unique zoo houses more than 400 exotic animals and is known for its captive breeding program of the giant anteater. Other programs monitor and protect the lion-tailed macaque, Bali mynah, small clawed otter, Siberian tiger, and the white rhinoceros. The zoo offers easy viewing opportunities of all its animals in including the polar bears and monkeys.

Reid Park is one of Tucson's most popular parks for picnicking and family games. It has tennis courts, swimming pools and golf courses. The formal rose garden will please all flower lovers.

Reid Park Zoo is open from 9:00 A.M. to 4:00 P.M. daily except Christmas. Enter Reid Park off 22nd St. east of Country Club Rd.

For information call 520-791-4022.

TOHONO CHUL PARK

Tohono Chul Park, toward the northwest edge of the city, offers thirty-seven acres of Sonoran Desert flora and fauna for you to enjoy. There are outer trails which lead you through the natural desert plant and animal habitats. You will see several species of native birds including the interesting roadrunner and Gambel 's quail. Small javalinas make their appearance at night and coyotes show up looking to catch a roadrunner or other small creature.

The inner trails take you to several gardens, the café and the tearoom. The Demonstration Garden shows you how to landscape with desert plants and how to conserve water. The Succulent Ramada includes plants that store water. In the Pincushion Ramada there are varieties of flowering cacti.

The Greenhouse offers the opportunity to purchase desert plants and seeds. Many of these seeds have been produced by the plants in the park.

In the Exhibit House are environmental exhibits, arts and crafts items, paintings, sculpture, and a botanical library.

Tohono Chul Park is open daily from 7:00 A.M. to sunset. The Exhibit House is open Monday through Saturday from 9:00 A.M. to 5:00 P.M. and from 11:00 A.M. to 5:00 P.M. on Sunday. The park is located at 7366 N. Paseo del Norte.

For information call 520-575-8468.

FORT LOWELL MUSEUM AND PARK

Established in 1866 to protect the citizens of Tucson from the Indians, Fort Lowell was a garrison rather than a stockade. The early soldiers rode out to make contact with the Indians when needed, rather than waiting for an attack. Today the officers quarters, storehouse, and traders' store are preserved and on view in the location where the fort was moved in 1873 to protect the citizens from the "outrages of a depraved and drunken soldiery". In 1866, one-fourth of the United States Army was stationed in Arizona. It was also here that Geronimo surrendered. A visit to Fort Lowell Museum will give you a glimpse into an era of hardships, excitement and survival of the white settlers of the West. The museum is open from 10:00 A.M. to 4:00 P.M., Wednesday through Saturday. The museum and park are located at Craycroft Road and Fort Lowell Road.

For information call 520-885-3832.

TUCSON BOTANICAL GARDENS

Arizona's sunny and usually arid climate is home to many extraordinary plants. Viewing these plants and learning about their unique life cycles and flowering habits can be a fascinating experience for visitors from other parts of the United States and abroad. A portion of the gardens is devoted to the solar powered Xeriscape Demonstration Garden which exhibits low water use plants and water conservation methods. The Gardens is open daily from 8:30 A.M. to 4:30 P.M. and occupies five-and-a-half acres at 2150 N. Alvernon Way. Adult admission is $4.00.

For information call 520-326-9255.

ARIZONA-SONORA DESERT MUSEUM

The Arizona-Sonora Desert Museum provides tourists with information about the Sonoran Desert. The museum, which ranks among the nation's top-ten zoological attractions, is named after two states, Arizona, USA and Sonora, Mexico. It exhibits flora and fauna native to these two states. Because of the large acreage of the museum we suggest you allow several hours to walk museum paths, learning and understanding the nature of the Sonoran Desert.

The excellent *Life Underground* exhibit includes a cutaway view showing burrow and cave habitats of small desert creatures..

Bats are helpful to southwestern agriculture by eating many insects. On Saturdays during July and August you can go on a Nightstalker walk to hear bat calls and see wild bats that have been caught by guides. You can experience the fascinating world of nighttime in the desert. There is a charge for these walks.

Another popular attraction is the bird aviary which allows visitors to sit in the midst of many species of birds watching them build nests, search for food, and feed their young. Don't miss the unique hummingbird aviary—one of the most popular exhibits.

Inside the museum buildings guests are offered information about the desert and an opportunity to view its inhabitants including rattlesnakes and scorpions. In the Earth Science complex you will find a display of crystalline-shaped and beautifully colored minerals. On the way out explore the well-stocked museum gift shop while you look for that special book, rock sample, or Arizona-Sonora Desert memorabilia.

The museum is open from 7:30 A.M. to 6:00 P.M., March through September, and 8:30 A.M. to 5:00 P.M., October through February. Adult admission is $8.95. Children from six to twelve pay $1.75. Located at 2021 N. Kinney Rd., west of Tucson. The museum is open every day of the year including holidays.

For information call 520-883-2702.

SAGUARO NATIONAL MONUMENT

Next door to the Arizona-Sonora Desert Museum is the Tucson Mountains unit of the Saguaro National Monument. People from all over the world come to see the large assortment of saguaro cacti, indigenous to the Sonoran Desert. Visitors to the monument can walk comfortably along the marked trails; motorists are provided with convenient pullouts and picnic areas. Make sure you have your own supply of drinking water. After hours of exploring the monument you may see an extraordinary sunset, a challenge to your photographic skills.

The western unit of the monument is located off N. Kinney Road and is open twenty-four hours a day, seven days a week. Admission is free.

The eastern unit, the Rincon Mountain Area Saguaro National Monument, specializes in exhibits about deserts, saguaro cacti and local creatures such as rattlesnakes, tarantulas, etc. This monument is open from 8:00 A.M. to 5:00 P.M. daily except Christmas. Admission is $4.00 per vehicle or $2.00 per biker. A fee is charged for the Scenic Drive Tour. The Rincon Mountain unit of Saguaro National Monument is located at 3693 S. Old Spanish Trail.

Western unit–for information call 520-883-6366.
Eastern unit–for information call 520-733-5100.

OLD TUCSON STUDIOS

Originally a movie set built in 1939 by Columbia Pictures producers seeking western authenticity of early Tucson, Old Tucson Studios now entertains millions of visitors each year. When you walk through the dusty streets among saloons, the sheriffs office, jail, and the general store you are going back in time to those Wild West days. There is a street from old Kansas City, an old Mexican plaza, an Indian trading post—all authentic enough to

Gila Woodpecker, courtesy of Arizona-Sonora Desert Museum

be used as movie sets. Begin your day by watching the eighteen-minute video, *Hollywood in the Desert*, which tells of the movie making history of Old Tucson.

Old Tucson Studios is an excellent reproduction of an old western town and its way of life. Stay until evening to experience the specific mood created by weak old-fashioned lighting accompanied by western or Spanish music and the smell of western cuisine wafting through the air. As you sip a drink and relax in the Royal Oak Saloon, you may be startled by a noisy Indian attack. Guests are provided with many live shows such as shootouts, bank robberies, music, and dance performances.

For our readers who travel with children, we suggest Old Tucson Studios as the best and most exciting way to introduce youngsters to customs and traditions of the Old West. The Studios provides many attractions for children, from a real stagecoach ride to child-driven cars. Try a real burro ride. Young visitors learn about the Old West while enjoying a fun-filled day.

Wear comfortable shoes and dress for the outdoors. Old Tucson Studios sells plenty of food, beverages, souvenirs, and wonderfully large ice cream cones.

Adult admission is $14.95. Open daily except Thanksgiving and Christmas. Hours are from 10:00 A.M. to 6:00 P.M. Old Tucson Studios is located at 201 South Kinney Road.

For information call 520-883-0100.

One of many Old Tucson Studios attractions   *Spanish Village movie set*

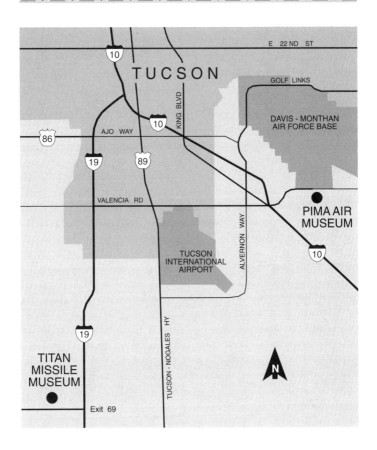

PIMA AIR AND SPACE MUSEUM

The Pima Air and Space Museum provides a look into the color-ful history of America's aviation, with an interesting collection of over 180 aircraft, from the 1903 Wright brothers' *Wright Flyer* to the world's fastest aircraft, the *SR-71*. The museum, filled with old planes, aircraft engines, flight suits, and other airborne gear, gives visitors an opportunity to experience the evolution of avia-tion. The exhibit that inspires the most interest is the four- engine *DC-6* which was used as Air Force One for presidents Kennedy and Johnson. Touring the plane, you will see the desk and chair where the president and others struggled with the Missiles of October Crisis and other difficult situations as they soared above the clouds. You can also peek into the press and secret service compartments.

The Pima Air and Space Museum is open every day except Thanksgiving and Christmas from 9:00 A.M. to 5:00 P.M. and the

last admittance is at 4:00 P.M. Adult admission is $7.50. To get there drive east from Tucson on Interstate 10, take the Valencia Road exit, and go east two miles to the museum entrance.
For information call 520-574-0462.

TITAN MISSILE MUSEUM

Another part of the Pima Air and Space Museum is the Titan Missile Museum which is the only Intercontinental Ballistic Missile (ICBM) complex open to the public. Fifty-four Titan missile sites were located in the United States—eighteen in Arizona, eighteen in Arkansas, and eighteen in Kansas. All have been destroyed except for this site which has been preserved as a museum. It stands today, as it stood on alert for nineteen years, accurate in every detail except for the empty booster and re-entry vehicle in the silo.

One-hour guided tours begin every half hour. Walking shoes are required (no high heels). The tour descends fifty-five steps to a level thirty-five feet underground where you can see the launch control center and go through a 200-foot-long tunnel to the 146-foot silo containing an actual Titan II missile.

Special tours may be arranged for the physically challenged via an elevator. Reservations are suggested; however, walk-ins are also welcome. There is an admission charge of $5.00. Open hours are from 9:00 A.M. to 5:00 P.M. The last tour is at 4:00 P.M. The museum is located twenty minutes south of Tucson in Green Valley. Take exit 69 west off Interstate 19.
For information call 520-625-7736.

B & B CACTUS FARM

Experience the unusual, colorful, and exotic world of cacti, succulents, and desert plant life. Located approximately twelve miles east of downtown Tucson, and surrounded by majestic mountain scenery, the outdoor gardens, greenhouses, and spectacular display area at B&B Cactus Farm provide hours of enjoyment for visitors and residents alike.

For more than fifteen years, the owners have devoted their time to nurturing and caring for desert plant life. Today, B&B proudly features over six hundred species and varieties of cacti and succulents from all over the world.

Barrel Cactus, typical of those sold at B&B Cactus Farm

The exciting array of desert plant life combined with the sunny Tucson climate and the backdrop of spectacular mountain scenery add up to a uniquely pleasant experience. You'll enjoy walking along greenhouse paths, among towering cereus cacti and fascinating hybrids that you may be seeing for the first time.

Designer cactus gardens featuring individual plants, plant assortments which make memorable centerpieces, and decorator accents, will intrigue and inspire you.

B&B Cactus Farm is located at 11550 East Speedway. *For information call 520-721-4687.*

GALLERY IN THE SUN

Considered one of the Tucson landmarks, DeGrazia's Gallery in the Sun, containing original DeGrazia art is located in a beautifully decorated adobe structure which was designed and built by the artist. Ted DeGrazia's art and the gallery's architecture, set in the beautiful southwest desert, combine to give visitors a pleasant and unusual experience.

Near the Gallery in the Sun stands DeGrazia's Mission in the Sun. The artist built this little chapel in honor of Padre Kino and

"San Diego Indians Learn to Sing" by Ted DeGrazia,
courtesy of the Gallery in the Sun

dedicated it to Our Lady of Guadalupe. Inside the adobe structure, the artist expressed his vision of beauty, simplicity, and faith. When you walk into rooms filled with sunshine flooding through the roof that opens to the sky and view beautiful DeGrazia murals on the interior walls, you feel the uniqueness of this chapel.

The Gallery in the Sun is the largest and most complete collection of DeGrazia art in existence. Viewers will be delighted with the variety of subjects expressed in the artist's work, from Indian lore through legends, celebrations, documentaries, all the way to bullfighting and rodeos. The walk through creatively decorated courtyards and many rooms, while viewing the art, contributes to the special ambiance associated with DeGrazia's art.

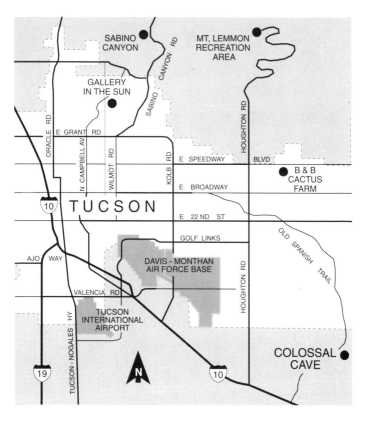

For visitor convenience and maximum enjoyment, museum officials rotate the exhibits throughout the gallery which allows people to see the artists bronzes, ceramics, stone lithographs, serigraphs, and jewelry as well as oils and watercolors. The museum is located at 6300 North Swan Road in Tucson and is open daily except major holidays from 10:00 A.M. to 4:00 P.M

For information call 520-299-9191.

MOUNT LEMMON

At 9,157 feet, Mount Lemmon peaks above the others in the Santa Catalina Mountain Range. All year the ski lift takes tourists to the top to enjoy the splendid array of wildflowers covering the meadows in spring, and thick white snow exciting skiers in the winter. One hundred and fifty miles of hiking trails wind through aspen and pine-covered slopes waiting for visitors as well as Arizonans to enjoy the cool breezes, fresh forest smells, and glimpses of wildlife. Trout fishing and picnicking add to the range of activities one can enjoy only an hour from downtown Tucson. Mount Lemmon is located forty miles north by way of the Catalina Highway from northeast Tucson.

For information call 520-576-1321 or 520-576-1542.

COLOSSAL CAVE

One of the largest dry caverns in the world, this limestone cave is an underground spectacle. Stalactites, stalagmites, and shapely calcite columns abound throughout the caverns, and the more spectacular formations are lighted by hidden lights. Soot-blackened ceilings, bones, and artifacts near the entrance attest to the cave's long history as a home for ancient people and many tribes of Indians. Deeper within the crystal halls is evidence that outlaws hid themselves and their loot in the caverns. Cave explorers have never found the end of Colossal Cave but they continue to search in remote areas many miles from the entrance.

The view from Colossal Cave's entrance is one of the most spectacular in southern Arizona. No special clothing or gear is needed for a comfortable visit to the cave's interior. In the middle of the summer the cave, with its year round temperature of seventy-two degrees, provides escape from Arizona's heat. Children are fascinated by the cave. Tours last from forty-five to fifty minutes and cover one-half mile and 363 steps. This tour is not recommended for those who have artificial joints, severe respiratory conditions or difficulty climbing stairs.

Monday through Saturday the cave is open from 8:00 A.M. to 6:00 P.M. On Sundays and holidays it is open an hour longer. Adult admission is $7.50. The cave is located off Old Spanish Trail, fifteen miles east of Camino Seco. You can also travel Interstate 10 nineteen miles east of Tucson to the Vail-Wentworth exit where you will turn north.

For information call 520-647-7275.

BIOSPHERE 2

Biosphere 2's futuristic appearance is incorporated into the foothills of the Santa Catalina mountains. Completed in late 1991, the largest self-sustaining ecologically-closed system ever built, Biosphere 2, amazed and intrigued its visitors as they toured around it listening to the guide explain how the eight people liv-

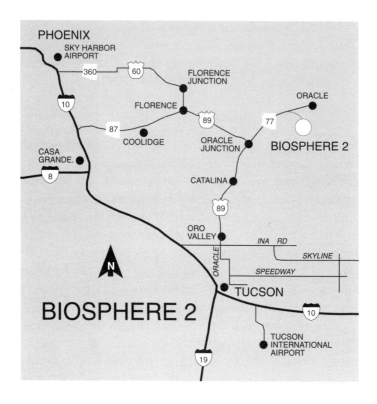

ing inside the hermetically sealed glass and steel structure could support themselves for the planned two-year confinement. They lived in the seven million cubic- foot enclosure, containing a rain forest, savanna, marsh, ocean, desert, farm, and micro city, provides everything that is needed for survival of thirty-eight hundred species of plants and animals—the air they breath, the food they eat and the water they drink. It was intended to be a miniature version of the Earth. It almost worked.

It was impossible to for the eight human beings to grow all their own food, maintain the flora and fauna in the environments and run all the equipment necessary for recycling air, water and nutrients. A few things didn't go as planned and there wasn't much time for the intended scientific research.

Today the project is being rethought by scientists from Columbia University and Arizona State Universities. The reality of an enclosed controlled environment of such magnitude is a scientist's dream. There may be be much agricultural experimentation conducted at Biosphere 2 in the future.

Working on the next century–Biosphere 2

Currently Biosphere 2 is being used as a classroom for science students and as a museum for tourists. Visiting this remarkable place is as interesting now as it was during its first experiment.

A shuttle bus takes you from the parking lot through a park-like setting to the entrance gate. After the interesting tour of the facilities, you may relax and dine in the Biosphere cafe, enjoy the hands-on exhibits at Biofair, or even spend the night at the Biosphere hotel.

Adult admission price is $12.95. Biosphere 2, open daily except Christmas from 8:30 A.M. to 6:00 P.M., is located two hours south of Phoenix or one hour north of Tucson near Oracle, off Highway 77.

For information call 520-896-6200.

HIKING AROUND TUCSON

Sabino Canyon. Frequently visited by tourists and popular among local residents, Sabino Canyon, in the Santa Catalina

Mountains, provides a number of short easy hikes. The canyon is closed to automobiles, but you can take a ride on a guided shuttle which will take you up to the wilderness edge. You can hike through this beautiful area observing native flora and fauna. Then either hike back down to your car or to the shuttle pick up point. To get there, exit from Interstate 10, go east on Grant Road to Tanque Verde Road, then go east to Sabino Canyon Road and north to the visitor entrance.

Bear Canyon/Seven Falls. Take a shuttle from the Sabino Canyon Visitor Center to Bear Canyon trailhead to begin the two-and-a-half-mile hike up Bear Canyon. The biggest attraction is Seven Falls which is considered the most beautiful falls in southern Arizona. Be prepared to get your feet wet because the trail crosses the stream several times. Estimate your hiking time properly, allowing yourself enough time to make the last shuttle.

Tanque Verde Ridge Trail. For most out-of-state visitors this typically southwestern scenic trail, winding through saguaro cacti, satisfies their desire for a taste of the Sonoran desert. It is an excellent place for a leisurely stroll. In about an hour's time, you can reach an elevation of 3,600 feet and enjoy a beautiful view of Tucson. For those of you who are anxious to burn unwanted calories, the rest of the trail offers a very difficult hike to Rincon Peak. To get to Tanque Verde Ridge Trail take Broadway east from downtown Tucson to Old Spanish Trail, then turn right and go about four-and-a-half miles to the park entrance.

Arizona Trail. For experienced hikers only, this trail will eventually stretch from Utah to Mexico. At present the trail begins south of the American Flag Ranch, about a mile past the end of the pavement on the old road between Oracle and Mount Lemmon. Catalina State Park north of Tucson is the area where this trails begin.

ADVENTURE SIGHTSEEING AROUND TUCSON

The Tucson area provides a number of privately owned stables. A trailride into the surrounding countryside gives you the flavor of real cowboy lifestyle and outdoor old-western cooking. Each stable offers its rides in a different area of the desert and at different times of day and night. It is advisable to call the stables in advance for reservations.

Desert High Country Stables, Inc.
520-744-3789.
Pusch Ridge Stables
520-825-1664.
Tucson Trailrides dba Pantano Stables
520-298-9076 or 520-298-1983.

If you're not afraid of heights and are brave enough to be lifted in a basket you can experience a one-of-a-kind adventure by taking a balloon flight over the Sonoran Desert. Because you are higher than any hiker can climb, the views end only with the horizon, giving you an opportunity to judge for yourself why so many people fall in love with this rugged area.

Balloon America
520-299-7744
Southern Arizona Balloon Excursion
520-624-3599

If you don't want to ride a horse and you're not into ballooning, you can always take a jeep tour which is one of the best ways to see the Sonoran Desert.

Mountain View Jeep Tours
520-622-4488

SAHUARITA NUT PROCESSING

After leaving Tucson and heading south, take a quick side trip east at exit 75 to Sahuarita. This is where locally grown nuts are processed. You will be able to buy Arizona grown pecans and pistachios and tasty confections made with nuts.

Return to Interstate 19 and go south to Tubac and then on to Tumacacori National Historical Park.

PICACHO PEAK STATE PARK

This impressive landmark rising out of the desert in all its black majesty can be seen more than fifty miles away. It has made its place in history as the most-western battle site of the Civil War.

Today it serves a more peaceful purpose as a great place to stretch your legs and have a picnic. Two trails accommodate every kind of hiker from the leisure walker looking for spring wildflowers to the rock climber looking for serious challenges. The campgrounds and RV sites entice visitors to spend a day or two enjoying the variety of desert cacti and flowers and exploring hiking opportunities. During wildflower season, April and May, the park is full of tourists and photographers supplying national media with gorgeous wildflower shots.

Picacho Peak State Park is right off Interstate 10 between Casa Grande and Tucson.

For information call 520-466-3183.

TOHONO O'ODHAM INDIAN RESERVATION

The Tohono O'odham Reservation occupies a large territory beginning 136 miles south of Phoenix and stretching south to the Mexican border. Beautiful Sonoran Desert landscape and a variety of unique attractions make this a special place to visit.

You will want to visit the village of Schuschuli, the world's first totally solar electric village. You can explore Ventana Cave or Forteleza Ruins and then marvel at the famous Mission San Xavier del Bac, known as the "White Dove of the Desert." Perhaps one of the most important attractions is Kitt Peak National Observatory, the world's largest observatory.

Be sure to stop at the local trading posts where Indians and visitors make their purchases and engage in conversation as they pass the time on a warm afternoon. The tribe is known for its beautiful basketry and pottery. The Tohono O'odham, formerly known as Papago, run a successful agricultural enterprise which supports modern housing, electricity, water, and their local government. To get to the reservation take Highway 86 west from Tucson or Highway 85 south from Interstate 10.

For information call 520-383-2221.

THE AMERIND FOUNDATION MUSEUM

This museum was developed as an archaeological research center in 1937. It houses collections of White Mountain Indian baskets, religious figures carved by Indians influenced by the early Spanish missions, Plains Indian costumes and beadwork, and

The blooming desert at Picacho Peak

early Navajo weavings. You will want to visit the art gallery housed in a separate building to view the paintings by William Leigh and the sculpture by Frederic Remington. The Foundation's goal is to increase the world's knowledge of ancient cultures by interpreting Native American history. A visit to Amerind is both educational and fun for the whole family.

Open hours are from 10:00 A.M. to 4:00 P.M. daily, September through May, and from 10:00 A.M. to 4:00 P.M. Wednesday through Sunday, June through August. Admission charge is $3.00 for adults and $2.00 for seniors and children. The museum is located east of Tucson off Interstate 10 at exit 318, on Triangle T Road in Dragoon.

For information call 520-586-3666.

SMITHSONIAN INSTITUTION'S
FRED LAWRENCE WHIPPLE OBSERVATORY

This observatory is a thirty-five mile drive south of Tucson. Its key feature is a multiple mirror telescope. The lengthy but interesting tours begin at 9:00 A.M. and last until 3:00 P.M.; therefore, children under six are not permitted. The guided tours are conducted on Monday, Wednesday, and Friday from March through November and include a video taped program and

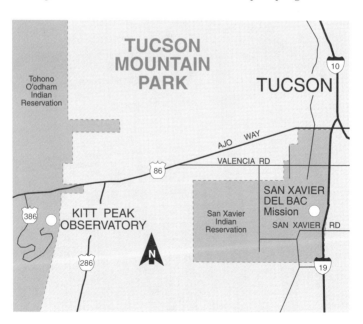

guided tour. The observatory is located at the top of Mount Hopkins at the end of a one-lane dirt road. The observatory bus will take you up this road after you have viewed the introductory tape in the field office at the base of the mountain. You can get to Whipple Observatory's field office by taking Interstate 19 south from Tucson to exit 56, Canoa Road. At the foot of the exit ramp turn left. Then turn right on the frontage road and go about three miles to Elephant Head Road, where you will turn left and cross the Santa Cruz River. About a mile past the river turn right onto Mount Hopkins Road and travel seven miles to the field office. Reservations are needed for the guided tours.

For information and reservations call 520-670-5707.

KITT PEAK NATIONAL OBSERVATORY

High above the Tohono O'odham Reservation, the white domes of Kitt Peak National Observatory stand out like sentinels searching the sky. Inside these domes are twenty-four telescopes, responsible for some of America's impressive space discoveries.

Many universities and the National Science Foundation, operating and supporting the observatory, enable many astronomers and astronomy students to explore the heavens, recording data in a variety of ways. Some of the equipment gathers radio waves emitted by stars, and sends the information directly into computers. The huge McMath solar telescope with a five-hundred-foot-long shaft transfers the solar image from a receiving mirror onto a thirty-inch surface where scientists can study its activity. This is the largest instrument for solar research in the world.

Make a day of visiting the world's largest astronomical observatory; enjoy the visitor facilities and self-guided tours. Take your sweater and a picnic lunch, because it can become cool and there are no food facilities. The Visitor Center is open daily, except for Thanksgiving, Christmas, and New Year's Day, from 9:00 A.M. to 4:00 P.M. In the gift shop you will find excellent Tohono O'odham baskets for reasonable prices. On weekends there are guided tours of the observatory. Admission is free. To reach the Observatory travel forty miles west of Tucson on Highway 86, then south for twelve miles on Highway 386.

For information call 520-318-8726.

MISSION SAN XAVIER DEL BAC

The two hundred-year-old Mission San Xavier del Bac rises mystically from the barren desert floor, with a dramatic mountainous background. The mission is called "The White Dove of the Desert" and is one of the most striking and photographed missions in the country.

With roots reaching far back to Father Eusebio Kino's days, the mission can be thought of as a symbol of Arizona. Father Kino's ministry to the people of the village of Bac, located on the present San Xavier Reservation, started in 1692 and still serves today's Native Americans. Mission construction was begun in 1700 but not completed until 1797. Lacking materials and funds, but having the desire to create a church as elegant as those in Spain, Father Kino's successors used Indian made paints and dyes to simulate elegant marble tiles. They even painted chandeliers and other ornaments on the walls, because they didn't have real ones. The baroque-style art was used to present the story of Christianity to the Indians.

Recently cleaned of years of candle soot and preserved, the murals reveal beautiful paintings using vermillion, copper green, and Prussian blue. It is thought that expensive imported pigments were used to create the murals. The paintings and sculpture were done by skilled Mexican artisans. Some of the designs on the interior walls of the mission church were painted by the O'odham people, the local Indians. Many legends surround the old church as well as many unanswered questions, such as, "Why was the second bell tower never finished?" The most popular legend talks about ornate carvings of a cat and mouse on each side of the entry doors. The legend says that when the cat catches the mouse the world will come to an end.

A trip to the mission provides excellent exterior photographic opportunities and exposure to a fine example of Spanish Colonial architecture. Photographing the interior is more difficult because of poor light and numbers of people. The mission is crowded with local people attending mass on Sunday as they have done for the last two hundred years. While you are there enjoy authentic Indian cooking and crafts. The mission is located off Interstate 19 at San Xavier Road, nine miles south of Tucson.

For information call 520-294-2624.

"White Dove of the Desert"–Mission San Xavier del Bac

MADERA CANYON

Driving up Continental Road to the picnic grounds, you will pass through changes in climate similar to those you would encounter driving from Arizona to Canada. Madera Canyon, at the base of Mt. Wrightson in the Coronado National Forest, is one of the outstanding areas in the country for bird watching. One can frequently see five to seven species of hummingbirds including the Broad-billed, Magnificent, Blackchinned, Costas, and Broadtailed. Greybreasted Jays, Acorn Woodpeckers, and Nuthatches are easy to spot. Rarer species, including the Elegant Trogon, draw birders from as far as Europe and Australia.

Trail maps are available. Bring drinking water or purification tablets, because the water in the streams and springs is not safe unless boiled or chemically purified. Provide yourself with layered clothing. Temperatures can be very chilly at these high altitudes, especially after the sun goes down. There are several parking areas with nearby picnic tables and other amenities. There are also cabins for rent. Madera Canyon is located off Interstate 19 about halfway between Tucson and Nogales.

TUBAC

Tubac claims to be the home of the first schoolhouse in Arizona, the first newspaper, the first Spanish land grant, the first state park and, most important, the first European settlement. Much of the original settlement is evidenced by the Presidio Museum, the old St. Ann's Church, and the surrounding adobe walls. When the Presidio was moved to Tucson in 1776, the citizens of Tubac became vulnerable to Apache Indian attacks until 1787, when a garrison of soldiers arrived. The village was abandoned many times and when it came under United States control it was nothing but a ghost town of adobe ruins. Revitalization of the town came in the 1800s with the mining industry. Tubac survived into the twentieth century and has become a mecca for artists of all media. The work of these artisits is the big draw for tourists. Dusty streets of Tubac lead you on a journey through southwestern art and craft shops and galleries.

Modern Tubac is a conglomeration of more than fifty art galleries and studios., a mecca for artists of all media and a big draw

"Sitting Bull's Visions", cast paper sculpture by Allen Dale Eckman, courtesy of Galleria Bernardi, Tubac

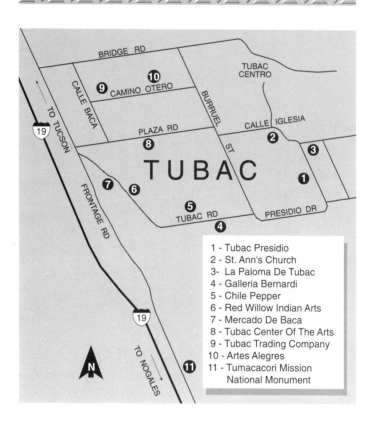

1 - Tubac Presidio
2 - St. Ann's Church
3- La Paloma De Tubac
4 - Galleria Bernardi
5 - Chile Pepper
6 - Red Willow Indian Arts
7 - Mercado De Baca
8 - Tubac Center Of The Arts
9 - Tubac Trading Company
10 - Artes Alegres
11 - Tumacacori Mission
        National Monument

for tourists. Galleria Tubac represents what Tubac has to offer. Galleria Tubac calls itself the "gallery with a split personality" because is has a southwestern fine arts gallery and a year-round Christmas gallery. The gallery shows watercolors, oils, and bronzes of twenty-five artists. Informative hosts take you on a tour of their displays explaining the media and meaning of the art pieces as well as background of the artists.

The Turquoise Tortoise gallery carries the cast paper sculptures by Allen Dale Eckman which were previously shown by the Galleria Bernardi. These are fascinating works of art executed with great skill and sensitivity.

For those who enjoy western art, old-western-town appearance, Mexican cuisine, casual atmosphere, and warm desert breezes, Tubac is the perfect place to spend a day exploring galleries and studios and talking to artists and shop keepers. The town is located forty-five miles south of Tucson off Interstate 19, exit 40, at Chavez Siding Road.

For information call 520-398-2704.

TUMACACORI NATIONAL HISTORICAL PARK

Father Kino visited the village of Tumacacori in 1691 at the invitation of the Pima Indians, also known as the O'odham people. Father Kino introduced horses to the Pima and established a mission outpost there, which in 1753, was moved to its present site. Father Francisco Guiterrez arrived in 1794 and was determined to build a church that would rival San Xavier del Bac in beauty. The church was never finished but was occupied until 1848 when the Pima parishioners were forced to leave because of Apache raids, lack of financial support, and Mexico's fight for independence.

The mission, no longer in use, is an excellent example of Spanish Colonial Baroque architecture with adobe walls nine feet thick in places. The cool, dark interior elicits a feeling of awe and reverence. It is weather-beaten and crumbled from attacks and neglect, and is quite picturesque. At the Visitor Center there is a beautiful garden and an excellent gift shop. When you arrive, be sure to spend some time in the small museum learning about the mission's history, before venturing out to the mission itself. The mission park is open from 8:00 A.M. to 5:00 P.M. daily except for Thanksgiving and Christmas. There is an admission charge. During the first weekend in December, you can enjoy the two-day *Fiesta de Tumacacori* celebrating the cultural heritage of several Indian tribes. Enjoy Mexican National performances and his-

Preceding page and photo above: Tumacacori Mission

toric Anglo-American activities. Tumacacori National Historical Park is located off Interstate 19, forty miles south of Tucson.

JUAN BAUTISTA DE ANZA
NATIONAL HISTORIC TRAIL

Just three miles north of the Tumacacori mission is the very old town of Tubac, now an art colony and delightful place to visit. If you are a hiker, you can hike the four-and-a-half-mile Juan Bautista de Anza National Historic Trail connecting the mission to the presidio in Tubac. The trail runs along the Santa Cruz River, and is noteworthy because it is part of the trail that 240 Tubac people traveled to California in 1776. They were led by the presidio's commander, Juan Bautista de Anza, and were instrumental in the founding of San Francisco.

PATAGONIA

Surrounded by some of the most spectacular ranch land in the state, Patagonia, an old mining center, provides a quiet lifestyle for local residents and hosts many tourists. When you are passing through the town you might want to stop and visit the Stradling Museum of the Horse. Among its possessions are a four-hundred-year-old Mexican ox cart, harnesses, saddles, and other equestrian paraphernalia.

Patagonia loop, a fifty-five mile scenic drive, heads east out of Patagonia on road FR 58 and then north on FR 799 to highway 83. It takes you from Patagonia into the Patagonia Mountains, into the San Rafael Valley, through the Canelo Pass and northward to Elgin and Arizona's wine country.

The biggest visitor draw to the Patagonia area is Patagonia Lake, created by damming Sonoita Creek. The lake provides many recreational activities such as fishing, boating, water skiing, picnicking, and camping. The high elevation of the park attracts people seeking cooler temperatures in the middle of summer.

Patagonia Lake State Park is well-equipped with modern facilities. To reach the lake, take Interstate 10 east from Tucson, then go south on Highway 83, and then west on Highway 82.
For information call 520-287-6965.

ARIZONA'S WINERIES

Take Highway 82 northeast out of Nogales to the Arizona Vineyards for one of the best winery tours in the U.S. In Elgin on Lower Elgin Road you will find the Callaghan and Terra Rossa vineyards. Next travel to Sonoita where you can follow the signs to a more high-tech winery that produces excellent estate bottled wines from Arizona grapes. The next stop should be the R.W. Webb Winery, built in 1980. Take Highway 83 north out of Sonoita until it connects with Interstate 10 and then exit between Sonoita and Vail.

For information call 520-287-3685.

NOGALES

On each side of the border between the United States and Mexico sits a city named Nogales, separated from its counterpart only by a border fence. Both cities are a bit worn and dusty and enjoy a long time friendship. Even Pancho Villa couldn't disturb the neighborly ties between these cities with his disruptive activities along the border in the early part of the twentieth century. The towns were named for two walnut trees (Nogales means *walnut* in Spanish.) that straddled the border.

Nogales, Arizona, with a population of about 20,000, features the interesting Primeria Alta Historical Society Museum, located in the old city hall. The city hosts a few special events, and provides an opportunity to tour a bootmaking shop where you can have beautiful leather cowboy boots custom made. This small city also provides parking space for those who want to walk across the border to shop for arts and crafts that come from all over Mexico.

Nogales in Mexico is a city of 200,000 and is crowded with fine shopping and eating opportunities along the two main downtown streets. All shops accept American money, and many shop keepers enjoy bargaining. You may still find bullfights on Sunday afternoons.

Nogales, Arizona is located in the Patagonia foothills where Highway 19 meets Highway 82 about sixty miles south of Tucson. For places to stay the night call the Chamber of Commerce at *520-287-3685.*

For information call 520-287-3685 or 520-287-4621.

BISBEE

Once a booming and powerful mining town, today's Bisbee is occupied mostly by retired people. Rich history, unique location, and old mines attract millions of visitors each year keeping this historic town alive. It all began in 1880 when Judge DeWitt Bisbee, along with a group of San Francisco business men, financed the Copper Queen Mine. The mine later merged with neighboring Phelps-Dodge and Company forming a rich and powerful mining giant. The high price of copper at this time, provided mine workers with generous salaries which they spent in Bisbee saloons and gambling dens. By the early part of the 1900s Bisbee had grown to a population of twenty-five thousand and was the largest and wealthiest city in Arizona and the largest mining camp in the world. During the Mexican Revolution of 1910, General Black Jack Pershing and Theodore Roosevelt used Bisbee as a base for attacks on Pancho Villa.

The last mining operations in Bisbee were stopped in 1975 because of falling copper prices. Since then, mines have switched to being hosts to tourists, and provide mine tours with a glimpse into the past. The slopes of Mule Mountain, on which Bisbee is built, bear such a resemblance to towns in Greece or Spain that Hollywood has used the location for several movies.

Stop at the Chamber of Commerce in the center of town for a map and then take a walking tour among the old homes that cling to the hillsides as if waiting for some natural disaster to befall them. Bisbee has survived floods and fires and will continue to survive.

Visitors enjoy warm climate, unique ambiance, mine tours, fine cuisine, and shopping for antiques and mineral specimens . Today's Bisbee has all the modern conveniences amidst the charm of the older homes and shops. Bisbee is located off Highway 80, southeast of Tombstone.

For information call 520-432-5421.

BISBEE ATTRACTIONS

Queen Mine and Lavender Pit Tours. Tours begin daily at the Queen Mine Tour office next to Highway 80. Take an underground tour deep into a copper mine or view the open pit Lavender Mine which will astonish you with its size.

The Copper Queen underground mine tour takes seventy-five minutes. There are five tours throughout the day. The first one begins at 9:00 A.M. and the last one begins at 3:30 P.M. Take a sweater because the temperature in the mine stays at about forty-seven degrees. You are allowed to take pictures but you will need a flash.

It is strictly coincidence that the Lavender Pit Mine, named after Harrison Lavender, also has a lavender-colored appearance. There is an admission charged for tours to both mines. Reservations are required.

For information and reservations call 520-432-2071.

Bisbee Mining and Historical Museum. Located in the old two-story headquarters building of the Copper Queen Mine, the museum offers exhibits of historical photographs as well as old mining equipment displayed outside of the building. The manager's office, with its oak interior, takes visitors back in time to moments of big business dealings. The museum is open between

Copper Queen Hotel   *Remains of Bisbee mining days–Lavender Pit Mine*

10:00 A.M. and 4:00 P.M. daily. There is an admission charge.
For information call 520-432-7071.

Muheim Heritage House. Built in 1898 by banker Joseph M.
Muheim, a wealthy Swiss immigrant, the elegant house is decorated with its original furnishings. It is open for guided tours
between 1:00 P.M. and 4:00 P.M., Friday through Monday, allowing visitors to see how comfortably the wealthy people of Bisbee
lived. There is a $2.00 admission charge for adults.
For information call 520-432-7698.

Copper Queen Hotel. Originally built in 1902 to host high
ranking visitors such as mining executives, politicians, and dignitaries, the hotel still serves the public. For its time, it was an
exclusive looking building with stucco exterior and tile roof. You
will enjoy staying in one of the rooms filled with rich history and
memorabilia. You might even bathe in a claw-foot bathtub.
Room 10 once provided accommodations for western movie star,
John Wayne. The saloon and the dining room have been restored
to their original elegance.

The hotel is located at 11 Howell Ave. Rooms range in price
from approximately $75.00 to $135.00 per night.
For information call 520-432-2216 or 1-800-247-5829.

TOMBSTONE

The wild and woolly past of a "town too tough to die" lives on in
well-preserved Tombstone, offering tourists the ambiance of a
wild-west town that is real, not built for movies. Tombstone, an
excellent example of our early western heritage, was once the
fastest growing city between San Francisco and St. Louis. At its
peak in 1880, Tombstone had a population of ten thousand people supporting silver mining efforts by providing stores, saloons,
blacksmiths, and barbers.

The notorious *Gun Fight at OK Corral* really did take place,
with the Earps and Doc Holliday shooting it out against the
Clantons. Three of the Clantons (Frank and Tom McLaury and
Billy Clanton) were shot by the Earps and are buried in Boothill
Cemetery. There were more shootings and reprisals among the
remaining gunslingers until the President of the United States
threatened to impose martial law on the town. The end of vio-

lence did not save Tombstone. Natural disasters took their toll — fire burning one third of the town, and flooding creating havoc in the mines. When mining ended in the early 1890s the population dropped to 150. The town struggled on, and gradually tourists began to arrive wanting to see where all the outlaws had hung out, and the town got its second wind.

A stay in Tombstone is a chance for the whole family to relive Arizona's exciting past. In October, *Helldorado Days* in Tombstone attracts thousands of people for a really wild time. You'll want to witness a shootout performance, visit the museums and gift shops, and see the sights we've included on the next few pages.

Tombstone is located off Highway 80, seventy miles southeast of Tucson.

For information call 520-457-2211.

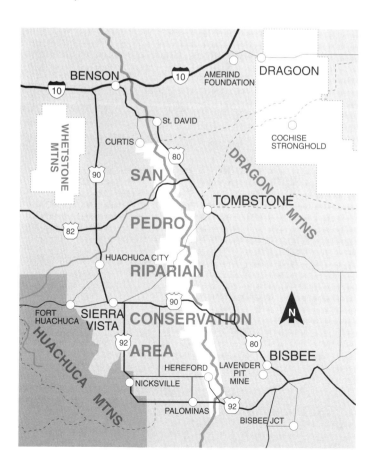

TOMBSTONE COURTHOUSE
STATE HISTORIC PARK

This 1882 impressive brick structure with Greek pediments, prominent cornerstones, and a unique tower was once the courthouse of Cochise County and is now a museum and gift shop. Inside the museum you will find the original judge's bench and prisoner's dock, restored sheriff's office, various versions of the OK Corral shootout, and memorabilia of Wyatt Earp and others. Outside, behind the courthouse, is the reconstructed gallows from which seven outlaws were hung.

The gift shop is stocked with a comprehensive collection of books on Arizona and local history. The Tombstone Courthouse and State Historic Park is located at 219 East Toughnut Street. *For information call 520-457-3311.*

OK CORRAL

The corral has become a tourist attraction because of the movie, *Gunfight at OK Corral*, starring Burt Lancaster and Kirk Douglas as Wyatt Earp and Doc Holliday. Actually the film was made in the stage set town of Old Tucson and the gunfight really

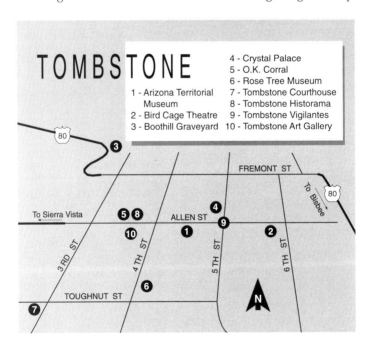

occurred at Fremont and Third streets, not right at the corral. The fight was the result of a long and bitter struggle for power between the law enforcing Earp brothers and the cattle rustling Clanton gang. After the gunfight, efforts of remaining Clanton gang members to continue their unlawful ways provoked a threat of federal interference in hope of ending the violence.

As you explore Tombstone be sure to see the Corral and the Fly Photographic Studio with unique early photographs of Geronimo's surrender. The OK Corral and the Fly Studio are located between Third and Fourth streets on Allen Street.

For information call 520-457-3456.

BOOTHILL CEMETERY

Enough occupants of this cemetery died with their boots on to justify this place of burial being named Boothill. Many of the 250 people buried here were outlaws or victims of outlaws as their grave markers attest. You will read some interesting markers, including George Johnson's that says "Hanged by mistake". The cemetery is located on Highway 80, one-half mile north of town.

For information call 520-457-9344.

Main attraction at Boothill Cemetery   *Following pages: Shootout in Tombstone*

ROSE TREE INN MUSEUM

One of your most pleasant moments in Tombstone may be viewing the hundred-year-old Lady Banksia rose bush which vines over eight thousand square feet of lattice-covered patio. The bush began its life here as a cutting sent from Scotland in 1885 and is known as the world's largest rose bush.

Right next door is the Rose Tree Inn, which houses a lock collection and lovely antiques. It is located at Fourth and Toughnut Streets.

For information call 520-457-3326.

CRYSTAL PALACE SALOON

Still colorful and in business, the Crystal Palace Saloon maintains its original look of elegance and glitter. You'll enjoy good drinks, western music and maybe kicking up you heels in a dance or two. It is located at Allen and Fifth Streets, just a block away from the Silver Nugget Museum and the old Bird Cage Theatre which once provided the whole range of entertainment from vaudeville to prostitution. The Crystal Palace Saloon almost backs up to the famous *Tombstone Epitaph* newspaper office, exhibiting the original hand-operated Washington printing press on which the first edition of the *Tombstone Epitaph* was printed in 1880.

For information call 520-457-3611.

FORT HUACHUCA MUSEUM

Fort Huachuca was established as a temporary military post in 1877 and became a permanent post in 1882 when it was needed to protect against the Apache raids. Located on the only active military post remaining from territorial days, this outstanding museum has artifacts and photos from Pancho Villa border skirmishes to Apache uprisings, and a room remembering the Indian scouts. There is also much about early life at the fort displayed in strikingly realistic ways. Some of the buildings date back to 1879.

Fort Huachuca, now a worldwide military electronics and communications center, is located west of Tombstone and south of Interstate 10 off Highway 90.

For information call 520-533-3638.

"The Advance : General Nelson A. Miles and the 9th Cavalry on Patrol",
by Frederic Remington, courtesy of The Desert Caballeros Western Museum

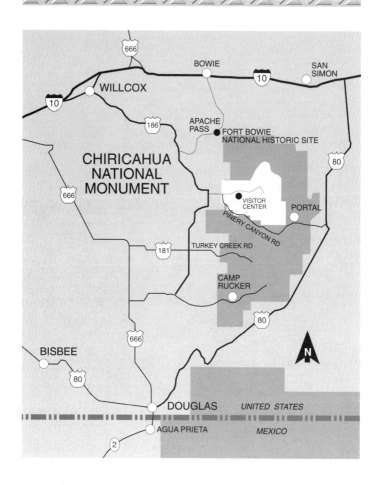

CHIRICAHUA NATIONAL MONUMENT

Rocks balancing on top of each other, golden spires glowing in the sunrise, giant "standing up rocks"—these are the Chiricahuas, formed from volcanically welded tuff, eroded during the passage of time. The huge volcanic explosion, twenty-seven million years ago, created these columns which once served as hideouts for Apaches, including Geronimo, whose surrender allowed settlement of the area. Now these rock spires stand magnificently as an eighteen-square-mile national monument which provides excellent hiking, camping, and picnicking facilities. Wildlife in these parts run the range from delicate hummingbirds to curious coatimundi and fearless black bears.

There are twenty miles of hiking trails and eight miles of steep, winding road leading you through the park and enabling

Wonderland of rocks at Chiricahua National Monument

you to be surrounded by these fantastic rock formations. We recommend hiking the trails for the ultimate experience of absorbing the grandeur of these column-like formations. You might feel a little uneasy as you look up at the precariously perched rocks , appearing to wait for a light touch or slight earth tremor to send them crashing to the ground.

This is truly an awesome experience. Take your camera and shoot your pictures before the sun suddenly drops behind the canyon walls. The colored leaves throughout October are striking and the flowers from July through September are truly a photographers delight. This is a uniquely beautiful part of Arizona that is off the beaten track of the majority of tourists.

Exhibits in the Visitor Center offer historical and geological information of the area as well as interesting artifacts of the Chiricahua Apaches. Take a free tour of Faraway Ranch, the house built by a Swiss family in 1886; and see one of the oldest log cabins in Arizona, built in 1862.

Admission to the Chiricahua National Monument is $4.00 per vehicle. It is best to fill up your gas tank in Willcox or Douglas because there are no gas stations near the Chiricahuas. The Chiricahuas are located off Highway 186, thirty-seven miles southeast of Willcox.

For information call 520-824-3560.

Faraway Ranch

HIKING IN THE
CHIRICAHUA NATIONAL MONUMENT

Heart of Rocks Trail. This trail, winding on top of a mesa, is one of the best trails for panoramic views of the rock formations which are called "Disneyland of Rocks". The seven-mile round trip hike is considered difficult but exhilarating and take a full-day. Carry plenty of drinking water. The hike originates at the Massai Point parking area.

Echo Canyon Trail. This three-and-a-half mile trail takes you on a fantasy journey through a labyrinth of towering rocks. The tight passes, high walls of the canyons, and lush flora engulf you in their beauty. For the essence of the Chiricahua National Monument, this is the best trail to hike. The trail starts at the Echo Canyon parking area.

Legendary Apache warrior, Geronimo,
courtesy of Finn Foto

FORT BOWIE NATIONAL HISTORIC SITE

To enrich your knowledge of the struggles between the Indians and the settlers in the late 1800s, we suggest you add the trip to Fort Bowie to your adventure in the magnificent Chiricahua National Monument.

For protection of the Apache Pass during their war with the Chiricahua Indians, the army built Fort Bowie, a useful stronghold in their battles with Cochise and later, Geronimo. After the surrender of Geronimo, who frequently hid out in the Chiricahua mountains, everything was peaceful, and Fort Bowie was abandoned in 1894.

There is a small Visitor Center at the fort where you can buy books and information about the battles with these great Indian chiefs and their warriors. Fort Bowie is located on Apache Pass Road, twelve miles from Highway 186 or eight miles down Fort Bowie Road from Interstate 10. Both roads are dusty but viewing the ruins of the fort and getting a feel for its history are worth it. After you have parked your car you will hike a one-and-a-half mile foot trail before reaching Fort Bowie.

For information call 520-847-2500.

DOUGLAS

Sitting on the Mexican border, Douglas, once dependent on copper mining, is now a manufacturing center employing mostly Mexican Nationals from Agua Prieta, across the border. Copper smelting shut down rather recently (1987) and would have left a lot of people unemployed had it not been for the cooperation of the two towns in attracting manufacturing businesses. Douglas has grown only slightly, to a population of thirteen thousand, but Agua Prieta has more than tripled its population in the last ten years.

If you're going through Douglas, do make the time to go into the Gadsden Hotel to see the elegant marble and gold leaf columns, unusual stained glass skylights, Victorian chandeliers, and the beautiful marble staircase. Reaching forty-two feet across the mezzanine, the magnificent authentic Tiffany stained glass mural will capture your attention.

Originally built in 1907 to house and entertain high-level copper executives and other dignitaries, the Gadsden has been through fire and then restoration to become Douglas's outstanding tourist attraction. The hotel is located at 1046 G Ave. Douglas is twenty-five miles east of Bisbee off Highway 80.

For information call the Gadsden Hotel at 520-364-4481.
or the Chamber of Commerce at 520-2477.

JOHNSON HISTORICAL MUSEUM OF THE SOUTHWEST (SLAUGHTER RANCH MUSEUM)

Take Fifteenth Street in downtown Douglas, head east for five miles to where the pavement ends. This is now the Geronimo trail, a well-graded dirt road which carries you for about eleven miles to the entrance of the Slaughter Ranch and the San Bernardino National Wildlife Refuge.

In 1884, two years before Geronimo surrendered, John Slaughter and his wife acquired 65,000 acres of grassland which he developed into one of the largest cattle ranches in Arizona. The Slaughter house, full of memorabilia, old furniture, and photographs of Slaughter and others is open to the public.

The museum is open daily from 10:00 A.M. to 3:00 P.M. There is an admission charge.

For information call 520-558-2474.

PRICE CANYON RANCH

Located near the southeastern corner of the state, the Price Canyon Ranch, a working cattle ranch, provides an opportunity to explore the life of the cattle rancher, marvel at the Chiricahua Mountains rock formations, bird watch and study Indian lore. While a guest of the ranch you can hunt for deer, javelina and bear during their seasons. Trailrides and one to twelve-day pack trips are popular adventures.

Cattle round-up times (minimum of three days) occur twice a year, from October 5th to 15th and May 5th to 15th.

Guests are given the opportunity to participate in general ranch life. Horseback riding can be an every day occurrence for all ages. Meals are served in the one-hundred-year-old main ranch house and accommodations are in one and two-room bunk houses with bath. Other accommodations include the more

spacious and comfortable "People Barn", apartments, or the trailer and camper sites with full hook-ups. Make reservations at least three weeks in advance and then don your cowboy hat and boots for a terrific family vacation.

The road to Price Canyon Ranch turns north off Highway 80 between Douglas and Apache.

For information call 520-558-2383.

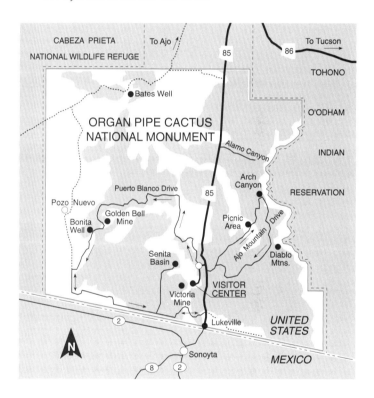

ORGAN PIPE CACTUS
NATIONAL MONUMENT

Twenty-nine species of cacti have adapted to this harsh climate and thrive at Organ Pipe Cactus National Monument, along with creatures such as kangaroo rats, jackrabbits, rattlesnakes, and owls. Use your flashlight to spot a few of these creatures that come out in the cool of the night. If you're on one of the scenic drives at dusk, watch out for the rabbits that like to run across the road. After the sun goes down in May, June, and July the south-facing slopes are in bloom with the pale lavender flower of

Petroglyphs, occurring throughout Arizona

the Organ Pipe. In March and April, after a wet winter, wild-flowers cover the slopes in a splendid array of colors providing exotic subject matter for photographers.

The levels of elevation throughout Arizona's largest (330,690 acres) national monument offer distinct plant groupings. Rangers conduct guided tours and give slide talks. For your pleasure, the Visitor Center has several exhibits of flora and fauna of the Sonoran desert. An even greater pleasure, is to hike the trails into the desert gardens or take either of the dirt-road scenic drives.

The United Nations has designated Organ Pipe as an International Biosphere Preserve. It is a unique place to spend some time enjoying the beauty of the Southwest.

To reach Organ Pipe Cactus National Monument go south from Gila Bend on Highway 85 or west from Tucson on Highway 86. The community of Ajo is the last opportunity to replenish your traveling supplies. There is a gas station at the junction at Why, a little further south.

For information call 520-387-6849.

HIKES AND DRIVES THROUGH
ORGAN PIPE CACTUS NATIONAL MONUMENT

Ajo Mountain Drive Trail loops around the park for twenty-one miles giving you many opportunities to see spectacular Sonoran Desert scenery from your car. You can stop in many places for a closer look or to photograph spring wildflowers. Driving up the winding one way dirt road toward Arch Canyon you are exposed to a vast array of organ pipe cacti on the mountain slopes. Half way through the drive you arrive at Arch Canyon which takes its name from the stone arch towering over the trail. If you are a photography enthusiast, this is the perfect place to challenge your skills as the red sandstone walls of the canyon become alive with colors emphasized by late afternoon sunlight. The views are so picture perfect that patient photographers camp for a few days waiting for just the right light.

Puerto Blanco Drive, a one way, fifty-three-mile dirt road takes you past spring wildflowers, shrubbery, and saguaro cacti backed by the Puerto Blanco and Sonoyta Mountains.

Distinctive Organ Pipe cactus

The length of the drive, desert environment, and the fact that you cannot turn back, make it necessary to have plenty of drinking water. If you stop to shoot photographs or hike on any of the trails be sure you have sun protection and sturdy shoes. Before you enter the Puerto Blanco Drive stop in at the Visitor Center for additional information. This is, at least, a half-day adventure.

Bull Pasture Trail is a self-guided hiking trail taking you two miles into the beautiful Ajo Mountains for an unbelievable view. You must wear sturdy shoes and have drinking water and sun protection with you.

Desert View Nature Trail is a short circular route leading to vistas of Sonoyta Valley and the pink granite Cubabi Mountains in Mexico. Trailside signs describe features along the way.

Cross-country hiking in the open desert can be enjoyable, but first discuss your planned route with a park ranger.
For information call 520-387-6849.

Ocotillo shrub brushing the sky   *Magic of the desert*

QUARTZSITE

It is strange to see more than five hundred thousand people and their motor homes gathered in the middle of nowhere for the world's largest annual February Gemboree rock and mineral show. Quartzsite is the place where people meet each year ignoring the barren scenery and enjoying each other's company.

Quartzsite does have a history as a stagecoach stop in the mid–1800s. Facilities have improved over the years. There are now restaurants, gas station, beauty salon, grocery, and a motorhome and RV sales office. The resident population is approximately eighteen hundred.

Transient people who gather in Quartzsite in the cooler months say they have a wonderful time. The biggest events occur during late January and early February when there are around six thousand booths set up to display remarkable gems and minerals as well as antiques. Evening dancing on the open dance floor is active and full of fun. Quartzsite is located where Highway 95 crosses Interstate 10.

For information call 520-927-5600.

ROCKHOUNDING TIPS

Rockhounding, a modern form of treasure hunting, is a popular hobby, form of relaxation, and for some, a profession. Many Arizonans and visitors engage in rockhounding challenges to find unique and beautiful specimens to enjoy, display, and trade or sell at various gem and mineral shows throughout the state. Arizona, a state in which rocks are well exposed, is a paradise for geologists and amateur rock hunters. Scant soil and little vegetation aid in making it possible to see rocks and mineral out-croppings from a short distance.

The discovery of gold in Arizona brought many of the early settlers. Mining towns sprang up and had their heyday when gold was plentiful, but today they are classified as ghost towns. Rockhounds still use those locations to experience the excitement of panning for gold. In many of those locations wheat-sized nuggets of gold can still be found. To find anything from a nugget the size of a pea to the tiny speck that prospectors called "colors" gives a modern gold digger quite a thrill. The easiest way to distinguish gold from other minerals is to use the color method. Gold has a unique color which appears the same in sunlight or shadow and at any angle. Another positive test is the streak test in which you drag your nugget across a clean steel surface. If the nugget leaves a black streak, it is not gold. If it leaves a streak of fine gold specks, you know it is gold. For those of you who want to experience gold panning, the necessary equipment can be purchased in the larger hardware stores and in most rock shops.

According to the Arizona Department of Mineral Resources, the most general classification of rocks is by method of formation. The three basic categories are igneous, sedimentary and metamorphic.

Igneous includes felsite, basalt, obsidian (Apache tears), granite, pegmatite and porphyry. The word igneous means "pertaining to fire". In geology it means rocks which have been formed by the cooling of once-hot magma. In general igneous rocks are hard, do not contain fossils, are not layered, and are bound together by interlocking crystals.

Sedimentary includes shale, sandstone, conglomerate, breccia, and limestone. Sedimentary rocks are made up of fragments of other rocks, sometimes contain fossils, and are lighter and

ROCK TABLE	REMARKS, WHAT TO LOOK FOR
Igneous	
Felsite	Mineral particles too fine to see. Usually parallel streaks.
Basalt	Often has small openings or vugs.
Apache Tears	Occurrs as inclusions in perlite.
Granite	Hard, tough, composed of quartz, feldspar, mica, others.
Pegmatite	Similar to granite, but large distinct crystals.
Porphyry	Rock with 25% or more crystals in a fine grained ground mass.
Sedimentary	
Shale	Soft, laminated, usually gray. Hardened mud.
Sandstone	Breaks through the cement, showing grains.
Conglomerate	Rounded pebbles and rocks cemented together.
Breccia	Rough, angular rocks and pebbles cemented together.
Limestone	May contain fossils. Can be scrathed easily with knife.
Metamorphic	
Schist	Usually breaks with wavy surface.
Gneiss	Usually streaked light and dark. Not platey like schist.
Quartzite	Resembles sandstone, but breaks through the grains.
Marble	Sometimes white, sometimes with dark patches.
Slate	Splits easily along cleavage planes.

softer than others. They are formed by layers of gravel, sand, or clay washed down into lake beds and ocean floors or laid down by ice or wind. Those materials are then cemented under pressure and later raised up again by the movements of the earth.

Metamorphic includes schist, gneiss, quartzite, marble, and slate. Metamorphic rocks are those which have been changed from the form in which they were originally laid down. Some of them bear a recognizable resemblance to the original rocks. Metamorphic rocks generally show bands of light and dark minerals, will split easily into layers, and are hard and crystalline.

For further information or suggested reading materials, contact Arizona Department of Mineral Resources, 1502 W. Washington Street, Phoenix, AZ 85007, 602-255-3791.

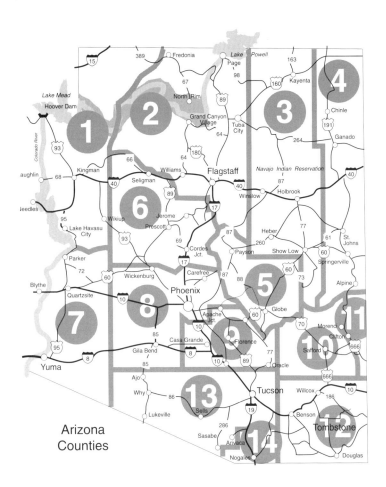

Arizona Counties

LOCATIONS OF ROCKS & MINERALS

ROCKS AND MINERALS	Mohave 1	Coconino 2	Navajo 3	Apache 4	Gila 5	Yavapai 6	Yuma 7	Maricopa 8	Pinal 9	Graham 10	Greenlee 11	Cochise 12	Pima 13	Santa Cruz 14
Actinolite	●					●	●		●	●	●	●	●	●
Agate	●	●	●	●	●	●	●	●	●	●	●	●	●	
Amethyst	●				●			●						●
Apache Tears	●					●		●						
Azurite	●					●	●	●			●	●		
Barite	●					●	●	●		●		●	●	
Beryl	●					●	●	●						
Bornite	●	●										●	●	
Calcite	●					●	●		●			●		●
Chalcedony	●	●	●	●	●	●	●	●	●			●	●	●
Chalcopyrite	●		●			●	●	●	●			●	●	
Chrysocolla	●					●	●	●	●			●	●	
Cinnabar	●					●	●	●						
Copper	●					●	●		●			●		
Cuprite	●					●	●	●	●			●	●	
Epidote	●				●	●	●	●		●	●	●	●	●
Feldspar	●					●	●	●	●			●		
Flurorite	●							●		●		●	●	
Galena	●					●	●	●		●		●	●	●
Garnet	●	●				●	●	●	●		●	●	●	●
Goethite	●					●	●	●	●			●	●	
Gold	●					●	●	●	●			●	●	●
Gypsum	●		●			●	●	●	●			●	●	
Hematite	●	●			●	●	●	●				●		
Jasper	●		●	●	●	●	●		●	●	●		●	●
Magnetite	●	●			●		●	●					●	
Malachite	●	●	●			●	●	●				●	●	
Marble	●					●		●	●			●	●	
Onyx	●	●			●	●	●	●						●
Opal	●					●	●	●				●		
Peridot				●	●									
Petrified Wood	●	●	●	●			●		●			●		
Pyrite	●					●	●	●	●		●	●	●	●
Quartz	●					●	●	●	●	●		●	●	●
Rose Quartz	●							●						
Serpentine		●			●				●		●	●		
Silver	●					●	●		●	●		●		●
Tourmaline	●	●				●	●	●					●	●
Turquoise	●				●			●	●			●	●	●
Uraninite		●	●	●	●	●								

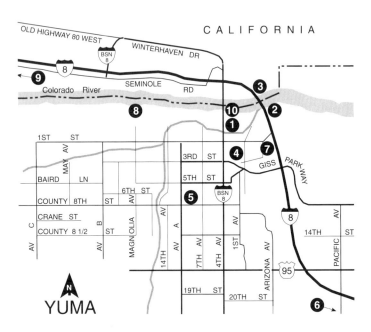

1 - Fort Yuma Quartermasters Depot
2 - Yuma Territorial Prison
3 - Fort Yuma Quechan Museum
4 - Century House Museum and Gardens
5 - Erlich's Date Garden

6 - To the Peanut Patch
7 - Yuma Art Center
8 - Yuma Crossing Recreation Park
9 - To Sand Dunes
10 - Steamboat Landing

YUMA

Living in the lower Colorado River area and bound together by the same language, the Quechan, Cocopah, and Mohave Indian tribes were known as the Yumans. The actual city and county of Yuma developed in rich Old-West fashion through its mountain men, soldiers, river men, railroaders, the Quechan Indians, and the inmates of the famous Territorial Prison. Development of this area can also be credited to Spanish priests who built missions, the Mormon Battalion who established the first wagon road in this region, Kit Carson who guided American troops during the Mexican War, and gold seekers who crossed the river to go on to California.

In the mid–1800s, shallow-draft steamboating on the Colorado River made Yuma the major riverport for Arizona, bringing goods which were then dispersed across the territory.

The activity of the fort brought much of the development to

Yuma which is now a multi-cultural community of 55,000 residents and is ideally located less than twenty minutes from Mexico, and three hours from San Diego or Phoenix.

FORT YUMA QUARTERMASTERS DEPOT

During the 1870s and 1880s, at the height of the Apache Wars, the activity of bringing in supplies for military posts throughout the region created a busy way of life at the depot, until the arrival of the steam engine. Many of the original depot buildings still exist and are in the process of restoration.

Trained guides will interpret history, bringing to life an exciting era of Arizona's past. There are craft demonstrations and story telling to delight everyone. To get there take the Giss Parkway exit off Interstate 8 to 2nd Avenue. Admission is $3.00.

For information call 520-329-0404.

YUMA TERRITORIAL PRISON

Many myths and legends surrounding the Yuma Territorial Prison have led people to believe it was a hellhole of brutality and unbelievably poor living conditions for the 3,069 prisoners housed there during its thirty-three years as a prison. In fact, it was considered to be a model prison of its time and beat the city of Yuma in getting electricity in 1885.

Even though the prisoners were treated humanely, many tried to escape, with forty-two being successful and eight dying from gunshot wounds. Other prison deaths resulted from tuberculosis, a common illness at the time. No one was executed at the prison, but punishments of the ball and chain or the dark cell did occur. Among those imprisoned for crimes which ran the gamut from polygamy, adultery, and murder to grand larceny were twenty-nine women.

Amenities for the prisoners took the form of job training in useful trades, and a library from which many learned to read and write. Crowded conditions forced the legislature to decide to move the prisoners to Florence, and in 1907 the last prisoner vacated the Yuma prison. Before the establishment was renovated and opened for tourists it was used as the Yuma High School and later vandalized by people looking for building materials.

while listening to a very knowledgeable tour guide gives you a feeling for the more rough sides of our early Arizona history. In the museum area there are archival photographs, relics, and written stories of the prisoners. The Yuma Territorial Prison is located off Interstate 8 near the Giss Parkway exit and can be seen from the freeway. It is open daily. Admission is $3.00.

For information call 520-783-4771.

FORT YUMA QUECHAN MUSEUM

If you appreciate Indian or military history, you'll want to visit this museum, located on the Fort Yuma Indian Reservation, directly across the Colorado River from the Territorial Prison. It is headquarters for the Quechan Indians and specializes in the history of the Quechan people. To get there take Picacho Road to Indian Hill Road on the California side of the river.

For information call 520-317-1802.

YUMA RIVER TOURS

While in the Yuma area, take an enjoyable boat tour along the lower Colorado River or cruise upstream to the imperial National Wildlife Refuge. The guide will tell you about mining camps, steamboat landings, petroglyphs, and other historical sites. There are two-hour, half-day, and full-day tours. The price is $32.00 per person.

For information and reservations call 520-783-4400.

YUMA VALLEY RAILROAD

Try the Friday night special of a railroad trip along the Colorado River and a cowboy dinner with Indian fry bread served on the Cocopah Indian Reservation.

For information call 502-783-3456.

MORE YUMA ATTRACTIONS

Century House Museum and Gardens. A day in Yuma can be enjoyed in the Century House Museum and Gardens and the Adobe Annex, both located in the 200 block of Madison Avenue. They were built in 1871 and 1890 respectively and house photographs and artifacts of the lower Colorado River life of that

Yuma Territorial Prison sizzling in the Arizona sun.

time. The Century House, a spacious nineteenth-century mansion, still has its impressive aviary and garden of exotic and desert plants and is well worth a visit.

For information call 502-782-1841.

Erlich's Date Garden. Satisfy your sweet tooth with a visit to Erlich's Date Garden to taste samples of several date varieties and to see how they are grown. The garden is located at 868 Eighth Street.

For information call 520-783-4778.

The Peanut Patch. Other tasty delights are processed at the Peanut Patch facility year round. To see the peanut harvest, be there between October and December. The Peanut Patch is located at 4322 E. County 13th St.

For information call 520-726-6292.

Imperial *Sand Dunes Recreation Area.* Going west from Yuma on Interstate 8 for about ten miles, you arrive at one of the playgrounds of Arizonans. The sand dunes are actually in California but we have chosen to include them because many Arizona photographers try to catch the ever changing dunes in that perfect early morning or late afternoon light. Many people have a wonderful time hiking the dunes or driving all-terrain-vehicles during cooler weather. The winds blow away their tracks recreating unspoiled, picture-perfect sand dunes again.

Drawing of a Papago design

PRONUNCIATION

So that you will feel more comfortable while you are here, we have included the typical pronunciation and a brief definition of many words unique to Arizona and the Southwest.

Ajo (AH - hoe) - meaning "garlic" in Spanish, is the name of a small town in southern Arizona.

Anasazi (Ana-SAH-zee) - meaning "the ancient ones", is the name of very early Arizona Indians.

Apache (Ah-PAH-chee) - a tribe of Indians who moved down from the north and settled relatively recently in Arizona.

Canyon de Chelly (Canyon du SHAY) - a national monument in Navajoland.

Chinle (Chin-LEE) - a Navajo town located near the entrance to Canyon de Chelly.

Chiricahua (Cheer-i-COW-wa) - a uniquely beautiful mountain range in southeastern Arizona., also the name of an Indian tribe.

Cholla (CHOY-ya) - Many varieties of this cactus grow in Arizona.

Coconino (Co-co-NEE-no) - a name most often seen on the Coconino National Forest signs.

Gila (HEE-la) - a Yuman Indian word meaning "salty water".

Guadalupe (Wa-da-LU-pay) - name of a town south of Phoenix.

Havasupai (Hah-vah-SOO-pie) - meaning "people of the blue-green water", also the name of a beautiful canyon which branches from the Grand Canyon and is home to the small tribe of Havasupai Indians.

Hohokam (HO-ho-kaam) - meaning "those who have gone", a name given to an ancient tribe.

Huachuca (Hwa-CHOO-ka) - name of a mountain range and a military fort in southern Arizona.

Hopi (HOE-pee) - a northern Arizona Indian tribe.

Javelina (Ha-va-LEE-na) - a wild pig or boar.

Jojoba (Ho-HO-bah) - a desert shrub with edible nuts from which oil is extracted for use in cosmetics.

Kykotsmovi (Kee-KOTS-mo-vee) - meaning "place of the mound of ruins". It is the Hopi tribal administrative center at Third Mesa.

Mesquite (Mess-KEET) - a desert tree which produces seed pods used by early Indians to make flour.

Moenkopi (Mu-en-KO-pee) - meaning "place of running water", a village on Third Mesa.

Mogollon (MUGGY-own) - edge of the Colorado Plateau referred to

as the Mogollon Rim.

Navajo (NAH-VAH-hoe) - the largest Indian tribe in Arizona.

Nogales (No-GAH-less) - meaning "walnuts". Arizona and Mexico have adjacent border towns named Nogales.

Ocotillo (O-co-TEE-yo) - name of a tall desert bush with red spring flowers.

Oraibi (Oh-RYE-bee) - meaning "place of the Orai stone", a village of Third Mesa.

Papago (PAH-pa-go) - an Indian tribe that is now known by its original name of "Tohono O'odham".

Pima (PEE-ma) - the first Indians encountered by the Spanish missionaries. Originally they were part of the Tohono O'odham people.

Sagurao (Sah-WHAR-oh) - very tall cactus, often with "arms".

San Xavier (Sahn Ha-VEER) - San Xavier del Bac, the "White Dove of the Desert" mission south of Tucson.

Sichomovi (Si-CHO-MO-vee) - meaning "hill where currants grow", a village of First Mesa.

Sinagua (Si-NAU-wa) - meaning "without water", an ancient tribe of north-central Arizona.

Shungopovi (Shung-O-PO-vee) - meaning "tall reeds growing by the spring", a village on Second Mesa.

Tempe (Tem-PEE) - city just east of Phoenix, home of Arizona State University.

Tohono O'odham (To-HO-no ah-toon) - meaning "people who have come out of the desert earth", original name of the Papago tribe.

Tubac (TU-bahk) - an historic place as Arizona's first settlement.

Tucson (TOO-sahn) - second largest city in Arizona.

Tumacacori (Too-mah-ka-COR-ee) - impressive abandoned old Spanish Mission south of Tucson.

Tusayan (TU-sigh-yan) - name of a Sinagua Indian ruin and name of a community near the Grand Canyon.

Wahweap (WAH-weep) - name of a large marina at Lake Powell.

Wupatki (Wu-PAHT-kee) - meaning "tall house" in Hopi. It is a large ruin north of Flagstaff.

Yaqui (Ya-KEE) - a small Indian tribe located near Tucson.

Yavapai (YA-vah-pie) - meaning "people of the sun", an Indian tribe in central Arizona.

Yuma (YOO-ma) - name of a city in the southwestern corner of the state, also the name of Indian tribes from the same area.

CALENDAR OF ANNUAL EVENTS

As a visitor to Arizona, you will discover that there are many festivals and events throughout the year. There is something to satisfy everyone's interest, from Indian ceremonial dances and rodeos to rock and gem shows. We have arranged the selected events alphabetically by city within each month and have included general information relating to dates, times, and adult admission charges. Admission for senior citizens, students and children is usually less. The publishers believe this information to be correct at the time of going to press. You will need to call to verify exact dates, times, and locations.

JANUARY

- **Alpine's** *Annual Sled Dog Races* at Williams Valley Recreation Area. Donations are appreciated. From 9:00 A.M. to 2:00 P.M. Call 520-339-4330.
- **Casa Grande's** *Annual Arizona Old-Time Fiddlers Jam &Country Store Bazaar* at the Pinal County Fairgrounds, seven miles east of town. Enjoy old-time fiddlers, entertainment, arts & crafts, and classic car show. Free. Call 520-723-5242 .
- **Glendale's** *Glendale Glitters* spectacular light show in downtown Glendale. November 27 - January 16. Call 623-930-2299.
- **Phoenix's** *Annual Frybread Festival* at the Heard Museum. On the last weekend of January try Indian fry bread with beans and salsa or with honey and powdered sugar. The festival is during regular museum hours. Call 602-252-8840.
- **Phoenix's** *Annual World of Wheels Automotive Show* at the Civic Plaza. A comprehensive and impressive show. Admission is $8.00. Call 602-262-7272.
- **Sedona's** *Annual Red Rock Fantasy of Light* at Los Abrigados Resort and Spa. Through mid-January. Call 520-282-1777.
- **Quartzsite's** *Annual Cloud's Jamboree*. Enjoy jewelry, rocks, and gems. Free, 9:00 A.M. to 5:00 P.M. Call 520-927-5600.
- **Quartzsite's** *The Main Event Annual Gem and Mineral Show.* Call 520-927-5213.
- **Scottsdale's** *Jaycees Parada del Sol Rodeo and Festival*. Enjoy

the world's longest horse-drawn parade and a rodeo that features the top names in rodeo. Event is held at Rawhide. Call 480-990-3179.

- **Scottsdale's** *Phoenix Open PGA Golf Tournament*. Call 602-870-0163 or 480-945-8481.
- **Wickenburg's** *Annual Antique Guild Show* and Sale at the Community Center. Admission . Call 520-344-3800.

FEBRUARY

- **Apache Junction's** *Annual Lost Dutchman Days.* A community celebration emphasizing the Lost Dutchman legends of gold in the Superstition Mountains. There is a Bluegrass festival and rodeo. Free. Call 480-982-3141.
- **Casa Grande's** *Annual O'odham Tash (People Days).* Powwows, Indian ceremonials, largest all-Indian rodeo, sports tournaments, and arts & crafts. This event takes place the third weekend in February and attracts 150,000 people. There are over 900 events. There is an admission charge for some of them. Call 520-836-4723 or 520-836-2125.
- **Flagstaff's** *Annual Winterfest* lasts for eleven action-filled days and features championship sled dog races and star gazing at Lowell observatory, among more than ninety other events. Enjoy skiing, ice skating, snow shoeing, wine tasting, concerts, and snow softball. Call the Flagstaff Visitors Center at 1-800-842-7293 or 520-774-9541.
- **Florence's** *Annual Tour of Historic Florence*, one of the oldest communities in Arizona. Tour is from 9:00 A.M. to 4:00 P.M. Admission is $5.00. Call 520-868-5216 or 520-868-9433.
- **Globe/Miami's** *Annual Historic Home and Building Tour and Antique Show.* Tour begins in downtown Globe and ends at the Antique Show. Fee is $6.00. Tour starts at 9:00 A.M. Call 602-425-4495.
- **Mesa's** *Annual Territorial Days* at Mesa Southwest Museum. Enjoy old-time pioneer arts and crafts festival, demonstrations of pioneer crafts and activities. Free. Call 602-644-2230.
- **Phoenix's** *Annual Sports, Vacation, & RV Show* at the Civic Plaza. All kinds of sporting vehicles, resorts, vacation spots, tents etc. Admission fee is $5.00. Call 602-262-7272.
- **Phoenix's** *Annual World Championship Hoop Dance Contest* at the Heard Museum. Hoop dancing is a fast-paced form of

Native American dancing. Free. Call 602-252-8840.

- **Quartzsite's** *Annual Pow Pow*. Gem and mineral show. More than five hundred tailgaters and dealers displaying, buying, and selling. Free. The event lasts from 7:00 A.M. to 7:00 P.M. Call 520-927-5600.

- **Scottsdale's** *Annual All-Arabian Horse Show*. Almost two thousand horses and riders come from many states and foreign countries. Enjoy the pageantry, bazaars, and culinary treats set up for your pleasure. The admission is $5.00 and the show begins at 8:00 A.M.
  Call 480-951-1180 or 480-945-8481.

- **Scottsdale's** *Annual Gem and Mineral Show*. Free admission. Call 480-945-8481 for date and location.

- **Tubac's** *Annual Festival of the Arts*. There are more than 125 visiting juried artists, entertainment, demonstrations, and food. Enjoy this old town, its art community, and the Tubac Presidio State Park. Free.
  Call 520-398-3269 or 520-398-2704.

- **Tucson's** *Annual Arizona Mineral and Fossil Show* at the Executive Inn from 10:00 A.M. to 8:00 P.M. Free.
  Call 520-792-1212. for the date.

- **Tucson's** *Annual International Gem and Mineral Show*, the world's largest, held at the Convention Center.
  Call 520-791-4266 or 520-322-5773.

- **Tucson's** *Annual La Fiesta de los Vaqueros* held at the Tucson Rodeo Grounds. Watch top-level rodeo contestants.
  Call 520-792-1212.

- **Tucson's** *Annual La Reunion el Fuerte* held at Ft. Lowell Park. You will be able to tour nineteen historic sites and enjoy the entertainment. The event is from 1:00 to 4:00 P.M. Call 520-885-3832.

- **Wickenburg's** *Annual Gold Rush Days* give you a taste of the old west with a rodeo, gold panning, western dances, arts and crafts, gem show and a mucking and drilling contest. Call 520-684-5479.

- **Yuma's** *Annual Silver Spur Rodeo Parade*. More than four hundred entries. Starts at 9:00 A.M. Call 520-783-3641.

- **Yuma's** *Jaycee's Annual Silver Spur Rodeo*. Admission is from $4.00 to $8.00. The grand entry is at 1:30 P.M.
  Call 520-782-2567.

MARCH

- **Chandler's** *Annual Ostrich Festival*. See the Ostrich races and enjoy international food and big-name entertainment. Free. Hours are from 10:00 A.M. to 10:00 P.M. Call 602-963-4571.
- **Cottonwood's** *Annual Verde Valley Gem and Mineral Show* at Mingus Union High School. Jewelry demonstrations in mounting, carving, and lost wax. Admission $1.00. The event begins at 10:00 A.M. Call 520-634-7593.
- **Page's** *Annual Page/Lake Powell Hot Air Balloon Regatta Air Affaire*. Thrill to the beauty of the balloons and the excitement of power aerobatics, parachute teams, and military static displays. Admission $5:00. Call 520-645-2741.
- **Phoenix's** *Gem and Mineral Show* occurs the first weekend in March and is an annual event featuring rare rocks. Interesting people become involved in the pleasure of gems and minerals and produce fascinating works of art. In one form or another probably all 650 of the minerals native to Arizona will be displayed at this Gem and Mineral show. It is held at the mountain preserve on E. Dunlap. Call 623-939-9293.
- **Phoenix's** *Annual DesertFest at the Desert Botanical Gardens*. Enjoy the planting and landscape demos. There are children's activities, succulent sale, entertainment, and desert food demos. Admission is $4.00. Open 9:00 A.M. to 5:00 P.M. Call 480-941-1225.
- **Phoenix's** *Annual Heard Museum Guild Indian Fair and Market Best of Show Competition.* On the museum grounds, 5:30 to 8:30 P.M., $15.00 per person. Call 602-252-8840.
- **Phoenix's** *Annual Heard Museum Guild Indian Fair Market*. The first weekend in March from 9:30 A.M to 5:30 P.M., $5.00. More than four hundred of the best Native American artists will sell their craft art and fine art. A variety of authentic Native American dances will be performed. There will be delicious Native American foods for sale. Call 602-252-8840.
- **Phoenix's** *Annual Desert Classic Invitational Team Roping*. Five hundred of the best team ropers and rodeo contestants in the U. S. vying for more than $200,000 in cash and prizes. Call 602-254-4393.

- **Phoenix's** *Grand Canyon State Woodcarvers Annual Desert Festival Award Show & Sale* at the Civic Plaza features carvers from all over the U.S. and Canada. Admission fee is $1.00. Call 602-267-7272.

- **Phoenix's** *Annual Solar & Electric 500 Auto Race* at the Phoenix International Raceway. This is the world's premier racing showcase of alternative-energy transportation. There is racing in four categories. Call 602-953-6672.

- **Phoenix's** *Annual Spring in the Mountains Trek* at one of the Mountain Parks, for hikers, mountain bikers, horseback riders, and bird-watchers, 7:00 A.M., $2.00 fee, breakfast available for $6.00. Call 602-495-5078.

- **Picacho Peak's** *Annual Civil War Battle Re-Enactment* at Picacho Peak State Park. Experience the reenactment of the only battle fought in Arizona. Soldiers dress in uniforms of the North and South. They ride horses and use black powder arms. Admission is $3.00 per vehicle. It all begins at 11:00 A.M. Call 520-466-3183.

- **Scottsdale's** *Annual National Festival of the West.* Enjoy a cowboy festival with music, cowboy poetry, gunfights, movie stars etc. From 10:00 A.M. to 6:00 P.M. Admission is $5.00. Call 602-996-4387.

- **Superior's** Boyce Thompson Arboretum hosts its *Annual Welcome Back Buzzards Day.* Celebrate the annual return of the flock of turkey vultures to their roosts in the Eucalyptus grove.It begins at 10:30 A.M. Call 520-689-2811.

- **Tempe's** *Biannual Old Town Tempe Spring Festival of the Arts* on Mill Avenue. This is the second largest arts and entertainment festival in the Southwest. There is a special children's area. Free. From 10:00 A.M. to 6:00 P.M. Call 480-967-4877.

- **Tombstone's** *Annual Territorial Days.* Free. Held the first weekend of March. Call 520-457-2211.

- **Tucson's** *Desert Botanical Garden Spring Plant Sale.* Purchase cacti, succulents, orchids, and drought-tolerant plants. Call 520-326-9255.

- **Tucson's** *Archaeology Fair* at the AZ State Museum. See the special displays by art museums, Native American tribes, and others. See demonstrations of prehistoric crafts and take guided tours of the museum. Free. 9:00 A.M. to 4:00 P.M. Call 520-621-6302.

APRIL

- **Casa Grande's** *Annual Ride the Ruins*, a twenty-five mile bicycle challenge beginning at O'Neil Park and ending at the Casa Grande Ruins, $10.00 or $12.00 participation fee. The ride begins at 8:00 A.M. Call 520-421-8600 or 520-836-2125.
- **Cave Creek/Carefree's** *Annual Fiesta Days* rodeo, dance, parade, arts & crafts festival, antique and classic car show. Admission is about $6.00. Call 480-488-3627.
- **Cave Creek's** *Annual Magic Bird Fiesta Daze Arts & Crafts Festival,* fine arts, crafts, American Indian art, international food bazaar, kids' funland, gold panning. Call 480-488-2014.
- **Glendale's** *Annual Peacock Jazz Festival* at Sahuaro Ranch Park. It is generally held on a Saturday from 5:00 to 10:00 P.M. Free. Call 623-435-4108.
- **Globe/Miami's** *Annual Copper Dust Stampede Rodeo* at the Gila County Fairgrounds, rodeo, parade, and jackpot roping. Admission is $4.00. Call 520-425-4495.
- **Phoenix's** *Annual Guild Native American Students Arts and Crafts Show* at the Heard Museum. Native American students from throughout the United States exhibit and sell fine art and craft art. Call 602-252-8840.
- **Phoenix's** *Annual Children's Fair* at Heritage Square, puppet theatre, stage entertainment, story telling, hands on activities. Free. Call 602-262-5071.
- **Phoenix's** *Annual Bank One Salsa Bowl*. Salsa made by dozens of restaurants is available for you to taste in the indoor concourse of the Bank One building at 201 N. Central. Help decide which is best, hottest, mildest, most unique, and best over all. Free. 11:00 A.M. to 1:00 P.M. Call 602-221-1005.
- **Phoenix's** *Annual Kid Connection Expo* held at the Civic Plaza, all things relating to kids, from food to toys to new teaching methods. Admission is $6.00. Bring your children. Call 602-262-7272.
- **Scottsdale's** *Annual Thieves's Market Street Bazaar & Wild, Wild Best Days*, Fifth Avenue, food, fun, family entertainment, bargains, cowboy shootouts, pony rides, and Native American dancers. Free. Call 1-800-737-0008.
- **Scottsdale's** *All Indian Days Annual Powwow*. From all over

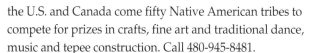

the U.S. and Canada come fifty Native American tribes to compete for prizes in crafts, fine art and traditional dance, music and tepee construction. Call 480-945-8481.

- **Seligman/Topock's** *Annual Route 66 Fun Run,* dance, BBQ, car appearance judging. Participants drive their restored or new cars along old Route 66 and join in the festivities and dancing during the last weekend of April. Participation fee and packet is $44.00. Call 520-753-5001.
- **Superior's** *Spring Plant Sale* at the Boyce Thompson Arboretum. Admission is $3.00. Call 520-689-2811.
- **Tempe's** *Annual ASU Spring Competition Pow Wow*, contest, social dancing and singing by Indian tribes from Canada and the United States, fry bread, and arts & crafts. Call 602-965-2230 or 480-894-1662.
- **Tucson's** *Annual Fourth Avenue Spring Street Fair*, festival atmosphere with many arts & crafts and food opportunities. Admission free. Call 520-624-5004.
- **Tucson's** *Annual San Xavier Pageant & Fiesta,* focusing on the O'odham and Spanish cultures, Native American dances, Mariachis, Waila Band, reenactments of history, and plenty of food. Free. Call 520-622-6911.
- **Tucson's** *International Mariachi Conference* features excellent mariachi and folklorico performers, parade, workshops, art exhibit and more. It's held at the Convention Center. There is an admission charge. Call 520-884-9920.
- **Tucson's** *Annual Spring Sale of New Desert Plants* at the Arizona-Sonora Desert Museum. Free. 10:00 A.M. to 3:00 P.M. Call 520-883-2702.

MAY

- **Ajo's** *Annual Cinco de Mayo* at Ajo Plaza celebrating Mexican independence with food, games, Hispanic folk dance, arts, crafts, and entertainment. Free. From 9:00 A.M. to 3:00 P.M. Call 520-387-7742.
- **Camp Verde's** *Annual Verde River Catfish Contest* lasts from noon to noon. Register at Ralston's Outdoor Sports. Fee is $5.00. Call 520-567-0535.
- **Cottonwood's** *Annual Greater Cottonwood Antique Aeroplane and Auto Show* at the airport. Call 520-634-2868.

- **Flagstaff's** *Annual Zuni Artists Exhibition at the Museum of Northern Arizona.* On exhibit are the finest contemporary Zuni arts and crafts. Watch the artists demonstrations and dance performances. $5.00. From 9:00 A.M. to 5:00 P.M. Call 520-774-5211.

- **Glendale's** *Annual Starwatch* at Thunderbird Regional Park. Bring lawn chairs, blankets, flashlights, and refreshments to enjoy the hands-on workshop with telescopes, slide presentations and lectures. Free. Call 623-435-4508.

- **Guadalupe's** *Annual Fiesta de la Flores* provides food, entertainment, Folklorico dancers, mariachis, dancing and Mexican festivities. Free. Call 602-730-3080.

- **Jerome's** *Annual Paseo de Casa*, parade of homes is held the third weekend of May. There is an admission fee. Call 520-634-2900.

- **Lake Havasu City's** *Annual Western Outdoor News Lake Havasu Striper Derby* at the Ramada London Bridge Resort, Two-person teams, $50,000 in prizes, the largest event of its kind anywhere in the West. It happens the weekend before Memorial Day. Call 714-546-4370.

- **Mesa's** *Annual Cinco de Mayo Fiesta* at Mesa Southwest Museum. Enjoy entertainment, crafts, and authentic Mexican food. Free. 10:00 A.M. to 10:00 P.M. Call 602-644-2242.

- **Nogales's** *Annual Fiestas de Mayo International Parade.* It begins at 9:30 A.M. on the first Sunday in May. Call 502-287-3685.

- **Page's** *Annual Cinco de Mayo* at the city park. Enjoy the evening activities of dancers, folk singing, food, exhibits, art, and music. Call 502-645-2741. Saturday evening closest to May 5th.

- **Page's** *Annual Lake Powell Rodeo* at Vermillion Downs. It's an all Indian rodeo featuring calf roping, bull and bronc riding, bulldogging, barrel racing and more. Call 520-645-2741.

- **Payson's** *Annual PRCA Sanctioned Rodeo* features bareback, saddle bronc, bull riding, steer wrestling, calf and team roping. Competitors are cowboys and well-trained horses from all over the country. Admission is $7.00. The event begins at 1:00 P.M. Call 520-474-4515.

- **Phoenix's** *Annual Jaycees Rodeo of Rodeos Parade* down Central Avenue features the best professional rodeo cowboys in the country. It starts at 8:30 A.M. Call 602-263-8671.
- **Phoenix's** *Annual Jaycees Rodeo of Rodeos.* Call 602-263-8671.
- **Prescott's** *Annual George Phippen Memorial Day Western Art Show & Sale* at the courthouse plaza. Free. The event lasts from 10:00 A.M. to 5:00 P.M. Call 520-778-1385.
- **Sedona's** *Annual Hopi Show* features Hopi Artists, dancers, cultural activities, and food. Admission is $4.00. The event begins at 10:00 A.M. on Mother's Day weekend.
  Call 520-282-7722.
- **Tombstone's** *Annual Wyatt Earp Days*. Enjoy a chile cook-off, gunfights, and other old west festivities. Free. It all begins at 10:00 A.M. on Memorial Day weekend. Call 520-457-2211.
- **Tucson's** *Annual Cinco de Mayo* celebrating Mexico's victory over the French. The celebration is in Kennedy Park. Enjoy Folklorico dancers, music, artists, and food.
  Call 520-292-9326.
- **Tucson's** *Annual Folk Festival* at El Presidio Park takes place in early May. Delight in continuous live musical performances. Three stages offer contemporary folk, blues, bluegrass, folk-rock, ethnic rag-time and gospel music, a children's show, food and crafts. Free. Call 520-326-9021 .
- **Williams's** *Annual Rendezvous Days* happen on Memorial Day weekend. Enjoy the re-enactment of springtime mountain men rendezvous, a black-powder shoot out and horse-related events. Call 520-635-4061.

JUNE

- **Prescott's** *Frontier Days* & *Rodeo* may occur at the same time as *Territorial Days* and provide you with fireworks, crafts, food, and a carnival. End of June through July 4th. Call 520-445-2000 or 1-800-358-1888.
- **Flagstaff's** *Annual Gem and Mineral Show* is held in the Grand Ballroom of the Little America Hotel, the first weekend of June. Call 520-774-2648.
- **Holbrook's** *Old West Days* occurs the first weekend of June and provides lots of excitement, including footraces, bike rides, and Native American dancing. Call 520-524-6558.

JULY

- **Flagstaff's** *Annual Festival of the Arts* draws crowds to its cooler climate to enjoy symphonic, chamber, and pop music concerts, dance, art exhibits, poetry, films, and live theater. The festival usually begins in late June and continues into August. Admission to events ranges from $8.00 to $20.00. Call 520-774-7750 or 1-800-266-7740.

- **Flagstaff's** *Annual Hopi Artists' Exhibition* at the Museum of Northern Arizona features, pottery, jewelry, baskets, kachina dolls, native dances, and ongoing demonstrations. This is the oldest continuing Native American show in Arizona. Adult admission is $5.00. Call 520-774-5211.

- **Flagstaff's** *Annual Navajo Artists Exhibition* at the Museum of Northern Arizona. Enjoy the exhibition and sale of jewelry, sandpaintings, baskets, pottery, and more. You'll be fascinated by the native dances and demonstrations. Admission is $5.00. Call 520-774-5211.

- **Payson's** *Annual State Championship Loggers/Sawdust Festival* where competition is tough in log rolling, cross cutting, and greased-pole climbing events. Call 520-474-4515 or 520-552-3068.

- **Prescott's** *Annual Frontier Days* features the world's oldest rodeo and parade. Call 520-445-3130 or 520-445-2000.

- **Prescott's** *Annual Bluegrass Festival* held at Watson Lake the third weekend in July. Call 520-445-2000.

- **Scottsdale's** *Annual Evening on Marshall Way and Summer Spectacular Art Walk* begins one block west of Scottsdale Road between Indian School Road and 5th Avenue and lasts from 7:00 P.M. to 9:00 P.M. Free. Call 602-945-8481.

- **Tucson's** *Annual Herb Fair* at the Tucson Botanical Gardens. From 8:00 A.M. to noon. Free. Call 520-326-9255.

AUGUST

- **Elgin's** *Harvesting of the Vine Festival* features wine tasting, tour of the vineyard and winery, music, and dancing from 11:00 A.M. to 5:00 P.M. Admission is $12.00. Call 520-455-5613.

- **Flagstaff's** *Annual Festival in the Pines* features more than 200

performances from pop to jazz, from magic shows to dances. There is plenty of food and special events for children. Admission is $5.00. This event is held the first weekend in August at the county fairgrounds. Call 520-779-7611.

- **Holbrook's** *Annual Quilt and Doll Show*. See hundreds of Arizona-made quilts and dolls. Call 520-524-6407.
- **Payson's** *Annual PRCA Sanctioned Rodeo* is the world's oldest continuous rodeo. Competitors are top cowboys and well-trained horses from all over the nation. The parade is free. There are admission charges to the rodeo and dances. Call 520-474-4515.
- **Sedona's** *Annual Arizona Woodcarver's Association Show and Sale* at Tlaquepaque. Appreciate the beauty of wood and the artistry of the carvers. There are original woodcarvings of all kinds. Free. Call 602-938-5702.
- **Tombstone's** *Vigilante Days* excites you with street shows, hangings, bar fights, and shoot outs. Enjoy the starlight concert and dancing. Feel the ambiance of this old and well-known Arizona town.Call 1-800-457-3423.

SEPTEMBER

- **Payson's** *Annual State Championship Oldtime Fiddlers Contest.* A lively contest of fiddlers from around Arizona and elsewhere. Call 520-474-4514.
- **Sedona's** *Jazz on the Rocks*. Thrill to the excitement of the state's top jazz festival. This event is so popular that you will need to call for tickets several months in advance. Call 520-282-1985.
- **Statewide**, *Fiestas Patrias* is the celebration of Mexican independence. Enjoy the gaiety of the fireworks, Mexican food, folklorico dancers, and mariachi band. Call 520-235-3101.
- **Window Rock's** *Navajo Nation Tribal Fair*, world's largest Indian fair offers an inter-tribal powwow, rodeo, arts, crafts, and food. There will be traditional singing, dancing, and drumming by numerous North American tribes. Everything begins at 10:00 A.M. Admission is $4..00. Rodeo admission is additional.The fair takes place during the first ten days of September. Call 520-871-6702 or 520-871-6478.

OCTOBER

- **Lake Havasu City's** *London Bridge Days* brings you festivities with English costumes, entertainment, and a parade, all to commemorate the dedication of the London Bridge. The event takes place the last full week of October. Call 520-855-4115 or 1-800-242-8278.

- **Mesa's** *Annual Mesa Powwow* offers competition for more than 3,000 Native American dancers and craftsmen. Native American crafts which include jewelry and weavings will be for sale. The powwow will be in front of the Mesa Southwest Museum in downtown Mesa the second weekend in October from noon to 11:00 P.M. on Saturday and noon to dusk on Sunday. Free admission. Call 480-644-2169.

- **Bisbee's** *Annual Haunted Mine Tour* Ride a train into the mine to see and hear the spirits of miners past tell of local legends. Queen Mine. Call 520-432-5421.

- **Phoenix's** *Annual All Indian Rodeo* at the State Fairgrounds occurs during the State Fair, the last week of October, and is free with the cost of admission to the fair. Call 602-252-6771.

- **Sedona's** *Annual Sedona Arts Festival,* occurring the second weekend in October, is a celebration of culinary, performing, and visual arts reflecting the culturally rich native and pioneer heritage of Sedona. From 10:00 A.M. to 5:00 P.M. Admission is $5.00. Call 520-282-8949.

- **Tombstone's** *Annual Helldorado Days*, the Oldest Gunslingin' Celebration. Call 520-457-2211.

- **Tucson's** *Annual La Fiesta de los Chiles,* generally occurring the third weekend of October, is a celebration honoring the chile pepper. There is music, crafts, food, and more. It is held at the Tucson Botanical Gardens, 2150 N. Alveron Way from 10:00 A.M. to 5:00 P.M., Saturday and Sunday. There is an admission charge. Call 520-326-9686.

- **Tubac's** *Anza Days* offers entertainment, a dance, food, and the main feature— the reenactment of the expedition from Tubac to what is now San Francisco. There are basket-weaving and cotton-spinning demos. Free admission. Call 520-398-2252.

NOVEMBER

- **Bisbee's** *Annual Festival of Lights.* Call 520-432-5421.
- **Bisbee's** *Annual Historic Home Tour.*
  Call 520-432-2141.
  Both of these Bisbee events occur on Thanksgiving weekend. There is a charge for the Home Tour.
- **Phoenix's** *Annual Cowboy Artists of America Exhibition* at the Phoenix Art Museum. This well-known show begins in mid–October and extends into mid–November.
  Call 602-257-1222 or 602-257-1880.
- **Wickenburg's** *Annual Four Corner States Bluegrass Festival and Fiddle Championship* occurs the second weekend of November. Call 602-684-5479.

DECEMBER

- **Phoenix's** *Annual Pueblo GrandeIndian Market* at South Mountain Park Activity Center offers the artistry of more than five hundred Native Americans. Prices range from $2.00 to $10,000.00. Do your holiday shopping.
  Call 602-495-0900 or 602-955-4722.
- **Phoenix's** *Annual International Christmas Exhibit* of decorated trees, ethnic dolls, and creches illustrates Arizona's welcoming spirit and genuine interest in visitors from all over the world. The exhibit is usually held in the Bank One Center concourse in downtown Phoenix and is open most of December. Call 602-221-1005.
- **Phoenix's** *Luminaria Night* at the Desert Botanical Gardens is the first weekend of December from 5:30 to 9:30 P.M. Enjoy food and musical performances. Call 602-941-1225.
- **Phoenix's** *Traditional Arizona Christmas* at the Pioneer Arizona Living History Museum north of Phoenix off Interstate 17. Enjoy the wagon rides, caroling, and luminarias. Call 602-993-0212.
- **Phoenix's** *Victorian Holidays* at Heritage Square happens the second weekend in December. Call 602-262-4734.
- **Phoenix's** *Annual Fiesta Bowl Parade* on Central Avenue. Enjoy the excitement of bands, horses, floats, clowns, and all the extras. Call 480-350-0911.

SELECTED BIBLIOGRAPHY

Bahti, Mark. *Southwestern Indian Arts and Crafts.* Las Vegas, Nevada: KC Publications.

Bromberg, Erik (1986). *The Hopi Approach to the Art of Kachina Doll Carving.* West Chester, Pennsylvania: Schiffer Publishing Ltd.

Chronic, Halka. *Roadside Geology of Arizona.* Missoula: Mountain Press Publishing Company.

Dittert, Alfred E. Jr. & Plog, Fred. *Generations in Clay.* Flagstaff: Northland Publishing.

Hoffmeister, Donald F. (1986). *Mammals of Arizona.* University of Arizona Press and the Arizona Game and Fish Department.

Kaufman, Alice and Selser, Christopher (1985). *The Navajo Weaving Tradition, 1650 to the Present.* Toronto: Fitzhenry & Whiteside Limited.

Meinzer, Wyman (1993). *The Roadrunner.* Lubbock: Texas Tech University Press.

Monthan, Guy and Doris (1975). *Art and Indian Individualists.* Flagstaff: Northland Press.

Patterson, Alex (1992). *A Field Guide to Rock Art Symbols of the Greater Southwest.* Boulder: Johnson Books.

Patterson, Alex (1992). *Hopi Pottery Symbols.* Boulder: Johnson Books.

Place, Chuck. (1992) *Ancient Walls.* Golden, Colorado: Fulcrum Publishing.

Robinson, Bert. *The Basket Weavers of Arizona.* Albuquerque: University of New Mexico Press.

Rodee, Marian (1987). *Weaving of the Southwest.* West Chester, Pennsylvania, Shiffer Publishing Ltd.

Smith, Robert L. (1982). *Venomous Animals of Arizona.* Tucson: The University of Arizona.

Trimble, Marshall (1986). *Roadside History of Arizona.* Missoula: Mountain Press Publishing Company.

Wright, Barton (1977). *The Complete Guide to Collecting Kachina Dolls.* Flagstaff: Northland Press.

Wright, Margaret Nickelson (1982). *Hopi Silver.* Flagstaff: Northland Press.

INDEX

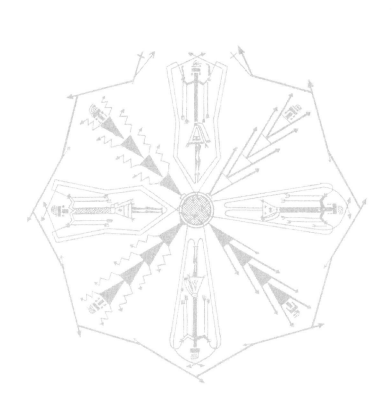